GOOD FORTUNE
NEXT TIME

LIFE, DEATH, IRONY, AND THE ADMINISTRATION OF VERY SMALL COLLEGES

GOOD FORTUNE NEXT TIME

LIFE, DEATH, IRONY, AND THE ADMINISTRATION OF VERY SMALL COLLEGES

WILL WOOTTON

Mandel Vilar Press / Dryad Press

Library of Congress Cataloging-in-Publication Data

Names: Wootton, Will, author.
Title: Good fortune, next time : life, death, irony, and the administration
   of very small colleges / Will Wootton.
Description: Simsbury, Connecticut : Mandel Vilar Press ; Takoma Park,
   Maryland : Dryad Press, [2017]
Identifiers: LCCN 2017036771 (print) | LCCN 2017037985 (ebook) | ISBN
   9781942134374 | ISBN 9781942134350 (paperback)
Subjects: LCSH: Wootton, Will. | College administrators--United
   States--Biography. | Education, Higher--United States--Administration.
Classification: LCC LA2317.W72 (ebook) |
LCC LA2317.W72 A3 2017 (print) | DDC
   378.1/11--dc23
LC record available at https://lccn.loc.gov/2017036771

Paperback ISBN: 978-1-942134-35-0
E book ISBN: 978-1-942134-37-4

Mandel Vilar Press / 19 Oxford Court / Simsbury, Connecticut 06070
www.americasforconservation.org / www.mvpress.org

Dryad Press / 15 Sherman Avenue / Takoma Park, Maryland 20912
www.dryadpress.com

To Lulu
Wife, Mother, Lover…Muse

Contents

1 A Gaggle of Gods • *1*

2 Many Dead, Many Dying • *11*

3 What the Work College Presidents Said • *25*

4 Matters of Governance, and Cocktails • *35*

5 Whores and Slaves • *51*

6 Going Once, Going Twice... • *73*

7 Search...and Destroy • *97*

8 The Dog Is Back. Kill the Dog • *117*

9 Depression is Preferred • *135*

10 My Father's Problem • *151*

11 Pennsylvania's Coastline • *175*

12 Vince, Me, and Rod Gander's Ghost • *191*

13 Regulate This! • *213*

14 A Twilight Zone for the Improbable • *221*

15 Lulu, a Grand Idea, a Mother of Irony • *233*

16 The Hill You Will Die On • *261*

17 Afterword • *269*

Acknowledgments • *275*

Index • *277*

Part two of the Sterling College mural: The stylized but not altogether inaccurate portrait of daily life on the Sterling Campus, its blue skies and verdant lawns, its structures, fields, animals, equipment, gardens, students, teachers, their learning, their work, and even its hard working president.

1

A Gaggle of Gods

This book began as a meditation in the style of a textbook, was put upon by unprovoked stories, developed memoirish tendencies, and finally found its footing as an excursion, back and forth through time, accompanied by a shifting host of characters and colleagues and *untenable situations*, few of which conformed, or ever would, to a linear, chronologically ordered world.

The goal of an excursion, this one at least, is to depart from where you are into whatever is out there and complete a rough circle of the territory, and then, sometime later — days, months, years, a half a lifetime later — arrive back at the start and resume life as normal, but enriched. The path eventually taken, as opposed to the course laid out, is defined by the terrain traversed and the traveler's compulsion to explore off trail.

I headed out following a college-level curriculum in nonprofit management, which consists of seminars and classes on such topics as mission, governance and leadership, marketing, fundraising and development, grants and foundations, ethics, finance, and regulation. All of this, to me, composed riveting, actually compelling, subject matter, even as I discovered its limits. Whatever my intentions to stick to the script, however focused I became on the subject matter at hand, it turned out the stories that emerged were more interesting and instructive to me than the subjects they arose from. I was off trail already. I didn't see these stories at first. They were underfoot, like an old, worn threshold tramped across without regard.

I didn't mean for my father to get so involved, nor did I intend to write so much about fishing. My wife Lulu's cancer didn't figure in at all. There was no reason to be thinking about the High Rockies and Colorado. My own anxieties and fears were not planned subject matter. Instead, I thought others — students, teachers, and professionals — might take something away from a purely academic view, especially those at the beginning of their career, or somewhere in the middle, or even themselves thinking of retiring and sharpening their quills.

It was more than a year after my self-inflicted retirement, at the end of 29 years embedded in the non-academic side of higher education, that I started writing. I'd run out of things to do, stuff to fix, nearby streams to fish. Not overly concerned with chronology, I discovered I was more comfortable moving from one subject to the next with little regard. I didn't take a lot of notes back then and what little dialogue there is is what was said, not necessarily what was spoken.

I wrote because I wanted to unravel what I had learned at Marlboro, Montserrat, and Sterling colleges, and where, after it all ended, I had arrived. The real excursion was over and done with, but to understand it required a return trip, a different sort of excursion where all sorts of new things would turn up, come together, or otherwise lead the way back. Like the first time, beyond the first step, I really had no idea.

In the early 1980s, when I started in the higher education business — nonprofit business, but business nevertheless — there were few supporting organizations. Entire development fields, those fields in which I romped and struggled, like planned giving and capital campaigns, were just beginning to mature. No one back then had conducted a multiyear, multimillion dollar fundraising campaign; no one knew how to. Those were years when anyone who could compose a few complete sentences, stand up straight, and possessed a handful of social grace and tolerance could get a position in college or university administration. When I began, the whole enterprise was expanding and adapting to decades of accelerated change around how higher education, public and private, fit the post-WWII social and economic structure of the nation, even as the millennium was in sight.

Today there are hundreds of academic programs in nonprofit administration and practice, and internship opportunities abound. Career paths are clearly delineated. Complex and proprietary computer programs and systems are widely available to help manage every aspect of higher education administration. There are case studies by the barrel, advisors by the boatload. As an industry, we've come a long way in just 30 years. At the same time, the thrill of experiential learning has been muted by so much deliverable, elemental knowledge. Such is progress.

Of many certainties, however, the most evident was that 25 of my 29-year career were spent at two of the smallest and most unusual liberal arts colleges in the nation, both of which happen to be in Vermont: Marlboro College in the southern part of the state, and Sterling College in the far northern part, and where I served as president from 2006 to 2012.

Marlboro with about 220 students in 2012 and Sterling with 114 when I began are distinguished not only by their size but also by their unusual curricula, their history, physical place, and people. To the general college aspirant it hardly matters because in the giant context of American higher education each was unknown, underendowed, underfunded, and, worst of all, practically unimaginable: a whole college considerably smaller than your high school graduating class. How could that be?

Each was further notable for having more than once skirted dangerously close to the sheer cliff edge of institutional oblivion. Today both remain so small that anyone who claims to know anything about higher education — and there are millions who do — would predict their near-immediate demise with an air of complete assurance, simply because of their obscurity and ridiculous, uneconomical, and clearly unsustainable size.

The United States has about 2,000 private, independent colleges and universities, and the same number of public institutions. Independents, however, are wildly diverse in comparison to their public counterparts. They include, for instance, small and midsize liberal arts colleges, research universities, church- and faith-based institutions, historically black colleges, single-sex colleges, two-year colleges, and colleges focused on law, medicine, business, the arts, and engineering, among other professions. Their student populations run from fewer than 100 to more than 30,000. All these statistics and many, many more are available through the National Association of Independent Colleges and Universities (NAICU), which is one of dozens of private and/or governmental organizations, associations, accreditation entities, even entire federal bureaucracies, that encompass and feed upon the higher education industry.

The average size of an independent U.S. college is just under 2,000 students. In the six states of New England, 38 percent of private institutions are under 1,000 students, and half of those have fewer than 500. Among them were my three, but I'll set aside Montserrat for the moment, where my time was brief.

Marlboro (somewhat erratically) and Sterling (somewhat compulsively) spent a lot of time figuring out how to stay small, how not to grow. They understand, as do some other Vermont colleges, that the diseconomy of scale is not the primary threat; that other equally forbidding threats are out there, including fiscal mismanagement, legal claims, lack of critical resources, shortfalls in admissions, board dysfunction, inept leadership, and increases in regulatory burden coinciding with any of the above. If it were as simple as being small they all would have succumbed decades ago, and this book would not exist.

Instead, whatever the size, type, or wealth of an institution, outside of the classroom all face nearly identical fiscal, political, and philosophical institutional challenges. They face them over and over, by decade, by year, by president. In this world, Sisyphus, rolling his boulder up a mountainside, would be a midlevel manager.

The difference is that at small institutions the margins for correcting institutional error are infinitesimally small compared with those margins at larger, wealthier institutions. That list of foreboding threats — any one of which, arriving at the right moment, could put a small college, or a weakened one, in a perilous spot, but would have virtually no overwhelming effect on a larger, bulkier, institution.

Because my colleges were for periods of time under tremendous, even crushing, stress, my career required what was for me an unnatural level of discipline and focus, a grim, sometimes frenetic determination and a sense of humor equal to the thickness of my skin. Also critical to my longevity was a consistent awareness — an itch in the center of your back — of the irony that enveloped these colleges and their presidents like a gaggle of minor Greek gods, mocking, sympathizing, punishing, rewarding, ignoring.

It was such ideas that I began writing about a year after my leave-taking as Sterling's president. I was suddenly energized and writing and researching daily. In six months, I had finished drafts of five or six chapters. However, except for my wife Lulu, who read, edited, and listened with patience, no one else had read a word. So I went to a friend, John Elder, who held a tenured teaching position at Middlebury College, and was an environmental writer and author of essays and books that I admired and cared for, *Reading the Mountains of Home* and *The Frog Run*, and asked if he would read the first few chapters and give me some idea where this book might be headed, because, suddenly, I was unsure.

I had gotten to know John several years before. In 2009, I desperately needed an active, engaged academic on the Sterling board's academic committee, which was suffering attrition. A pleasant and attentive man, John also possessed a level of academic gravitas effective in overawing non-academic trustees when they mucked about in the curriculum, where they did not belong.

John and I were having coffee at my place in Craftsbury, six miles northeast of the common, and he paid me a few compliments on what he'd read. Then he asked, "What is it? What are you writing?"

What would have happened if I'd said something like, "An artistic/literary memoir-less instruction manual for people interested in non-profit management, particularly in very small liberal arts colleges in Vermont." I'll never know because I blurted out "memoir."

That's what had happened. Whatever the topic underway — the importance of mission statements, for instance, or techniques for major gift campaigns — it quickly emerged as a story, or an outright diversion, usually about people, about me, inevitably based on my perceptions alone, which led to other personal stories, which led to chronology, and even to topics I had no interest in talking about. But there they were, like boulders and gullies, impeding the way.

John delivered an encapsulated, personalized lesson about the arc of a narrative and how the reader becomes interested in the writer, and, in a memoir, how the author changes, or is changed, over the course of the book. That is, how the actual writing of the book itself changes you, the writer. It made perfect sense.

But I didn't feel memoir. I couldn't help being more interested in nonprofit management, higher education, and, particularly, the rare and little understood role of the college president.

It's what I had been doing and loving for half my life. I loved the intensity. I loved the stress. I loved the size of the thing, no larger than a small ship — all the working parts at hand. I loved the frustration of working with presidents. I loved the storms that beset us. I loved the odds against survival. I loved the mission.

I desired to give students of the subject and other interested readers a look at that kind of professional life, but I came to realize I'd blundered into the briar patch of memoir and couldn't extract myself without getting all torn up.

John emphasized that understanding something about the author was as critical as the subject matter at hand. He was more instructive than that. He wanted to know, specifically, how it happened that for one year I was the editor, chief reporter, and paste-up/production manager of Boston Chinatown's bilingual newspaper, *Sampan*, which published monthly, with English printed on one side and handwritten Chinese on the other.

That happened after graduate school in journalism at Boston University, 1979, I explained. Lulu was pregnant with our second child. I was looking for a job and the Chinese (now Asian) American Civic Association, publisher of Sampan to this day, was looking for a bilingual, bi-literate Chinese reporter/editor.

Bilingual, bi-literate Chinese reporters willing to move to Boston from New York or San Francisco for a position paying maybe a quarter of their current wages, at a paper of age but of irregular quality, were not to be found, not one of them. I, on other hand, a white, marginally experienced reporter, with some paste-up skills, but no Chinese, and no intercultural experience worth noting, had no wage expectations at all. Which made me a powerful contender, especially because the paper had missed its previous deadline and no one among the ill-paid part-time reporters and translators, or the publisher, was willing to take it on.

John then asked about those summers and falls in the French (Swiss, really) restaurant (in Vermont, not Switzerland) with chef/owner Hans, and Victor the Russian-speaking piano-playing sous-chef, and me the other sous-chef.

Well, those stories are all about Hans killing piglets with a large nail driven to the forehead, so he didn't have to waste a .22 bullet, and slugging down shots of frozen vodka as the dining room filled up with the Marlboro Music Festival pre-concert crowd. It was all about paper-thin air-dried beef, and haunches of veal, whole salmon delivered on ice, and of aspic and brown sauce, and garlic, and wine, and brandy, and the oft-delivered wild game we plucked, gutted, skinned, or otherwise illegally prepared for a party of six, a party of four, hunters who could shoot and fish, I guess, but not cook.

I can see where this is leading, Hans's kitchen: how that experience could reach well into the future, which now is my immediate past. The unremitting intensity of the job as president of Sterling — the unrelenting demands imposed from within and without, physically and mentally, the criticality of maintaining an attentive level of concentration through the storm around you, all the stuff flying at you; everyone jumps — or doesn't! — to the decisions you make every moment, the words you write and speak; it's all fear and the gripping excitement like a rollercoaster, it's all like cooking for 100 patrons; Hans shouting or laughing, wielding his giant chef's knife and long fork, the pans flying through the flames, the broiler hissing and spitting, the sauces and broths bubbling on the steel grill. The waitresses circling through the kitchen ordering and picking up. The dishwasher works tirelessly at the Hobart, taking the pans and returning them in moments, polishing the wine glasses and the silverware. The bartender responding to our calls for beer. One summer it was 130 degrees in the cramped kitchen and we had to put on jackets to go outside into the 80-degree summer evening for a smoke before the second seating.

And Colorado, John is saying, where's that going in the memoir?

Those are great stories, he says. He's talking about the ranch my father bought after a long search up and down the Rockies, looking to reclaim somehow the golden ring of his adolescence when ranching and horses, and pack trips, and the wilds of Wyoming and California, of the High Sierras were all still inexorably of his mind. He spent his career at *LIFE* magazine, becoming an editor, then an executive editor, and when he couldn't stand it anymore he started looking and finally bought Singing River Ranch, in Red Wing, Colorado. It was 1972, I was 23. My mother cooked and my sisters and cousins kept the cabins, or worked as carpenters or general ranch hands. I wrangled horses morning and evening, and took riders, often birders, high into the mountains and returned them safely to the ranch, a 2,000-acre dot at 9,300 feet in the Front Range of the southern Rockies, at the high tip of the Huerfano Valley. John's right, it's all there in my mind, the creeks and trout, the horses and hay fields and irrigation ditches, the peaks stretching out above the tree line, the high valley of unoccupied wilderness, ponderosa pine and aspen, and mile after mile, the whole great expanse watching over the dry gulch and pinion pine and juniper-studded foothills and the far-reaching plains to the eastern horizon.

Only I, and later Lulu and I before we married, ever spent months alone at the ranch, Mt. Blanca driving the winter weather, 30 horses to feed once a day: I'd load eight or so 60-pound bales in the ranch pickup and pound my way to the top of the upper hayfield, slip the truck into low gear, climb out the door and into the bed and let the old Dodge bump along downslope as I broke open the bales and tossed sheaves of hay to the gathering herd, which ambled along behind the truck. Then I'd climb back into the cab before we ran out of field and crashed down into the creek. That, chopping ice out of the creek for water, and surviving safely is all you had to accomplish in winter. The nearest neighbor was eight miles down the only road, and he was not all that put together. No television, a lone landline telephone tucked away in the main cabin, a single thin radio station drifting down from Pueblo.

How comfortable that was. Like an honorarium. To be secured deep within of the violent grandeur of the High Rockies in winter, alone in it and, beyond the daily chores of life, insignificance — just me, then just the two of us. Not too different from Sterling and Craftsbury Common in 2006, tucked away as we were in a near Internet-free zone, among the boreal forests and dairy farms of the Northeast Kingdom of Vermont.

If I think about it all like that, if I strip away the jobs and schools and careers, and bundle what is left — the two of us — and drag it through 15 household moves in 40 years, I begin to make out the origins, the place names that secure the stories of our two lives. Each place as intriguing as the other, and each move requiring a rebalancing of relationships, a refocusing of self. Stories are there, too, stories that become the future or inform the past, and others that define it. But aren't there always?

So it's a tough business, this kind of writing. And one needs all the help one can get to find those hills and gores of enlightenment where writing happens. If you don't have a friend like John Elder to stir things up, if you can't find guidance in the literature of your subject, which I admit I often could not, then a fish story may help; it's Ishmael's reflection: the Pequod, Ahab, Starbuck, and the entire crew are just days from their final, fatal encounter with the white whale:

> One often hears of writers that rise and swell with their subject, though it may seem but an ordinary one. How, then, with me, writing of this Leviathan? Unconsciously my chirography expands into placard capitals. Give me a condor's quill! Give me Vesuvius's crater for an inkstand! Friends, hold my arms! For in the mere act of penning my thoughts of this Leviathan, they weary me, and make me faint with their outreaching comprehensiveness of sweep, as if to include the whole circle of the sciences, and all the generations of whales, and men, and mastodons, past, present, and to come, with all the revolving panoramas of empire on earth, and throughout the whole universe, not excluding its suburbs. Such, and so magnifying, is the virtue of a large

and liberal theme. We expand its bulk. To produce a mighty book, you must choose a mighty theme. No great and enduring volume can ever be written on the flea, though many there be who have tried it.

Who can fault him? Who can do better? Here, it's only the lively pen that transcends the writer, when you get lost in a paragraph by following an unchosen subject to a conclusion you watch happen, instead of make happen. I don't think that sort of transcendence occurs much in books about higher education, hence the stories, hence the excursion, my mighty flea.

2

Many Dead, Many Dying

December 13, 1993

When Rod Gander, the president of Marlboro College and my boss, climbed down from the hissing, dripping 6 pm Amtrak train from New York City, I'd never before witnessed such a visage of depression and defeat. His whole body seemed smaller, shrunken inside his topcoat.

He started off across the crowded platform, and then stopped as passengers and porters flowed around him. He shook a cigarette from a pack and lit it with a lighter. He looked up, caught my eye, and without expression hunched his shoulders up and down, once, then waved his cigarette toward the exit and headed that way.

That was not good. In today's nomenclature, the college — his college, my college — was on a short and economically unsustainable path. We had two, maybe three payrolls in the bank. Rod's trip so carefully planned and prepared for — well, it had been a good idea and, really, there was no choice. Being out of money was not exactly a new condition for one of the nation's smallest liberal arts colleges. The visit to the Christian Johnson Endeavor Foundation was perhaps the last opportunity to put the college's case, a desperate case, there was no hiding that, in front of someone who could actually help, who had the money at least, if not yet the motivation.

Julie Kidd, whose family foundation she inherited from her father, was familiar with Marlboro through a relatively new member of the board of trustees and his wife. Because of them the foundation had already given Marlboro one grant

11

the previous year. But it was a one-time gift, she indicated. That she would entertain the sort of meeting Rod had asked for was like being invited to a party, a dinner dance, where you knew you didn't really belong.

Rod had spent the week before at his desk, writing a report to the foundation,
banging it out on his manual typewriter he'd brought from New York, stabbing
away at the keys with two stubby forefingers. As a former editor and the former
chief of correspondents at Newsweek, Rod wrote well and straightforwardly. He
had an ease I would have sinned to obtain. Instead and for the better, over 14 years
together at Marlboro I had the services, the almost exclusive services, of one of the
finest editors in journalism.

I was very respectful of that. In New York a generation of young journalists
was also respectful because Rod was a natural-born mentor and teacher, always
willing to share his extensive journalistic knowledge. He could also be sardonic, in
a gentle sort of way. Once we'd been discussing editors we'd worked for, the types
who, back then, in pencil deleted bits and pieces of your story and rewrote the same
words above, so to the next editor up the line it looked like he was actually doing
something. What's your definition of an editor, I asked him. "An editor," he said,
"is simply a mouse who wants to be a rat."

What we had pieced together was an economic plan, an explanation, of how
the college could survive the current threat and begin to prosper, if the foundation
became engaged. Still, whatever he wrote could not hide how awful the numbers
were, how alarming, how fearful. The projected deficit was like a tsunami, building every moment and speeding to crash into the college, which was protected by
the fiscal equivalent of a knee-high wall of sandbags.

Rod's secretary retyped everything, packaged up the six- or seven-page report,
and put it in the mail to New York. Rod called and made the appointment.

We'd asked for $750,000 over three years, a lot of money even by today's
standards. And we asked that it all be unrestricted: just cash to get us from one
very insecure place to another more secure place.

Outside the train station I hurried Rod into a small tavern and steak joint I'd
checked out earlier in case we had reason to celebrate. We slid into a booth. Rod
ordered scotch and I got beer.

"She didn't read it," he said.

"She didn't. . . " I said.

"She forgot, I guess, about the meeting."

"Did you have a meeting?"

"We did. I outlined everything as best I could. She was very apologetic. She said she'd read the report and call."

"When?"

Rod's shoulders went up, paused, then down.

That was it then, December 1993. Disillusionment and despair, in a bar booth next to the train station in dark, rainy, rundown downtown Springfield, Mass.

⸺⸺⸺⸺

During three decades in higher education I had to live a human life, as well. Work and career were accented by illnesses, deaths, injuries, births, surgery, fishing, hockey, automobiles, ratty old boats, dogs and cats, and farming. Farming because for some dozen years, Lulu, with my willing labor — so, it was "we" — operated a commercial cut-flower farm on our 16 acres in Marlboro, a few miles from the college.

I graduated from Marlboro in 1972, when the college was only 24 years old, and I was 23. That same year I met my sweetheart, Lulu Ballantine, who was an entering freshman. Her formal education was almost immediately interrupted due to, due to us beginning what's been going on for 40 years, following each other's passions in a divergent, entertaining sort of way. Together we have a son and a daughter, who are now longtime adults with their own children, two apiece, so there's a bunch of us.

Lulu, the youngest of five children born over five and a half years, came from a circus family. Her father, Bill Ballantine, a magazine and book writer and illustrator after service in WWII, eventually landed a career with the Ringling Bros. and Barnum & Bailey Circus, and became the creator and first "dean" of Ringling's Clown College. One of Lulu's brother's spent a decade or more with Ringling, then with a host of traveling shows; colloquially, mud shows. Her eldest sister, Bridget, was a Ringling showgirl, then trained as an aerialist, and one night, working for a mud show out west, she fell. Recovered, and with a show-born daughter, she married, happily, outside the circus. Lulu's mother, Roberta, a head taller than Bill, had come from a considerably more refined background in southern California. A showgirl herself for a while, she wrote an entertaining book called The Care and Feeding of Clowns, which was about how to eat well while crisscrossing the country on the Ringling train.

Roberta's southern California based family was underwhelmed, sometimes demonstrably so, at her union with an artist and writer. But it was a union that persisted until Bill's death in 1999. Roberta went on to author a complex, historically layered, 600-page treatise, *Marlowe Up Close: An Unconventional Biography, With a Scrapbook of His Ciphers*. The point of it was to convince the reader that Marlowe was Shakespeare.

After a decade of short-lived careers for both of us, we returned to Marlboro College in 1983, and for me graduate school at Boston University, where I earned a journalism degree. Before that move, I cooked in restaurants, worked in the woods with a famous old forester, Halsey Hicks, and put in my time on my father's Colorado ranch, still called Singing River. After a year as editor of Sampan, I was a freelance reporter in Boston until we abandoned urban life and, packing up our two small children, moved to the bucolic Amenia, New York countryside where Lulu and I taught and I coached hockey and lacrosse not very successfully in a private high school for dyslexic boys. After a couple of years, we were back at Marlboro and I was the alumni director and editor of the magazine, *Potash Hill*. In 1986 I became the director of development, but retained editorship of the magazine for another decade or more. Marlboro grew from a perilously low 167 students to just over 300 in my 19 years.

After those 19 years, as Marlboro's vice president of institutional advancement and a husk of my former self, burnt out, exhausted in a way where rest was ineffectual, I needed relief. I needed out. I resigned, and received a few months' pay and a big party and celebratory dinner. The trustees attended. Even my mother and my two sisters attended. I got to make a speech. I was 53 years old. I didn't have another job lined up. I hadn't spent one minute looking.

I took a while to figure out even where to look, and after so many years, how to look for a new job. I was trapped amongst the streams and swamps, the hills and swales of higher education. I had a "skill set" not unlike a hunter- gatherer with his collection of stone tools and knowledge of the local terrain. But how would I know, really, how serviceable my skills were, having lived solely with institutional crisis and fiscal catastrophe for, say, 17 of those 19 years?

Of independent colleges and universities there are those financially shaky, old, settled in their ways, and aging badly. There are colleges newly born, and others approaching adolescence, and still others finally nearing something like adulthood after 70 or 80 years of hard living. There are huge 20,000-student universities and colleges with thousands of undergraduates, and there are tiny places like Sterling and Marlboro, shrews dodging the footfalls of dinosaurs.

But we are all colleagues, absolutely, all part of the history and traditions of academia. Our mission statements could live together comfortably in an old shoebox. We talk the same language, know the same people. We fight the good fight. We live confidently under the broad umbrella of the liberal arts.

But higher education also competes, and not always nicely, for students, grants, philanthropists, and maybe most of all for status. We steal ideas, language, and personnel from one another with impunity. We will undercut the competition for a single student. We wouldn't hesitate to cut out a major donor from another's herd, like a cowboy on a quarter horse. Looked at from this view, we are more part of an industry than we are members of the same team, or even the same movement, or anything like that. It's an industry in which each member is focused on replicating itself, and protecting its assets while growing in size, or stature, or geographical reach. I tell you, if private colleges and universities were all bobbing around on a giant, stormy sea and one of us started to sink under the waves, well, too bad for that guy. It's that sort of industry.

I'm not saying the whole enterprise is fractal, only that higher education in America, particularly the liberal arts approach to undergraduate studies, works about the same way whatever the size of the institution, on both faculty and administrative levels. All colleges are nonprofit institutions (except the online for-profit education mills, of course). And college professors look pretty much alike everywhere, their various rankings, degrees, and colorful academic hoods serving to individualize members of the same species. All colleges are run by a president — a character as hard as steel round shot — being crushed from above by a wedge-shaped board of trustees to whom he or she is responsible, and ground away beneath by the roiling magma of faculty, staff, students, and community. All have professional people running complex programs in fundraising and development, finance, enrollment, plant and operations; all the pieces needed whether the student body is 10,000, 1,000, or 114.

When colleagues assemble at conferences, or meet in regional associations, the issues they face are similar and familiar; the frustrations, identical; their stories of students, nearly interchangeable. The quality of instruction across higher education, studies have shown, is roughly equal across type of college. That's as it should be, as colleges produce graduates who go on to become teachers in colleges.

As a whole, the industry is robust, though the likelihood of failure and death is real but seemingly reserved for some and not others. The huge land-grant universities, for instance, aren't going to go broke, and if they were to, they're still not going to close. State and community colleges may shift around, merging and unmerging among themselves, but there is little chance of a single president or group of overseers directly causing the actual demise of one. The publics are protected by politics, cronyism, alumni, and history, and that adds up to security, if not always to excellence.

Among the couple thousand independent liberal arts colleges, the Ivy League and the smaller potted Ivies are cushioned by enormous endowments and their own gold-plated histories, shaped from a studiously cultivated alumni, their alumni parents, and alumni children. There must be another thousand regional institutions, including faith-based colleges and universities that are fiscally and institutionally sound and have been for generations.

However, death, and its dismissive cousin, death-by-merger, is reserved for the old and infirm, the shrinking, the undernourished, and the timid, and for the young, the experimental, and specialized. To this segment of the industry, death visits often enough, and threatens often enough, to keep people like me habitually wary.

In Vermont, Windham College succumbed in the early 1980s, as did the fledgling Mark Hopkins College before the decade was out; then Trinity College of Vermont, a Catholic women's institution, in 2000, and Woodbury College was absorbed by Champlain College in 2008. In Massachusetts, Atlantic Union College closed in 2011, Urban College of Boston in 2012, and in 2012 New Hampshire's Chester College went under. Famously, Antioch, in Ohio, succumbed after more than a century (it reopened after some years, unaccredited and struggling). Recently Sweet Briar, in Virginia, announced its closure, but the alumni and others rescued it, at least for the time being.

Most recently and dramatically, in 2016, 200-student Burlington College, in Burlington Vermont, died a painful and public death by fiscal overextension and stunningly inept leadership, after more than 40 years in operation. A rescue team of experienced administrators parachuted in, fought the good fight for a couple of years, but it was too late.

Unlike those examples, the death of an institution often begins with a merger. These are not partnerships or collaborations. They are unequal, where the wealthier, larger institution absorbs, legally and completely, the smaller, weaker institution. One could argue, miserably, that mergers for the lesser participants are not death. If not, then they are transportation into some benign nether world, leaving behind their ledgers, cultures, and missions for storage in some vault in some other place.

There's another critical, personal aspect to endemic institutional fragility: in some perverse way for some of us long timers, it is the odds against a future (and a future paycheck) that makes it all worthwhile, that justifies spending one's effective working years at worthy places generations away from financial stability, demonstrated by periodic crises that threaten everything.

I did look eventually, with Lulu's encouragement, but the job I found in January 2003 required leaving Vermont. Worse, it meant leaving my two senior hockey clubs, and wintertime Tuesday and Friday nights spent at the rink. And the flower farm, its 16 acres, and its uninterrupted 180-degree ridgeline view. And, too, the campus where, cumulatively, I'd lived 22 years of my life, met my wife, enrolled our children, and learned what I thought at the time was about 90 percent of everything one needed to know about nonprofit higher education management.

Our children, Russell and Clara, who graduated the same year from Marlboro, were grown and out of the house. The flower-farming business was slowing down anyway, and Lulu could work summers and take art classes in the winter. We were both attracted to the notion of coastal living. I particularly because fishing for striped bass could easily be substituted for Vermont trout. So off we went, barely three hours away but far enough to land in the middle of Beverly, Massachusetts, on the North Shore of Boston, at Montserrat College of Art, home to 300 undergraduate refugees from traditional higher education. I was the new vice president for advancement, and second in command generally.

Everything was new to us and to me professionally. Not strange, but new and exciting. We rented, then bought a little in-town house where with some head bobbing you could see an orange marker out in the harbor. For the first time in our lives we ordered out food and wine and had it delivered to our door. I walked on sidewalks to work. We had trash pickup. Cell phones worked. We felt like we were living in imperial Rome.

The whole experience, from the paint-splattered studios and white-walled galleries to the shoreside mansions of art collectors and the parade of Yankee wealth, just out of grasp, was all so refreshing after the woods and hills of rural Vermont. And what finer students are there, really, than those whose learning is on display every day? Art college, leading to a BFA, is a clear example of the beauty and power of experiential learning, a practice too often missing from more traditional liberal arts institutions.

We thought it would be my last job, but it didn't last even a thousand days. Major problems, mostly with a micromanaging, budget-cutting president who was increasingly ineffective, were splitting the faculty and staff into camps and clumps of confused employees. And then there was me, impatient, even pushy. I thought I could do better, and it wasn't the first time I'd thought that, even at Marlboro I'd thought that, with both presidents. The truth is, at times I chafed against working for presidents, and, after a polite departure from Montserrat, promised myself I'd never work for one again.

Just two years before I returned to Marlboro in 1983, Rod Gander became its third president. He had been a summer resident with a streamside cottage in Green River, a few miles from the college. Chief of correspondents at Newsweek in New York, Rod was being pressured irrevocably toward the management side of journalism — he hated the idea, so he quit, 50 years old, and moved to Vermont with his wife, Isabelle.

He confessed to me he'd imagined a Vermont college presidency to be a gentle, rural sinecure from which he could write books. That forgivable fantasy crumbled mere weeks into his 15 years of service. Rod was a generation older than I, and we were much alike, but he was more worldly, smarter, and funnier. We were passionate about politics and journalism, the glory days of hockey, poker, fly-fishing, and Marlboro's desperate search for money and students. He repeatedly saved the college, seeming to yank $100,000 rabbits out of plain air. He was a friend and mentor, but there were times I thought I could see the way ahead for Marlboro better then he could. In 1996 Rod retired at 65, as he said he would, so as not to hang on and on as too many college presidents do. He wasn't quite done, and won an open seat in the Vermont senate in 2002, but then died shortly after his second term, in 2007, too young at 76, of cancer.

I had — the question came up and recurs — no inclination to apply for the Marlboro presidency. I don't recall even thinking about it. I was not qualified and certainly not qualified in the eyes of those doing the hiring, my board of 19 years. I wanted change, yes, but I was, after my career there, after my student years there, also wanting out.

Replacing Rod in July 1996 was Paul LeBlanc, still a few years from 40, without an ounce of Ivy League blood in him, and with absolutely no management experience except ideas he'd read about. He had a PhD from Framingham State and the energy of a gang of teenage boys, but I don't think he'd ever hired or fired or even bossed anybody around. His fiscal management experience was nil; his marketing opinions were, well, singular. And everything he knew about student admissions he'd learned in a three-hour meeting with a fellow who ran a successful office at one of the little Ivies, Hamilton or Williams, where full-pay freshmen begin lining up when they're in the seventh grade.

I like to joke I taught Paul how to be a president, something he doesn't fully deny and I'd never disabuse him of, but it's not true. All that lack of knowledge and experience intimidated him not one bit, and his smarts and charm and refreshing ambition carried him through each error and stumble of his first year, and then some. Innovative and bold, he believed in Harvard Business School's Clayton Christenson's ideas about disruptive technologies and innovating at the edges of an institution to avoid being hidebound by traditions and fear of change. A lot of that worked, and a lot didn't. But it had great effect on me and how I was thinking, and I could tell that this was going to be a wildly different ride than the one I'd been on.

I happily worked with Paul for four years, after assuring the board I'd stay at least one with Rod's successor. Paul carried on another two years, never at anything slower than 110 miles an hour. Today he's the hugely successful and entrepreneurial president of Southern New Hampshire University. And he's still a friend.

So, Montserrat turned out not to be my imperial Rome. Instead, I'd closely experienced a liberal arts model I was only vaguely familiar with, the professional college of art, which I became completely enamored of. And I learned much from a community and college that might as well have been 10,000 miles from the college of my immediate past, and the one of my immediate future.

In late summer 2005, I applied and survived a fairly typical months-long presidential selection process and became the new president of

Sterling College in Craftsbury Common, Vermont, a village almost as far north as one can go in Vermont before running into Canada.

The Black River flows on two sides of the common, rounding the southern flank on its way to Newport, Lake Memphremagog, and the Canadian border. The common itself would have made a fine medieval redoubt upon which to build a stout castle. Living there, whenever one leaves one almost immediately heads downhill, to East Craftsbury, Mill Village, or destinations beyond. Ninety percent of the structures on the common — the college, the high school, the residences, the iconic United Church of Craftsbury with its tall, thin steeple, the post office, even the round music bandstand — are white clapboard. There is no code that makes them so. They just are.

The search ended in December but I didn't begin actually begin until July first, the start of the fiscal year. A couple of things happened within a month or two of moving into North House, the president's house, smack in the middle of campus, attached to the post office, across the white-fenced common from the church and the surrounding houses. Besides white clapboard, what fills the eye are Holstein cows and their milking barns, hay fields and fields of corn, maple trees, hills upon hills, and the uncluttered 200-year-old common as large as two football fields. It is all at times achingly beautiful. The New England of your mind.

One of the first things that happened was I came to understand that I knew, at best, not 90 percent but maybe 30 percent of everything one needs to know about nonprofit management to be a college president. Then, in a little ceremony in my own mind, I forgave the three presidents for whom I'd worked for all their transgressions of common sense, their unwise decisions, blundered opportunities, or misguided choices I had so confidently made judgment upon. It was arrogance that made me do it, self-contained, but arrogance nevertheless. It had the consistency of pudding and, upon this revelation, slipped off without argument from me.

Sterling, now with about 125 students, is distinguished by a curriculum that weaves together traditional and experiential academics. It is also the nation's only genuine year-round residential college, conducting three semesters every 12 months. Students work hard, stay enrolled, graduate more quickly than normal, and, as a cohort, I swear, are mentally and physically the healthiest student population I've ever seen anywhere. Sterling also grows and raises a large percentage of its own food, and has the best, least expensive dining room in higher education.

All that and not a spare dollar, an endowment you couldn't trip over in the dark. For six years I paced the Porch of Worry at the rear of the president's house, the gods of anxiety at my side, whispering, urging me on. During those years, deeply formative ones for the college's curriculum, physical infrastructure, and fiscal profile, Sterling also delivered forth a disproportionate bounty of surprises, crises, opportunities, disappointments, and successes.

The second thing I learned, definitely a crisis, escaped its cage hardly a month into my six years. It's always comptrollers who bring the bad news. "You're not going to like this…" is how mine began.

Sterling's comptroller, who was soon to resign and leave me fiscally blind for months, did manage to work through the current budget and that afternoon came down the hall to my corner office. "You're not going to like this," she said. The college was facing a $350,000 deficit, and that was after having to raise $200,000. Before I could manage to fall over dead she added, "We also have some serious cash flow problems you might want to take a look at."

I took everything home, every number and audit we had, and within 24 hours confirmed this was no tsunami barreling toward the college. That was Rod's problem years and years ago. This was more like a cow-sized meteor streaking in from space and aimed to fall exactly on my head 11 months hence. It meant there was, again, no money, and, this time, no plan. And it was all mine.

———

Rod came into my office at Marlboro, down the hall from his, and plopped into the red, as opposed to the green, chair. It had been days since we drove back from Springfield to Vermont, and waited for Julie Kidd to call.

I was typing a story for the alumni magazine, Potash Hill. *I didn't turn around.*

"She called."

I stopped typing.

"She read it. She's going to do the whole thing. Two hundred and fifty-thousand a year for three years. Unrestricted."

The tsunami disappears like fog does, like it was never seriously there. I turn around and see Rod is practically floating from the weight off his shoulders. He's grinning. He starts to sing, holding up his palms — he knows the lyrics to hundreds of tunes, from the 1920s to the mid-1950s — "We're in the money.... The sky is sunny.... Old man depression you are through...."

"Yes," I said, "That's great. But what have you done today to save the place?"

"Not a thing," he said. "I'm waiting for tomorrow when I tell the board we're halfway to a balanced budget. Only another quarter-million to go. And it's only November. It reminds me of the newspaper hawker in Chicago. We'll have to send him to a new corner."

"What hawker?"

"Whatever the headlines were, he stuck with only one call, over and over, for years: 'Many Dead, Many Dying! Many Dead, Many Dying!'"

3

What the Work College Presidents Said

For each of the one million U.S. public charities, 100,000 private foundations, 370,000 other nonprofit entities, including some 2,500 colleges and universities, there is one short document that, if absent or ignored, can result in an organization stumbling around like a drunk on a ship. It is the mission statement, two words that generate 225 million hits on Google.

Colleges, universities, and other established nonprofit institutions always have a mission statement, and it is always applied in strategic ways, the inside front cover, when not the cover itself, of marketing brochures, alumni magazines, fundraising appeals, and grant submissions.

The simplest definition of a mission statement I found amidst those millions on Google was: "A formal summary of the aims and values of a company, organization, or individual."

There are practical reasons for having a mission statement. In higher education they can be thought of as a board-level, formal version of an "elevator talk" — a timely, succinct, positive statement of purpose and direction meant to inspire or inform. Equally, they serve as a test or an initial point of view to new institutional ideas or initiatives.

Well thought out and expressed, they can help keep an institution headed in the direction it wants to go, even as economies and generations reshape its world.

Not surprising, an understanding of mission statements, their uses and importance, is the first subject in the established sequence of courses at a couple hundred colleges and universities that treat non-profit management as a worthy academic pursuit. Whether a student's pursuit begins at a small liberal arts college or large university, at the undergraduate, graduate, or even doctorial level, nonprofit management is big business in higher education, and it all begins (and sometimes ends) with the mission statement.

On academia's heels is an expansive industry of workshops, certifications, presentations, books, and booklets that operate under the general banner *"How to Start and Run a Nonprofit Business."* Many are relatively quick reads and focus on those who want to "Change the World!" and their titles and texts are festooned with exclamation points as a way of demonstrating excitement! for an otherwise utterly prosaic subject. Among these many short works my favorites are the numerically based, as in, *The 10 Best of This! The 17 Most Important of That! The 101 Newest Ideas! Twelve Steps That Will Destroy Your Nonprofit, and You!*

Less quickly read are tome-length collections of essays by people often in the for-profit business of helping colleges and universities with almost any administrative task needed, from maintenance to financial investments. Most of these corporate strategists once served in the non-profit sector for years or decades, before recognizing that management advice was more profitable, and thus took up the mantle of consultant.

Spending an afternoon scanning the web for mission statements is a good way to go blind or to dent the mind, or both. Still, to understand we must look, however briefly. First, my three colleges:

> **Sterling College:** The Sterling College community combines structured academic study with experiential challenges and plain hard work to build responsible problem solvers who become stewards of the environment as they pursue productive lives.

This is a pretty good one, a single sentence well packed, informative and somewhat intriguing. Sterling juggles two mottos, as well: *Fovete*

Stirpes (Nourish the Roots) and, more popular, *Working Hands, Working Minds*.

> **Marlboro College:** The goal of Marlboro College is to teach students to think clearly and learn independently in a structured program of the liberal arts. Students are expected to develop a command of concise and correct English and to strive for academic excellence informed by intellectual and artistic creativity; they are encouraged to acquire a passion for learning, discerning judgment and a global perspective. The College promotes independence by requiring students to participate in the planning of their own programs of study and to act responsibly within a self-governing community.

Years ago Marlboro's statement ended after "to think." Now it seems to put most of the mission's burden on the students rather than the college and its faculty. However, I think it accurately reflects what Marlboro does, especially for a statement that, knowing the college all too well, was constructed democratically by hundreds of people and a heavy handful of committees.

> **Montserrat College of Art:** Montserrat College of Art, an independent institution of art, provides an intensive visual arts education that will enable students to sustain a lifelong involvement in art and design and to become informed, responsible members of society. In addition, Montserrat is committed to contributing to the cultural life of its surrounding communities. Through its degree, diploma, and community-based programs Montserrat offers. . . .

And here Montserrat runs off four more paragraphs that more usefully belong in marketing materials. This is a common error, and a result of the community of people responsible for shaping a statement who just can't stop explaining, can't stop showing off the good stuff.

Montserrat, too, had a very snappy and useful tagline: *Art Changes Everything*. (A tagline attempts to add drama or excitement, usually but not always without the use of an exclamation point. A motto, on the other hand, I understand as a mini-mission statement, providing a little more depth than a mere tagline.)

One could argue that Montserrat, Sterling, and Marlboro were cut from the same cloth, given their overall similarities in size and culture, and in curriculum and liberal philosophy. Their mission statements, however, identify distinct institutions. Extend that across higher education and you gain some insight into the incredible diversity, reflected in an absolute jumble of mission statements, of American higher education.

Two more:

> **Harvard College (1643):** "Let every student be plainly instructed, and earnestly pressed, to consider well that the main end of his life and studies is to know God and Jesus Christ which is eternal life (John 17:3), and therefore to lay Christ in the bottom, as the only foundation of all sound knowledge and learning." While this has certainly been updated, it strikes me as similar to any number of current mission statements of faith-based institutions.

There are about 1,000 sectarian colleges in the US, of which close to half are Christian. One of the smallest is Ecclesia College in Arkansas. Like very nonsectarian Sterling, Ecclesia is one of the seven federally recognized Work Colleges, which I'll explain in a moment.

> **Ecclesia College:** As an institution of higher learning, Ecclesia College mentors effective leaders to strengthen the foundations of society through the life and values of Jesus Christ.

Mission statements are different on the business side, the for-profit side, although they can read similarly. During a long afternoon reading corporate mission statements, what struck me was how little notice is given their genuine mission, which is to make a profit. I found very few corporate statements even noting the importance of providing shareholders healthy returns on their investment. So it is unclear to me the for-profit's statement's actual importance or usefulness.

I pay attention to this sort of nuance because I have a professionally engrained problem with profit. Not normal profit, but gross profit, accompanied and supported by politics and law, resulting in obscene wealth. This problem is a result of so many years in the administrative trenches of under-resourced (what a phrase) colleges. It's an attitude, as well, a pissy one, that profit above a certain level is an astounding, almost environmental, waste of good money.

It is like you are crawling, dying of thirst in the desert and you come upon a man who pours you a small glass of water — it's not nearly enough, you're going to need more — but before your very eyes he continues to pour, overfilling the glass, the water sloshing out and disappearing into the hot sand. That's the money, the water hitting the sand at his feet, instead of being preserved for you. The man does this because he is not paying attention.

What bothers me is how, by needlessly skipping the obvious, the corporate mission statement loses much of its credibility. It's not that business missions or goals are fake, but they are secondary to the reality of first and foremost making a profit. No profit, no product, no service. Mission over.

Colleges, on the other hand, or at least my kinds of colleges, can survive for years without turning a surplus, a nonprofit euphemism for profit. Living eternally in the shadow world of debt and doom, though, is not pretty. It's exhausting and wearing. That year after year there is too little money can be terrifying and normal at the same time. For presidents, endemic deficits are the phantom scolds, the all-consuming things following at a near whisper as you pace the Porch of Worry. Still, as fragile as things may be the mission is intact, even bounding along; so for the mission-driven mind the world is still right, looks pretty good because except for some money, everything's going well, the mission is being fulfilled.

It is early February 2009, and as a nation we are deep into the largest recession since the Great Depression; it is a Sunday afternoon in Washington, DC. I and the other six presidents of the seven federally recognized work colleges are sitting around a conference table in a private room in a Capitol Hill hotel, where hundreds of college and university presidents have assembled for the annual meeting of the National Association of Independent Colleges and Universities (NAICU).

The annual meeting is always held in the nation's capital so presidents can fan out like teams of sappers through the government and buttonhole their congressional and senatorial representatives about higher education issues and deep concerns. On Tuesday I'll head off with 8 or 10 other Vermont presidents for the offices of Senators Leahy and Sanders and Representative Welsh, where we will crowd into their conference rooms, listen to them talk, bring up our stuff, and depart within 15 minutes. But because I'm in the company of my fellow Association of Vermont Independent Colleges (AVIC) presidents, I can't start talking about work colleges, so I leave behind a formal letter with the higher-education staff noting the special concerns of this tiny consortium of seven.

Officially called Work-Learning-Service colleges, each of us receives a portion of a $7 million federal appropriation to help fund and administer a program where all residential students work and are paid for their work. Sterling's share, for instance, was about $80,000 in 2007, and the program cost the college about $200,000, most of that in student wages.

If the seven of us in our private room are at all representative of the hundreds of other attendees, then this is a hotel of misery and resignation. The typhoon of the great recession has swept over us, 99 percent of us, anyway, leaving our campuses torn apart, our students and their families in shock, and, most important in this hotel, our endowments in tatters. About 30 percent or more in tatters, if we average it out.

When Stanford or Harvard loses hundreds of millions, it's serious, of course. But when Berea and two of the other work colleges lose a third of their endowments, it is catastrophic because these colleges are tuition free. They have what you might call working endowments of considerable heft and age, and the money generated directly offsets the cost of free tuition. It's part of the mission.

So here we are:

At the head of the table sits Larry Shinn. He's a huge, heavy man with a big friendly face, glasses, a full head of hair, and he's president of the mother ship of work colleges, Berea, in Boone, Kentucky. He's chairman of this board, one of the original members, and he runs a masterful meeting, grinning, agreeing, contesting, and checking items off the agenda. Larry is, even more so than most college presidents, used to getting his way, of taking charge, of being sure.

Sandy Pfeiffer, president of Warren Wilson College in Asheville, North Carolina, attended the Harvard Seminar for New Presidents with me in 2006, as each of us began our presidencies. Most similar to Sterling with a full agriculture program and an experiential bend to the broader curriculum, Warren Wilson is older and wealthier. Some of Sterling's best students had transferred from Warren Wilson, something I pointed out to Sandy until Sterling hired one of his graduates as farm manager, instead of one of their own. Sandy is a trim man who keeps himself in good shape. And he seems a happy man, too, having finally achieved his longtime goal of becoming a college president.

Sandy and I represented the secular wing of the work college consortium.

Oren Paris, the youngest of us, became president of Ecclesia College, in Springdale, Arkansas, in 1997, when his father, the founder, retired and the son took over. That's the way it is sometimes done in Christian colleges, and it's probably as good a way as any to switch out presidents.

Mim Pride, long-serving president of Blackburn College in Carlinville, Illinois, and the only woman president in the consortium, was also an original member. There seems not a mean bone in her body; she lightly holds your elbow as you stroll down the hotel corridors. She was the group's historian, who regularly and concisely put into context what we were dealing with at any moment. "This all goes back to this..." she would say. And, "This stems from when...." To me, Sandy, and Oren, the newer presidents, the "this's" were very useful, but I think they drove Larry to impatience.

Joe Stepp, president of Alice Lloyd College in Pippa Passes, Kentucky, which like Berea is tuition free, stands almost seven feet tall and is a former college basketball star. He usually carries a dark, leather-bound Bible with him. It would rest on the conference table alongside our notes and briefing papers, budgets, and all that. He was very quiet and when he did speak he always seemed certain of his point of view, and would articulate how that point of view related back to his college and its mission and programs. He must have laughed at different times, though I have no recollection.

College of the Ozarks, Point Lookout, Missouri, was in some ways the most conservative college in the group. Jerry Davis, its president, was tall, thin, rough-faced, serious, and to me looked completely at ease whenever I saw him, while simultaneously appearing wary, watchful. Jerry spoke in an articulated southern drawl inevitably sweet to New Englanders, representing as it does thermal warmth and sunshine. He'd been a college president forever. "Hard Work U," Ozark's tag, guarantees students will graduate debt free, but they will also work 15 hours per week, the most hours among the work colleges.

And finally Sterling, the only member from New England and the one with the shortest workweek, ten hours.

At the conference table, we've taken care of business. The budget has been examined and passed. Our lobbyist has reported on the activities of various members of Congress who might help assure the work college legislation does not get eliminated in this belt-tightening year, like some small creature plucked from the jungle floor. We get our assignments.

———

Larry Shinn checked off the final agenda item, checked his watch against the time allotted on the agenda, and abruptly asked our full-time director and her part-time staffer to leave the room so the presidents could speak off the record.

After Larry watched the door close, he turned, "Tell me, everyone, if you would, if you are comfortable. . . ." he said, looking at each of us, "How much money did your endowments lose?" There was a moment of silence before Larry interrupted himself and said, "I'll start."

Before the 2008 crash Berea had just over one billion in the bank, and was the newest member and the least wealthy among the 100 or so colleges with a billion dollar endowment. After the crash, Berea had something over $700 million left. Instead of retiring as planned, Larry was committed to staying on and reshaping how Berea would work in the future, with far less money for the college, but no disruption in financing 1,500 students.

I was next. "Sterling had an endowment of about $850,000. We lost about $250,000 of that, so we are below corpus and won't have access to any funds for years."

And that's how it went around the table. Brief, resigned statements of huge financial loss and incalculable harm to our colleges, of the still threatening future, and of the inevitable and painful climb back we all must make while cutting expenditures, squeezing down a little further. Except for Warren Wilson, we all learned from Sandy, who was last to report and said, deadpanned, "We didn't lose a nickel, sorry."

"And? So?" said Larry, for all of us.

It was easy enough, Sandy said his college's financial advisors pulled out of the market four months before the crash, simply not believing that what was happening could keep happening.

Well, there wasn't much to say after that, but Larry had another question.

"Mim, Gentlemen," he said, "I would ask us this: would you change your mission to keep your institution alive?"

I don't know what the others were thinking during the silence that followed. But I was thinking, Larry hadn't asked us if we would abandon our mission, just change it. Abandon, no, I'd want no part of that. Only once before, when it looked like Marlboro was going under, really, this time, had this question came up. Just between Rod and me, driving someplace to meet someone. No, we agreed, if it went that far, if there were no more moves to be made, we'd feel better closing down, rather than being run over or taken over. The great experiment done, true to the last, your fault, my fault, no one's fault.

Larry went around the table.

I went first and said, "Yes, sure, I'd change the mission. I'd adjust it to reality, as it is now."

It was pretty much the same with everyone. Live to fight another day. Sure we're all about mission, but we're not crazy. And the question is hypothetical.

Until we got to Ecclesia and Oren Paris, last. I don't know what

Oren looked like when angry, but he sounded a little angry. He just shook his head. "No. no. Wouldn't change a word."

In a practical sense, there's not a lot of wiggle room in Ecclesia's mission statement. I wanted to ask Oren whether, perhaps, expansion of the mission might be acceptable. I mean, Harvard's current mission statement looks nothing like the first one from the 1600s; that is what you need to do if you want to live for hundreds of years.

But that wasn't the point for me. The economic damage was done. The reality, still at this moment, was overwhelming. Each of us (except for Sandy, the anomaly) was responsible for somehow patching back together everything that had been torn apart, and none of us had experience in doing that. What struck me was here we were at a very dark hour, worse than any of us had ever experienced, seven presidents representing over 5,000 students, a thousand or so teachers and staff, generations of alumni, the broader communities in which our colleges lived, as well as a few hundred years of higher education practice, and what do we do?

We sit around and worry about our missions, seeing how they still fit, measuring their worth against this yet again new world. If they are intact — if they are worthy — then the essentials of life are secure and we'll work through these problems with that in mind. Phew!

4

Matters of Governance and Cocktails

In addition to a single president, it takes four groups of willing participants to operate a college: students, faculty, staff, and trustees. That's a college today. In its ancient and simplest form, which some academics stridently believe still exists, only two groups were needed, students and teachers. But presidents and staff, some crude version of them in any case, must have evolved soon after because without them teachers and students alone would have starved to death. And finally, toward the end of this imaginary evolution of the entire beast, in wandered a few trustees, then small herds of them, all seemingly far removed from the axis of teaching and learning, but there they were, rather suddenly, at the top of the heap.

Well, sort of at the top. Who rules? Students, of course. They outnumber everyone else, they pay the money, and they demand attention. Faculty actually rule: it's their deep traditions, commitments, and learning that both maintain and propel the academy, unquestionably. Veterans of the president's chair have no illusions on this point — they rule, they lead, it is built into the position; leadership required on an hour-by-hour basis.

Well, yes, but the Association of Governing Boards (AGB) would have you believe that it is exclusively from boards of trustees that balanced, forward-looking policies and decisions descend upon the rest of the institution in a steady, relatively benign reign of authority and leadership, the result of a board's sober thinking, motivated committees, and expertise in being an effective board of trustees.

AGB, a nonprofit itself with over a thousand institutional members, predominantly independent liberal arts colleges, focuses wholly on academic governing boards and boards of institutionally related foundations. Their mission is to improve academic governance through publications, programs, and advocacy. AGB holds its annual National Conference on Trusteeship in different cities around the nation, it conducts and publishes studies and surveys, and it goes to battle with the Securities and Exchange Commission or the IRS when they push into AGB territory. If all that isn't enough, if you can't find solutions to your trustee problems in AGB's deep and searchable website, you can just hire them outright and a team of expensive-for-sure consultants will dive in and help.

So, you have questions in topics related to governance and the role of the board of trustees? You need go no further than the AGB homepage and their list of 10 *Governance Topics*, a few truncated samples of which are below. Click on any one and a world of facts and figures and well-written commentary appear before you. You can taste the dry adroitness and professionalism of AGB right away:

> Academic and Student Affairs: *A board's responsibilities for academic affairs cover the gamut...*
> Ethics and Accountability: *Expectations of trustees have undergone a dramatic change...*
> Finance and Endowment: *Trustees have no greater responsibility...*
> Fundraising: *Fundraising is one of board's most basic and important responsibilities...*
> The Presidency: *Today's higher education presidency is a constant mix of challenges that combines an expectation for exceptional executive leadership, academic innovation, fundraising prowess, and a public profile...*

With Governance Topics on its homepage, you can imagine how exciting things get further along. Over the years at various conferences and workshops I've run into a number of AGB consultants: great listeners, smart talkers, confidence builders, and business suits worn so comfortably you might wonder whether they even own other sorts of clothes. So, not demeaning, but in more rural areas we refer to such people as Suits. As in, "There are Suits on campus," or "It was a good meeting, full of Suits."

Between the Suits and the website, which represents a researched-based approach to institutional governance, AGB misses nothing in depicting a formal, studied, top-to-bottom, reasoned, orderly system of high-level academic governance but which is, unfortunately, completely unobtainable by normal human beings, enveloped as they must be in the deep cultures and turbulent realities of their institutions. To me, any schematic approach to governance in colleges so greatly diminishes the influencing twists and turns of culture, politics, relationships, egos, money, and the lack of money as to be misleading, even disorienting, although like a subway map, it may help get you there, but only through a rumbling dark tunnel.

Perhaps because of the tunnel effect, boards of trustees and even senior administrators are sometimes slow to understand the genuine depth of a fiscal crisis beyond its worrisome annual operating deficit, bad as that can be. With their focus on that, however, governance boards often do not perceive the loss of institutional muscle tone and the onset of institutional fatigue, which is a kind of community-wide disillusionment, bordering on depression that stems from a complex of poor decision-making, institutional rigidity, lack of attention, and self-deception.

At Sterling in the fall of 2006, for instance, the board as a whole was less than fully cognizant of the $350,000 deficit that appeared, apparently out of nowhere, the first month of my presidency. That was bad enough. But different, larger fiscal crises were brewing across campus: the college's two largest dormitories, Hamilton and Jefferson, were practically unlivable; a student attrition problem was draining money from the institution; and a severe maintenance backlog was expanding from debilitating to dangerous, to name just three.

When fiscal disruption is undeniable, like a threatening face smack up to your face, governance weakens and energy is turned into lamentations over lack of funds and what to do about it. A sort of restrained, slow-motion panic sets in and other concerns of governance and the board members who concentrate on those areas are shunted aside. Everything becomes short term. Bad policies and nervous egos are delivered up as if by uniformed couriers. Open doors become closed doors. The pathways of good or at least normal governance, once so clear, are torn up, their complexity and nuance revealed and troublesome.

What happens then? Well, luckily, a substantial degree of institutional governance swings through the president's office and is hurled back to the board of trustees for yet another go-around. Critically, when that happens the other parts of a college, like teachers and students, libraries and labs, field trips, all-nighters, grades, meals, books, Wikipedia, Google, and texting all move along *exactly as they should*, concerned but unbothered for the most part by the machinations of the board and president. I don't mean for weeks or semesters, but for years if necessary.

There's an expression that college presidents get the boards they deserve, which I don't understand because the board is in place when you arrive. Over years you will build or help build the board you deserve, that's certain, but at first you actually inherit the board your predecessor built and that carries his or her DNA, sometimes in bucket loads.

Bylaws, on the other hand, are an institution's unique step-by-step guide to governance, inherited by every president and every board except the document's originators. Bylaws evolve by amendments, but usually slowly and often catching up after the fact. When well attended to, one can follow the development of a college's governance history through its bylaws, and from that get indications of its culture over time.

The most confusing language in Sterling's bylaws seemed to indicate the president could not fire the vice president, as he was an officer of the college. To me, that was very strange. Everybody in a college works for the president, and the president works for the board of trustees; it's that simple. A vice-president responsible to the board cannot be on the staff, really, because he reports to the board. Nor is he a trustee but an informant, the ear of the board, where they get the scoop without going through the president, which doesn't make a lot of sense, one scoop being as good as another, which is why the practice is unheard of.

I went to the source, the vice president himself, our only Harvard-trained academician, Ned Houston, who was the longest-serving staff and faculty member at the college, and had served as the de facto president on a number of occasions. Ned was as iconic a figure to Sterling as the Common was to Craftsbury Common. Any biography of Sterling would have to be in part one of Ned, as well. He'd devoted his entire professional life and much of his personal life to Sterling, as had others, but just not for as many years or with such consistent effectiveness and, mostly, good humor.

After puzzling the thing through, we weren't sure whether I could fire him. Not liking messy bylaws, I would have preferred changing or removing that section, but the ensuing debate would only serve to take attention away from more critical matters. . . like gigantic deficits they were unaware of, student attrition they thought was normal, and dormitories festering with rot and mold.

It turned out the whole notion of tiny Sterling needing a vice president at all stemmed directly from the board's infighting, intriguing, and general dysfunction even as it struggled to establish itself as a two-year institution. Steve Wright, my predecessor's predecessor, assumed the presidency at the urging of the board, of which he was a member, only to be run out two and a half years later despite his effectiveness and (relative) popularity with the faculty. Bitterness lingered, and there followed a series of even shorter timers, some ineffectual and at least one disastrous before Jed Williamson, in his 10-year presidency (1996-2006), managed to provide a level of institutional and board-level calm, very much to my benefit. Steve Wright, the former commissioner of Vermont's Department of Fish and Wildlife under the Kunin administration and who still resides in Craftsbury Common, went on to a distinguished career with the

National Wildlife Federation, and thus attesting there is life after a college presidency.

So Ned's position was created so as Sterling presidents came and went, and board members came and went and bickered, there was in the vice president a firewall between the two sides of the college, the teaching and learning side, and the dysfunctional governance side.

Whether it was the unusual bylaw or simply the competence of Ned and Jed, it worked. By the time I arrived, those turbulent years were looked upon with and without bitterness, but mostly as growing pains, as a struggle the college survived and learned from. Ned carried on until his retirement a year after mine, but the VP position lives on in the bylaws, an historic relic not to be misjudged.

I'd seen them, performance reviews, over the years at Marlboro, particularly under President Paul LeBlanc (1996-2003), who to his credit was all for new management concepts and methodologies, including performance reviews, I suppose, as opposed to the considerably more patrician (but hardly passive) approach of Rod Gander.

Employees are reviewed by the boss; bosses by the president; the president by the board of trustees. I've been forced to review many people over my career, having been a boss for a long time. It's a tricky business, even more so with the unstructured methods we employed in the less-structured years before HR (Human Resources) offices took fashion and took over. Rod underwent of couple of reviews in his 15 years, but they were not rigorous things back then, at least not when the board and the president were sympatico. When Paul was all about reviews, I was, finally, selected for one. The head of the review committee was appointed. She took it on like a mission, alerting the community, seeking input, reflections, and answers to specific questions, and a number of interviews with me. Such complexities for something so simple.

Then everything went quiet. The report was in her hands, or being compiled by her hands, who knows? Months went by. Then, suddenly, she was gone. Another job. I don't recall. My review never saw the light of day, and I did not seek it out but suffered a tinge of loss.

As Sterling's president I was reviewed by the board after about seven months on the job. It was quick, informal, a simple interview with the board leadership, and I think scheduled just in case the new president turned out — which under normal circumstances very few of us do that quickly — to be worrisome or even disastrous.

However measureable, the performance level of a board of trustees doesn't come cheap. Let's look at some numbers to illustrate:

At Marlboro, averaging four meetings per year over 19 years, I attended 76 four-hour-long board meetings. Those meetings occurred during weekend-long board of trustee gatherings, which were full of other meetings. I would normally serve as the staff representative for three committees: development, governance, and marketing and as secretary to executive and finance. So that's another 304 two-hour meetings over 19 years, for a grand total of 380 formal board-level meetings. That boils down to six eight-hour workdays per year of actual seat time.

Marlboro's board-level governance model was easily recognized as standard, despite that much of the institution revolved around a town meeting system of operational governance.

Preparing for trustee meetings began weeks ahead of time, because each weekend-long meeting required producing a thick "Board Book" with agendas, past meeting minutes, notes on the upcoming meetings by the president or staff, the weekend's schedule, and documentation of all sorts: charts, graphs, spreadsheets, reports. Accommodations had to be made for trustees, their spouses when present, and all the participating faculty and staff to be fed, repeatedly, and usually well. And there was the inevitable formal or near formal dinner or two, always preceded by a cocktail hour. There was always wine with dinner, and student servers.

A Marlboro trustee's weekend starts Friday afternoon with the executive and finance committee meeting, followed by cocktails and dinner and conversation usually in and around the meeting's issues. On Saturday the full board meets in the afternoon following a morning of committee meetings. Work wraps up at five sharp, for cocktails and dinner at six.

The third and final step of a trustee's weekend is the cleaning up, paying the student helpers, running around to make sure staff members are writing up their committee reports, and sitting down with the president and what's left of the college liquor cabinet for a long debrief.

What's the value of all these meetings? Are they themselves cost effective? All independent liberal arts colleges I know of have boards of trustees, but there's nothing in law I'm aware of that requires them; most states document only the names of the officers of the corporation, a president, vice president, and treasurer.

Consider my six full workdays a year sitting at board and committee meetings, then estimate and add three hours of pre- and post-work for each meeting, and keep working through until the end, where I count a total of roughly 24 eight-hour workdays a year devoted exclusively to official board business. Just as roughly, that's where I earned 10 percent of my wages.

The figure doesn't include the thousands of other contact/work hours I devoted to the board and its members over the years; doesn't include the costs of food and liquor, or student wages; it leaves out the work hours of support staff in the development/events office. And it doesn't include any of the president's time, which probably exceeded mine by 10 or 15 percent.

Add all that up. Throw in some staff and dean hours devoted to pre-, post-, and the actual meeting — who knows? You easily come up with 40 eight-hour days per meeting, so figure about $6,500 staff costs per year. Now food and liquor, very roughly, $2,500 per meeting for another $10,000. Finally, throw in another $25,000 per year on the myriad other trustee-related activities, the hundreds of meetings and communications, the sometimes extensive travel to or with board members.

So, quickly, little Marlboro College was spending *at least* $71,500 per year in feeding, housing, and supporting about 30 trustees. That's about $600 per member, per meeting.

A lot of money when you're losing money.

Expensive or not, good trustees, people with applicable knowledge, access, or skills you need to run a college or university, are difficult to get. Really good ones are also wealthy and philanthropic, as rare as buried treasure and long-lost works of art. On the other hand, letting go of the tired, the ornery, the aggressive, the know-it-all, and the useless to make room for more treasure, or expertise, or youth, or whatever, is as difficult as bringing people on to a board in the first place.

When a college has strict term limits for board members, usually three three-year terms, and a valued trustee reaches that limit, you want to keep her, but your own rules are in the way. The only institutional hedge is a bylaw providing reelection after a year's wait. If the call doesn't come, your trustee days are over. It's tricky for everyone. And still, waiting nine years to off a board member who is driving everyone nuts cannot represent good governance.

At colleges with unlimited terms where the underperformer threatens to be with you forever, you *really* have to be rid of them, ease them off the board at an end of a term or, eventually, an entire board can stultify.

It's an imperfect science, the whole thing.

Some few years before the turn of the millennium at Marlboro, without term limits, we — actually I — figured out how to keep the best and remove the worst. After long debate, the nominations committee decided that rather than almost automatically reelecting members every three years, we'd simply explain to those affected about the critical need to add new members. We'd point out their obvious commitments elsewhere, or whatever it was that kept them from attending meetings, or that directed their philanthropy elsewhere. We would emphasize their value and they would understand, and, of course, it was the decision of a committee. Nothing personal.

We could, in other words, counsel them off the board even after a single term, if that was called for.

In the late 1990s we had flagged five members who might be "released" off the board: they missed too many meetings, skipped a retreat, didn't join the annual fund, disrupted committee meetings, desperately wanted to get into management, or were simply passive to the point of annoyance. As for the counseling off, the vice chairman of the board was selected for this job. He was a stalwart trustee, long serving, a former dean turned investment advisor for, as I understood it, a single person. He was cheerful, positive, one of those really good ones, somewhat reluctant at this assignment, but willing, always willing. After all, what's a vice chairman for?

So, a difficult board management issue put to rest. A genuine middle road. You keep the good ones and let go the others, without offense. Excellent.

We armed the vice chair with all the information he would need for each of them, one file folder apiece. Let me know how it goes, I said. We're all anxious to hear.

Weeks went by, and no word. I emailed and asked, anything I can help with? Nothing.

The president called — no response.

Eventually the vice chair did call. I grabbed a pencil and got ready to write.

"Well," he said, "I've reached them all and the result is clear: don't send me to shoot them."

"Did you shoot any?" I asked.

"They're all back on. Just couldn't do it."

He just couldn't do it because to a man — these were all men — all were surprised at any implication that they were not anything but, if not ideal, then certainly conscientious and effective board members. Our vice chair was not there to argue. Our efforts were shaped by a pathetic hope that the self-evident was, in the end, self-evident.

———

But there was perfect, too, in a handful of gentlemen and two women among the long-tried members of the Marlboro board, back then, when possible closure of the college was quietly discussed, in the mid- and late-1980s.

There was Dick Taylor, a retired lawyer who lived at the UN Towers on the east side of Manhattan. Thin, polite, businesslike, he was in law school when drafted in 1942, ending up on Eisenhower's staff. He'd tell stories of delivering early morning debriefings to Patton, Montgomery, Bradley, and scores of lesser generals after spending the night with other lieutenants consolidating battle reports. He told us he and a few others hand-delivered Eisenhower's orders to delay D-Day by 24 hours.

John Straus's grandparents were the famous elderly couple who died together, refusing to part, when the Titanic went down. He lived in an enormous, dark apartment on the east side across from Central Park; he and his wife, whom everyone called Bunny, also owned a nearby country house in Bedford, NY, with a large pond and garages full of antique cars. John was the head of the student flying club at Harvard when WWII broke out. He ended up a flight instructor at a base in Louisiana, where he spent the war flying the newer, faster, more powerful fighter planes being developed, and teaching experienced pilots their nuances. Wealthy, pleasantly egotistical, predictable, and generous, John was, like these others, an ideal trustee.

Holbrook Davis, who owned a garden center on Cape Cod and admitted he'd flunk out of Harvard if he ended up there today, was the youngest of the WWII veterans and spent his service time in the navy. He was on board and on his way toward the kamikaze-filled skies over the Japanese islands when the war ended. The garden center kept him busy; the source of his wealth was his own and, primarily I believe, his wife's family. He was more conservative than many others on the board, and disdained the graphic humor students published in their occasional literary publications. One such cartoon cost the college thousands of dollars when "Brookie," as he was called, immediately refused to make a second annual fund contribution when I asked him.

"What do you think about that?" he asked, not angrily.

"I think it's a pretty understandable thing to do," I said.

Lil Farber, a small, intense, Jewish woman from New York City, with an easy laugh, had married and divorced a very wealthy Floridian after three children. She became a New York City photographer and collector of some note when she and her companion, Bern, moved to Newfane, Vermont, where she met Rod Gander and found herself on the Marlboro board. Six years later she became the first woman chair, just in time. Lil was the sort of person who was audited by the IRS every year because she gave away more money than she could afford to.

It was Lil who urged Rod to let go the then-current development director. Like me, Rod was practically useless when it came to firing people. But he managed it this time because Lil hounded him until he faced up to it. Then we searched high and low for an experienced fundraiser. We put out ads. We interviewed people. We called friends and colleagues. It dragged on. One day Rod said, "Why don't you do it?" And after a moment I said I would.

Six months later it was obvious that something about this arrangement bothered Lil. I asked Rod, but he just shrugged his shoulders. It was mystifying because I knew Rod had checked with her before offering me a job I hadn't applied for. It was 1987, I'd been back at the college for four years and felt hardly proficient in what I was supposed to be doing, and now struggled with a considerably more complex set of problems and issues, especially at the board and major donor levels. I wondered if there's been a miscommunication between Rod and Lil.

I lay low. Then one morning Lil called and asked to meet in Brattleboro for coffee at 10. Intrigue is part of the concentrated political world that is small organizations, so such an open-ended invitation was not out of the ordinary, and I said of course, and drove the 11 downhill miles to what I figured was going to be my fate.

In town Lil was nervous when we sat down. She did not order coffee or anything.

She said, "I have to tell you this. I know you're not going to like it. But now that you are the development director you have to . . . you just must . . . it's not going to work unless you do. . . ."

"Do what, Lil?" I interjected. She was so uncharacteristically distraught she shook her head, stood up, took my hand, and led me out the door onto Main Street.

"We're going to Mann's," she said.

Yikes! Mann's, just across the street, was the only men's clothing store in town, in southern Vermont for all I knew. I'd never been inside.

"You need better clothes. I know you can't afford them."

"Lil!" I said in alarm. We were on the sidewalk in front of Mann's. She had me by the elbow. "Really, you don't. . . ."

"I do," And in she pulled me.

It took well over an hour. It was hilarious. It was awful, with Lil waiting outside the short-curtained changing room, or handing me sweaters, or fingering silky ties. "I'm going to get you back for this," I called out.

I came away with a suit, some oxford shirts, a vest, three pairs of pants — trousers, that is — a pair of dress shoes, two ties, and a snappy blue sweater vest.

How word of this mortifying experience flashed through the administrative offices of Marlboro before I returned well after lunch, I have no idea but strongly suspect Lil reported to the president and the president delighted in spreading the story.

"So where are your new duds?" my secretary asked.

Then Rod walked in and sat heavily, grinning, in the green chair. "I sure wish Lil would take me out shopping," he said.

Even Lulu took advantage. "What, no socks?"

Most important, there was Jerry Aron, recruited by his old friend Dick Taylor who lived higher up in the UN Towers. Immediately after Japan's surrender Jerry, a 24-year-old junior officer, was ordered to secure the Tokyo telephone exchange. With interpreters and others he figured he'd personally go to the exchange and find out what it was, having no idea at all. He was brought to an enormous room where 300 kimono-clad telephone operators rose in unison, stepped to the side of their stations, and bowed deeply. It all looked secure to him. From there he went to Nagasaki.

We had a vital non-trustee, too, in Elizabeth McCormack. In the late 1960s Elizabeth was a Catholic nun and president of Manhattanville College, in Tarrytown, NY, when she fell in love with the college's comptroller, whom she had hired. That was Jerry Aron.

Rod Gander and Jerry Aron got along right off and built a friendship that shared humor and determination. Jerry marveled at the horrible condition of the college's finances and the devotion of the faculty and students to their academics. He used his short stature — he and Elizabeth were equal in height — and his gravelly voice to stand and lecture the other board members on the importance of the college and the inevitability of ultimate success.

The relationship between Jerry the trustee, Rod the president, and

Elizabeth the advisor was based on a genuine friendship built on an unspoken strategy that acknowledged only one way the college could get out of the mess it was in, and that was money. Big money. Millions of dollars. Nothing else mattered, after mission, of course.

When Jerry came onto the board, Elizabeth had been the personal philanthropic advisor to the Rockefeller brothers, with an office 60 stories up in Rockefeller Center, for many years. A lifetime trustee at Hamilton College, Rod Gander's alma mater, Elizabeth was soon to be appointed the chair of the board of the MacArthur Foundation. At that point she was, undoubtedly, one of the most influential women in America, all five feet four inches of her. And, of course, she knew a lot of powerful people, knew their interests, knew what they wanted and needed. No name-dropper, she was circumspection itself, except once when seated next to Harrison Ford at some event. "Now that's the way a woman wants to be treated," she said, showing off the photograph.

Marlboro had never met people quite like Jerry and Elizabeth. And neither of them had ever run into anything quite like Marlboro. It was a beautiful thing, the thin green line from Dick Taylor to Jerry, from Jerry to Elizabeth, from Elizabeth to Julie Kidd, then from Jerry and Rod and Paul LeBlanc to, ultimately — it took over a decade — the only thing that mattered, the big money that would anchor the endowment we were determined to create.

John Straus and Dick Taylor were board members when I was a student at Marlboro and both remained on the board after I'd gone, until indeed they were gone, or had "fallen in," an expression Dick Taylor used once, asking whether a certain individual had fallen in. Did he mean fallen into line? Or fallen into the grave, with a thud? I never got a clear answer.

The others, except for Jerry and Lil, had been on the board for many years by the time I returned in 1983 as alumni director and editor of *Potash Hill*. As other members came and went, these and a number of others became the hardcore trustees, who had been wrestling with fiscal problems for decades and who never panicked.

They are all gone now, except for Elizabeth, as are their cohorts, Fred Kunreuther, Ragnar Naess, Mary Jane Whitehead, all those old hands who, there's no other word for it, fell in love with Marlboro and gave time — decades — and money, and houses, and charitable remainder trusts.

Their memorial services were held at the college, as they had wished. I spoke at Rod's. A few years later, I spoke at Lil's. I sat with Fred in the local hospital the day before he died.

So yes, if you remember the question, boards of trustees are worth the money, the work, the patience. They work for free, after all, and what they put in of themselves individually and collectively as a governing body can have incalculable benefit to an institution. It's their place as much as anyone's. Just differently so.

But let me tell you: you spend years with these people, if you and they last that long. Professionally, you are "building relationships" but in reality you are committing to them institutionally and, whether you want to or not, personally. But they're not friends. Not the kind you invite over for dinner, or even out for a social cup of coffee. You know things about them, about their finances, their wills, their families, and their fears that their friends don't know. They don't know much about you. The strangeness of the relationship is revealed when you leave, when, after a couple of decades in their company you take a new job, and they stay as they were. You don't call them. They don't call you. There is a loss for both, but there is nothing to reach across with — the bind of the institution has snapped. It was all business, after all.

5

Whores and Slaves

When you ain't got nothing, you got nothing to lose, Bob Dylan sang in my head as I sat, staring at a stack of papers, reports, and notes from phone conversations about a huge, multiyear federal Department of Education grant. These sorts of million dollar grants were too big, too specialized, and too full of process and procedure for a single individual to wrestle down. At what Rod and I referred to as "real colleges" whole teams of people took on the sorts of federal grants I was interested in: specifically, the Title III, Strengthening Institutions Grant. It was massive, I learned from a discouraged development officer who'd floundered badly in his attempt and was quitting the race. It was overwhelming, impossible. Except for 350-student College of the Atlantic, one of Marlboro's toughest competitors, in Bar Harbor, Maine. They did it. A vice president, Ted Kaufman, designed and wrote a Title III application just two years before. In fact, he had written two successful Title III grants that changed the physical and academic infrastructure of that institution: building programs, modernizing, becoming electronic.

I spoke to Rod as he thumbed through my pile of research. Marlboro was closing in on desperation, so, I suggested, what's another thousand bucks to fly me down to Washington for a workshop? Just to see the reality of the idea, see if there was anyone, on the staff or among the grantees, who might help.

"You think you can put this thing together?" Rod asked.

"If Ted Kaufman and COA can," I said.

The rewards were tremendous, I explained. We should try. How hard can it be?

Title III: Round One

It is late fall 1990, about two in the morning when my forehead slams into the heavy metal table in the sleeper compartment of the Amtrak train. It wakes me up. Papers all over the place, yellow legal pads with page after page of writing, in pencil, two large three-ring binders, each half full, and a dozen titled file folders. The train has stopped. I don't know where or why because it stops all the time, in the middle of nowhere. I climb off, groggy, and smoke a cigarette. The conductor waves at me and I climb back on, sit down amidst the piles, and randomly choose a file folder, titled Activity Two: Rationale and Budget, Year Three: Columns.

I take up my pencil and begin again, meticulously completing each square in each of the five columns as I had already done for Years One and Two. If I could complete this section, then maybe I could sleep for a bit and as soon as possible start rewriting the 30-page narrative that described one of the two projects, to wire the campus for Internet, and to modernize the library's card catalogue. This round, it was a three-year, $600,000 grant. In Washington, it was also a culture and a well-established bureaucracy within Department of Education, an even larger bureaucracy.

The train is returning me to Albany, New York, from a small Illinois station somewhere between Detroit and Chicago. How would I know where? I took a cab from the small station to the four-floor motel and met the senior development officer for a large public technical college that was, in their successful grant, an important component of the retooling of the U.S. auto industry. I'd located him through a Title III staffer at the Washington workshop, who had warned me I was already late in beginning such an effort and most real consultants were booked solid. So Bob in Illinois was the only one willing to help me understand and write — and write in a way no one should be asked to write — the Title III application.

We had pushed the beds aside, called for two tables, and for 26 of the next

36 hours before I boarded the train back home, we sat across from each other writ-
ing, figuring budgets, working through levels of details and resource projections
only a decades-old bureaucracy could have developed, defended, and been proud of.

I had taken the train because I could work all the way out and all the way
back. Time was short. I had exactly 45 days in which to complete the 170 or so
pages required. My assistant at Marlboro, armed with an electric typewriter, spent
hours typing repetitive budgets, activities, results, etc. into small boxes within pages
of forms. I had moved a computer and printer, huge things back then, into the cel-
lar of our home so I wouldn't have to go to the college and be distracted by any-
thing. I did go in for an hour or two after lunch, my only break before a late after-
noon and evening in the basement. I worked 43.5 days and evenings, only taking
off Christmas Day and half the day before, to shop.

The proposal was due in Washington on a date in January. You get a mailed
receipt. Then you wait until March for the results of three readers. Starting at
100, it is then downhill: they grade your application moving down and nicking
off half a point here, a half point there. Then some sort of administrative review
follows and a staff member calls.

I picked up the phone, and just listened. I'd done miserably. Off the mark
entirely with an 87. The cutoff, she said, was 98.5. Only applications graded
above 98.5 were awarded.

I walked down the narrow, second-floor hallway of Mather House, a creak-
ing, ancient Vermont farmhouse that used to be a dormitory, and told Rod the
Title III application was a bust. We mourned for five seconds, being, now, pro-
fessional absorbers of discouraging news.

"You going to try again?" he asked.
"I am. I should. If we have the money."
"Are you going to start earlier this time?
"Next week," I said.

Colleges are meant to grow old, to live long, long lives. It's like survival
rates among humans: if a child survives the first few years the odds of
a long life increase. In young colleges born poor, infancy and its dangers
stretch on 50 years or more. After that, chances improve.

Or so we hoped, because as Marlboro approached its 50th anniversary we were making plans to launch the kind of fundraising campaign that could, under the right circumstances, generate endowment gifts.

I knew, Rod knew, the board of trustees knew, all the consultants and all the fundraising firms knew that having an endowment, a large, protected corpus of money usually assembled over generations of specific gifts, sometimes created from a single gift, was an institution's first bulwark against financial disruption, even economic collapse. The trick, of course, was an endowment's permanent nature: only its growth and dividends could be spent, which is why to be effective it had to be big.

Without endowment earnings absorbing some of the shock of bad times, or affording investment in good times, a college is dependent upon making a profit, a "surplus" in nonprofit terms. Ironically, the only way to be a fiscally secure nonprofit institution is to have enough wealth in the bank that you don't need to earn a profit.

The problem for Marlboro was how to get one, especially when posting significant deficits year in and year out.

An annual deficit — Marlboro's red ink ran anywhere between $100,000 and $300,000 a year — is like an old smelly dog with rotten teeth and patchy fur that refuses to die. Not a kindly, ancient, deserving old dog, but one that still bites and hates children and craps anywhere it wants. And the dog wasn't yours to begin with. Some idiot brought it on campus years ago, and now the damn thing causes nothing but trouble and refuses to leave. Worse, it appears at inconvenient times, snarling under the table during board meetings, or lying about in the sun attracting flies, prompting a prospective donor or a foundation representative to ask, in alarm, "What the hell is that?!"

Marlboro was starting to raise more money in the early 1990s, over $400,000 annually and growing. But the deficit ate it up each year, ate it as fast as we could make it, and we'd be in a hole again before the leaves turned red in the Vermont fall foliage.

Given everything the college had survived over the past decade, we were all determined to make the most of a 50th birthday. But what to do? We didn't have the experience or the constituencies to conduct a successful endowment campaign in celebration. We didn't have the money it takes to go out and make money, especially endowed money that sits in the bank. We needed money we could spend.

So we did what any other upstanding college would have done, we put together the ever-useful, fully authentic, "comprehensive campaign," meaning every dollar that comes to the college for the duration is counted toward the goal. Nothing is too specific. The individual area goals are shaped to stay away from the endowment and to feed the dog, feed it enough so it dies. That's the real goal, in what amounted to a practice campaign. Then we'd be ready for a real campaign, the campaign for endowment.

In the meantime, our *50th Anniversary Campaign*, 1991-1996 would have all the appearances of a big multiyear capital or endowment drive: first, an elaborate dance with the wealthier board members and a handful of others, looking for what they see in such an effort, all on the quiet for now. Second, an expensive "feasibility study" conducted one-on-one with a couple dozen of our most generous, or most wealthy, or best connected friends by the college's "outside counsel." Third, a handsome brochure and other documentation with goals and timeframes, the lead gifts, and the 100 percent involvement of the board. Then you make calls and ask, "I'd like to come down and talk with you about the campaign and the materials I sent last week." Then you go down and talk and ask for money, a specific amount, usually. You know quite a bit about this person — this couple — because although anonymous, the outside counsel has indicated to you how one might best approach this particular friend, parent, alumna, or neighbor. If they're not quite ready this time, you can come back. The campaign will run for five years and all kinds of good stuff is going to happen.

But not exactly on schedule.

Here's what happened. If you ever get into this business, try not to let it happen to you.

Every elaborate campaign, especially the type linking everyone, the whole college community on campus and across the globe, to an important and party-worthy milestone, like 50 years, is, in reality, aimed at very few people, in our case back then fewer than 40 individuals and couples. By itself, Marlboro's alumni body, one year achieving a remarkable 60 percent giving rate, still could not generate the kind of response that would earn Marlboro $5 million in five years.

It's a fundraising axiom: 98 percent of the money will be given by 2 percent of contributors to a big money campaign. More current perhaps: 99 percent of the money from 1 percent of the entire constituency.

In any case, after a lot of work designing goals and timeframes, and putting it together in a draft document, and leaving plenty of room for input from our top donors, we put our outside counsel on the road to interview some of those friends of the college, our most influential friends, and the board leadership.

This was Carol O'Brien, an independent consultant for just this sort of thing and the only one Rod or I ever met whom we trusted completely. It was her knowledge, her smarts. She was as kind as a mother, could listen to you when you weren't even talking, which somehow helped people open up to her beyond the dozen or so questions of the confidential interview.

Within a couple of weeks Carol called for a meeting and informed us, kind as a mother, that our *50th Anniversary Campaign* was dead in the water. That is, she said, until you can explain in detail how you are going to get the college out of its financial doldrums (such a gentle word she used). They want to help, are prepared to help, but not if their money is going down the rat hole again, Carol noted, quoting one anonymous interviewee. They wanted to know how the numbers add up. What is the plan? Where is your future? Only then will you have enough to get going, but not now.

We had to reconfigure everything. Rod had to come up with a plan, which he did. It was beautifully written and the numbers were orderly, clear, and everything in the five-page report added up to success, to coming out of the campaign debt-free, deficit-free. The whole thing was balanced precariously on a set of fiscal assumptions clearly stated and backed up with charts and graphs. But we knew what it was — a plan held together with gum and rhetoric and a single focus, the goddamn dog.

Title III: Round Two
Winter/Spring 1991
This time, I found Vince Norelli. An independent, full-time Title III consultant, from DC.

Good thing, too, because this time, because of a change in the Title III law, the grant was for five years and $1.7 million.

Vince charged a flat fee, $10,000, and he didn't write the grant but reviewed and edited every part you wrote, every section, subsection, list, table, timeline, budget, rationale, on and on and on. He kept you on task, so to speak, and he watched the clock and kept you up with it.

He paid meticulous attention to the wording of the Title III law, the evolutionary complexity of which rivaled the very best of federal bureaucratize, and to which the Title III staff was tethered. I got my ticket and flew to DC for every Title III workshop and to meet the staff, ask questions, and work with Vince.

Vince's best advice, his highest bar, was "to seek specificity until you weep," and, "to remove every excuse, every possible reason, for a reader to take off so much as a quarter of a point."

The reality of shaping such a complex proposal for Marlboro was made more complicated by the increase in the award and additional years. Most Title III applicants, a hundred institutions or so each year, were large enough so they could spend $350,000 each year with relative ease on a single large project. After a 50-page narrative, all one had to do was describe the project's budget, personnel, equipment, expenditures, and implementation in excruciating detail for each year, each month, of the five-year grant.

Title III applications at this level were going to run between 350 and 400 pages. I was not intimidated. I was obsessed by the prize. I was obsessed by the enormity of it. But Marlboro's problem was no single fundable project we could imagine would cost $1.7 million: the grant seemed too big, a mind-spinning reversal of Marlboro's diseconomy of scale. The solution was complex and dangerous. We would propose two or three projects, which could potentially confuse readers, anonymous judges who in the end were really the only people who mattered.

Title III Strengthening Institutions Grant was like a perfect diamond sitting, shining deep inside the bulbous, porous body of the U.S. government and the Department of Education. It was wonderful because it flipped the normal in grantmaking onto its head. Instead of seeking proposals for specific, precisely defined projects or initiatives desirable from the government's or the DOE's point of view, Title III said, you tell us exactly what you want to do, and justify it within the (admittedly hyper-distorted) language of the law and before the (uneven but entrenched) staff and administration, and we'll pay for all of it and its operations. That meant half of my wages and half of my assistant's — bottom-line money, for five years, like a gift, but one you have to keep working to collect.

And it was wonderful because not just anyone could apply. Title III had a poverty threshold based on the percent of your students who qualified for federal Pell Grants, above which institutions could not apply. So Title III workshops and annual conferences were full of Native American colleges, historically black colleges, Hispanic-serving universities, community colleges, and the occasional oddball college. No Ivies, no potted Ivies, no giant universities, only the rest of us.

We designed three major projects, and a couple of "initiatives" within each. At first Vince wasn't thrilled by the complexity of multiple projects, and we worked hours shaping them like interlocking puzzle pieces, inseparable from the whole, but simple, easy to follow, and airtight, my mind running out five years and back five years, over and over. We (a committee, of course) came up with this: lace the campus with underground fiber optic cable and terminals in every dormitory room and office in the college; build a computer lab in the library and computer stations throughout the academic buildings; develop two new academic components: a video/film teaching lab and new curricula and faculty in film; build a new foreign language lab capable of downloading learning resources from around the world.

I set up shop in my basement again and started working half-time there before going in to work and, with plenty of help checking, editing, organizing, and assembling the massive amount of detail and paperwork a perfect Title III application required. That's how Vince talked about it.

There was another reason, another motivation why I was willing to try again and Rod was willing to pay again, pay Vince, pay for four or five trips to DC, pay to take the chance. Except for Julie Kidd and her Christian Johnson Endeavor Foundation, we weren't doing very well in the foundation world. We had prospects, we thought, but not much earned money and a list of rejections from some of New York and New England's most prestigious foundations.

These large established foundations are not, in general, risk-taking institutions. They are, at their administrative base, more often controlling and elitist. Foundation principals, however, those who actually created a foundation or inherited one, like Julie Kidd, are much more likely to entertain, in their minds and pocketbooks, a place like Marlboro or Sterling. Getting to those individuals, however, by getting around a foundation's guidelines and its staff, is a separate and maybe black art, but a necessary one.

In any case, we had been running into stone walls, sometimes even with foundations that had supported Marlboro in the past. That's how bad it was. Marlboro was too small, one would say, rejecting even the notion of a written proposal. Another, a couple of others, would say, you are too poor; first let's see three years of balanced budgets. Good idea, but we could sooner fly to Mars for lunch.

There was also Marlboro's distinct lack of status that turned off foundation officers, who impress their trustees with grants that always succeed at well-known and safe entities, already with plenty of money. It's the good old boys, the same old gals, and rounds of dance parties I wanted Marlboro to be a part of whether we knew how to dance or not; at least we'd be in the right room.

But with federal grants, Title III grants, everybody was equal. It was competence based. If you could stick with it, if you could make it perfect, if you didn't miss a step in the invisible hierarchy, then you were in. Status meant nothing. Three years of deficits meant nothing. Size meant nothing.

Points meant everything.

We got 98.5. This time the cutoff was 99.

⁓

Recently I drew a timeline on a large piece of paper beginning with 1983 and ending, petering out is more like it, in 2002 when I finally dragged my ragged self off the Marlboro campus for good. I wanted to reconstruct the sequence of events and people that led from the college's lengthy hand-to-mouth existence to something closer to modest wealth compared with its earlier days, certainly, but also compared to many colleges today.

From 1983 until about 1991 it seems very little happened in the development department, which consisted of me, a gift secretary, an annual fund director, and an alumni director. We were working like mad, raising money, increasing the percentage of givers in each constituency and the amounts raised, but nothing much was happening, nothing changed. Upon reaching our hands, the money vaporized.

As the college grew thinner and thinner it seemed all we could do was chase after the few wealthy folks we knew, most of whom were on the board.

Besides that, we put as much into motion as possible. We developed systematic ways of communicating with alumni and other constituencies; we researched and wrote grants. We got on the road and visited people and asked them for money. We wrote letters. We doubled our phone bill and doubled it again. We joined the Consortium for the Advancement of Secondary Education (CASE) and went to workshops and conferences to learn more about what was still a young practice. We focused on major gift prospect development, meaning the art of finding wealthy, philanthropic people and introducing Marlboro to them.

I spent seven days in a New Jersey hotel being trained in planned giving techniques and tax law. Then I joined the Planned Giving Group of New England (PGGNE, pronounced, unfortunately, Pig-knee) and spent one day a month for the next 10 years in Boston, keeping up on the tax, legal, and ethical intricacies of, when combined, dying, giving, and receiving.

We hooked onto Title III and were holding on.

We were scrambling, bobbing and weaving, trying anything and everything, preparing for a future that could sputter and die at our feet, pretty much at any time.

So the earlier timeline on my piece of paper isn't empty but sparsely dotted with small notations of small successes in a linear forest of setbacks, stalled efforts, regulatory threats, and of course, the dog at our heels. But we were doing something right in reshaping the campaign and letting Carol O'Brien complete the study, which indicated five million over five years was a stretch, but achievable. So, without a lot of fanfare we finally launched the 50th Anniversary Campaign in 1992, a single notation on the timeline.

Then, right in the middle of that campaign, in 1994, trying anything and everything suddenly made a lot of sense because most of the stuff we'd been working on for years somehow came to fruition almost simultaneously, and kept fruiting for years, decades in some cases.

You couldn't see or feel these seminal happenings at the time. They were just part of the muddle, the scramble and good times, their impact not certain but welcome. But now, poised above a timeline, there appeared a confusion of circled notes and penciled lines and arrows clustering around 1994, like one of those rare springs where everything is blooming, everything old, young, high, low, out in the fields or bound up under canopy, blooming like it was about time it was blooming.

Julie Kidd, the Christian Johnson Endeavor Foundation, gave her three-year $750,000 gift in 1994, which did not eliminate the deficit by itself but had an immensely stabilizing effect on the college's finances, and established a relationship now entering its third decade.

In 1994 the college received its first charitable remainder trust, and after my New Jersey experience we launched a narrow but full-scale planned giving program, The Ramona Cutting Society, using one old college friend's $10,000 to create a pooled income fund, a "financial device" popular then, but unused today.

It was the year Jerry Aron wrote a letter to an old friend of his and Elizabeth's, Jerome Kohlberg, formally of Kohlberg Kravitz, the firm that, as I understand it, invented the corporate takeover, a practice that Jerome Kohlberg quickly grew tired of and so retired to run his 900 or so other companies, upscale organic farm, and nearby upscale rural restaurant, as well as his foundation.

Jerry was very proud of his letter and described it at a board meeting. He had a gravelly voice, a bald head, an Abe Lincoln beard, a handsome beaked nose, eyebrows that could talk, and hands that played a supporting role, rising and falling, resting on the table, grasped together like an exclamation point. He had a tendency to partially disappear into the large captain's chairs in the meeting room. He and Elizabeth were not particularly wealthy, compared to lots of the people they knew.

"When one man writes another man," Jerry intoned to the board, slowly, "and informs him of the fact he has just contributed a huge amount of money to an institution that he feels is worth every penny, then that other man sits up, because he knows the first man doesn't really have that sort of money, and he knows what's coming next." Jerry pauses. "The first man has to say how much. Well, that's me and Elizabeth and it is $100,000. That's what I wrote." Another pause. "And he asks straight if his friend, who is truly wealthy, might match his gift and then, maybe, get to know the college, come up and visit. Just because his friend asks." Jerry's hands rise up above his head, his lips curve down, his eyebrows arch up. "And he did match it. And he will come up. Here. With his wife. To see the college."

That's how Jerry got his friend to mail a $100,000 check, Jerry and Nancy Kohlberg's first gift to the college in 1994 in the middle of our anniversary campaign, and another at its end, $450,000.

Also in 1994 the college managed to build two new academic buildings, both, as it happened, for the visual arts and both examples of stirring up activity and keeping an eye out for opportunity. Construction of the college's first dedicated art gallery, for example, began with me hoping to patch up a much-soured relationship with a wealthy family: the mother an early trustee, the father a friend of the college, the son a graduate and eventual trustee, who managed the family's money.

The problem stemmed from a classic development blunder, one I later narrowly escaped at Sterling. So, again, if you are in this business, or thinking about getting into it, pay attention. But first understand that reconciliation with the disgruntled, the annoyed, the downright angry, even the wholly disaffected, is a specialized practice within fundraising, one I enjoyed and became fairly good at. Individually or in groups, impossibly unmovable or easily brought around, I discovered it is only from the disgruntled you learn the deeper truths of your organization, what you act like, what you look like through the eyes of the genuinely pissed off.

I didn't care if it came from the rich or poor, alum or neighbor, banker or butcher. When the disgruntled raised themselves up, I was there. Mostly, though, of course, to listen, to mildly deflect, to say how things are now or will be soon, to never, well, rarely, disagree. To not talk too much. To patch it up, work it out, turn it around, or, at least, set it on a course that leads toward rather than away.

There's no question, however, that it is more interesting when the disgruntled are disgruntled former or potential major donors. In a fundraising sense, your odds of achieving a large gift are immensely greater with a disgruntled man, woman, or family of proven means than they are with an equally disgruntled but relatively penniless former student or parent.

At Marlboro, the family in question wanted to fund a new facility, a large arts building, a Center for the Arts, to house four or five faculty, students, and their equipment and studio spaces, all presently ill-housed and spread around campus. They gave the college about $250,000. So far so good. Next, college creates committee, committee hires architects, and architects take charge. Everyone's excited: there are brainstorm-ings, workshops, field trips, drawings, "renderings," specs, site explo-ration. There is even a magnificently detailed scale model with walk-ways and little trees; it had its own domed cover with a brass handle on it. But holy moly someone wasn't paying attention and suddenly there's only $100,000 left. The donor imagined something closer to double that. He, the son who managed the money, was pissed. He was still pissed and his family was still pissed when I went to see him probably 10 years after this.

"You still have a $100,000 of our money. There's no more money coming for this project from this family," he said immediately after my first query, which was a suggestion he and the family give another $100,000 so we'd have enough to . . . didn't matter; it was not what he wanted to hear. I had another option or two in my back pocket, where they stayed.

So we talked and it became obvious that this fellow, this graduate just like me, and his family didn't want to be angry. They still wanted to help and be involved. Time had passed. The perpetrating committee was long ago disbanded, the former longtime president forgiven. We agreed on using the remaining funds to build a new gallery, attached to the theater, which they would name, but there would be no more money, at least not until this is done, on budget.

The funding for the second building came via an alumna from my era who, upon her father's death, became the steward of a small fund devoted to the arts, which, if we did things right, could grant us $80,000 for a new painting studio, and thus another boost to the reversal of the balkanization (as we liked to call it) of the arts on campus.

It was rough having to build a painting studio without running water, but such was the case until the college could construct a new septic system, still a few years and almost a million dollars in the future. Until then, no more hookups. But no faculty complaints, either, which, at Marlboro, meant unqualified success.

And in 1994 Title III finally gave way to persistence, the head-pounding type displayed by woodpeckers and crazy people. In the short term the grant's impact was immense, given the size of the college relative to the size of the grant, $350,000 per year for five years. Marlboro College was able to catch up with the rest of higher education in its electronic and communications infrastructure and practice, build two important academic programs, modernize the library systems, and provide computers and other technologies throughout the college.

Title III's details were critical at the time, but just as important was the sheer momentum the grant provoked in academic and administration capabilities. The dust it stirred up on campus was literal, too, as crews blasted their way through bedrock to lay fiber optic cable from one end of campus to the other. Good things were happening and everyone could see that in 1994. We had more to shape fundraising around, more to impress prospective students and parents, more for foundations to see we were serious people. Movement, activity, hubbub, money, opportunity.

Still, that year, 1994, just to test our sobriety, we posted a deficit in the hundreds of thousands of dollars. It took two more years to kill that dog.

Title III: Round Three
1993/1994
The final 405-page Title III application was indeed perfect. Tight, like a safe. Its dozens of budgets and sub-budgets, its detailed description and rationale for

truckloads of electronic equipment, its implementation timelines and schedules of NASA-level complexity and engineering, no one piece of it could be separated out, isolated, and questioned. It held together like a Greek phalanx, bristling with spears and banners declaring, Dare Not Nick Off Even Half A Point Or You Die!

The final application didn't differ very much from the previous one, although it had to be completely rewritten because that was easier and safer than trying to edit and rewrite. We also studied past applications, our own and others, to understand better what sparked readers to take off half and whole points and thus doom an application, dumping months of work in the trash bin. Often, readers were taking points off for things they were not seeing or not understanding, or, we found, not finding what should be there: the rationale for a new microchemistry lab, for instance, or the justification for the extraordinary cost of a secure computer server room.

So we developed a pattern of NOTES. Like that, all caps and boxed smack in the middle of a paragraph, or all alone between paragraphs to make its importance even more obvious. Thus: "NOTE: See server room bids and cost analysis, Project # 2, Section 2, Part A, page 276." And, "NOTE: For rationale and implementation plan for the new microchemistry lab See Project # 3, Section 12, Part B, Page 323."

There must have been 50 of these notes, all of them saying to the reader, "Don't think what you are thinking. It's all there, just follow the note."

But who knows what worked? I also attended practically every Title III workshop given over the previous year, flying to DC, meeting with Vince, going to the workshop on whatever — budgets, allowable expenses, federal audits (God forbid) — meeting up with Vince again and going out for drinks and sometimes dinner with a Title III staffer. By this time, after all, I'd been writing the grant and hanging around for almost three years.

It was late on the day the results were to be announced. Then it was evening. Vince didn't know, but informed me there were times in the past when the staff was a day or even two days late. I couldn't take it. I called one of those staffers and asked, when. She gave me a different answer, "Don't worry."

What a thing to live with for 24 hours, knowing, but not really knowing. And not daring to tell anyone, I mean, as the hours pass, what does "Don't worry" really mean? It could mean anything!

Such was my state of mind.

Rod got the official word the next day — we scored a 99 — and went out and bought a $100 bottle of brandy. It was June, there were no students or faculty around. The whole staff gathered around the picnic table and we drank the brandy out of paper cups in the hot afternoon, glad, at least, that it was over.

For the next five years I traveled to Washington on Title III business at least twice a year, and five or six times one year when the Clinton administration threatened to cut our annual appropriation in half.

Going down there, meeting time after time, year after year, with three or four hundred college presidents and chief development officers from independent colleges and universities of every stripe, community colleges, historically black colleges, technical colleges, Hispanic colleges, American Indian colleges, from every part of the nation and Puerto Rico, even the Pacific Islands, listening to their stories, hearing their problems and anxieties, was to me like standing before a gigantic window, a huge, living diorama, watching a part of American higher education I had been only remotely aware of. Not just a part, but the actual heart of American higher education, a heart that does not include the Ivy League or its children, or aunts and uncles. In comparison to the Title III crowds, the Ivies and their kind are like fancy resorts full of all the best stuff, but gated and guarded and somehow not as important or as interesting as I had thought they were.

And it's easy to admit, coming from the whitest state in the United States and one whose entire population is fewer than 650,000, the size of a single city in most states, rubbing elbows with all these people, most of whom were not white, was a cultural experience I found fulfilling and meaningful and completely unavailable in Vermont. Similar, but less fulfilling, and also not found in Vermont, was my discovery and exploration of a genuine, humongous, practiced, and self-confident government bureaucracy. What an impressive creature is the Department of Education, and to think it is just one among dozens concentrated around the Washington Mall like hulking building-sized zoo animals from another planet, imperturbable, harmless, unmovable, and even beneficial though perhaps not in proportion to their mass.

Three years after the close of the 50th Anniversary Campaign, after Rod's retirement and Paul LeBlanc's start, the Kohlbergs gave their $12 million: $10 million in endowment, another $5 million for faculty support and $5 million for student support, and another $2 million for the library wing. In doing so they officially kicked off our new campaign, the Campaign for Marlboro, with an initial five-year goal of, if I recall, $16 million in permanent endowed funds. Hard to recall because the goal changed numerous times as the whole effort, which concluded after my departure, fed upon itself and ultimately garnered upward of $25 million.

The Kohlberg's giving to the college continued for years, then a new generation carried on and still carries on, all on account of good stewardship on the part of three presidents, or on account of a single great letter from Jerry Aron, or because way earlier Dick Taylor thought Jerry Aron might make a good trustee. That was some fundraising.

─────

Spring, 1999, and Paul LeBlanc, almost three years into his Marlboro presidency, was at this moment like the rest of us, sitting still in a comfortable leather swivel chair at a conference table in a closed-door room in the relatively new offices of Chesapeake Asset Management, One Rockefeller Plaza, New York City.

We had been aiming for this exact moment, this once-in-a-lifetime opportunity, for years. At first not sure where it was or even if it existed, now it was before us, the penultimate piece of the financial puzzle, the financial scramble for existence that was Marlboro. We had already built the fundraising campaign to do what Marlboro had never had the strength to do before, run a genuine endowment campaign, where only large gifts were sought and when found went straight into the bank as permanent, restricted funds, with earnings only flowing to the college. That's why endowments have to be large to be effective. That's why we never had the muscle to launch such an effort. Until this moment, the need for cash today precluded any notion of seeking cash in the bank for tomorrow.

By this time, too, we knew how to conceive and conduct such a campaign, because we'd practiced by running the 50th Anniversary Campaign with its false start, with Carol O'Brian's feasibility study, with motivated trustees, and a full development staff.

This one, this campaign-in-waiting, The Campaign for Marlboro College, was ready to launch even as we stepped into the offices of Chesapeake Asset Management; in fact had been in operation for more than a year, quietly building commitments, building capacity, and waiting for the conclusion of the intricate dance among Rod, then Paul, and Elizabeth McCormack and Jerry Aron and, at the center of the party, Nancy and Jerry Kohlberg.

We waited because there's no use announcing a campaign without a goal, or with a goal you cannot achieve. Our idea, our strategy, had been to wait for the Kohlbergs to establish that goal by making the initial leadoff gift. They had, of course, and the sum, $12 million, stunned us. That's the kind of endowment giving that such campaigns are made of.

I was sitting across from Paul and the board treasurer, Dick Taylor. Jerry Aron was next to the head of the table, where a single oversized swivel chair was empty. We were there to meet Jonathan Smith and agree, at Elizabeth McCormack's recommendation, that he would be the investment manager of the largest gift in the college's history; at that time, the largest gift to a Vermont college in the history of the state.

Standing behind the empty chair, Mr. Smith had our complete attention. Not only was he on first impression crazy, but at the moment, he acknowledged, coughing and shaking his head, was fighting a terrible bout of flu. "It's meaningless, meaningless," he said, gagging violently, suppressing the need to cough. His face reddened, his eyes popping red. He sweated. His pale skin glistened. But he did not sit down. He slowly paced behind our chairs, holding forth about his firm and investments, what's important and the decisions that have to be made. Clearing his throat every third word, he eventually worked his way around the immense table to stand beside Jerry, and without looking reached out and put his hand on Jerry's bald pate and gently rubbed his hand back and forth while he continued to speak. Jerry sat and listened, quite content.

Half the time he shouted, or tried to with a voice now wracked with abuse, and it all came off as anger, extreme impatience and anger. You wondered how long he could keep it up before his head exploded. The table had room for 12, and at the far end, well spaced from the rest of us, sat two dark Suits. Investment brokers. They had pushed their chairs back a little from the table, as if to give themselves an extra quarter-second if they had to bolt for the door. On his first round, Jonathan Smith had quizzed these two on their various wheelings and dealings and the levels of their own personal investments in these named but to us unfamiliar vehicles. He stood behind them, asking his questions, looking around the table at us, his hands gripping the soft backs of their black leather chairs. Apparently the two gave the correct answers and appropriate responses; to their obvious relief, they were then dismissed.

Abandoning Jerry's scalp, Jonathan Smith lowered himself into his big swivel chair and said, "Okay, you must have questions."

Our board treasurer had a few, all technical. Then Jerry and Jonathan got into a relatively relaxed conversation about endowment investments at colleges generally. In speaking with Jerry, Smith seemed to calm down and everyone relaxed, even risked a laugh at something Jerry said, just what escapes me; I was watching Smith.

Amidst the relative gaiety, Paul saw his chance to pose his question, which was, he said, a concern on the part of the students and the Marlboro community as a whole. In choosing our investments, Paul asked, could we avoid investing in a number of. . .

And here it came: Jonathan Smith's head snapped around with an angry who-said-that?! glare, his eyes beginning to bulge again, even as his right hand rose high above his head and came down flat on the table and sounded like a shotgun blast.

"Whores and slaves," he growled, his voice shaking, his face explosive and red as an apple. "We don't do whores and slaves!" The growl spiked to a strangling, thundering shout. "Everything else is on the table! Everything!"

———

After another 20 minutes of Jonathan Smith again pacing around his conference table, expounding on how things work in his world, that is, the real world, of course, and once per round stopping to rub Jerry's head, he finally released us from One Rockefeller Plaza. Suppressing a gagging cough he ushered us to the much larger reception area over-looking the street three floors below, and with handshakes and a curt thank-you to Paul and everyone else, said his goodbyes. In a more expansive farewell, maybe for having delivered him $12 million, he gave a genuine full-on hug to Jerry, whose fringe of hair was then pushed further askew by a final head rub.

On the sidewalk, we were laughing like we've escaped a madman chasing after us with a spiked club. "Whores and slaves?" said Paul. "What the hell's that about?"

What was there to say? Jonathan Smith was our investment manager, our portfolio manager; there was no question from the start about that. He could have been a raving lunatic but he was Elizabeth's suggestion, he was Jerry's friend, he was a proven philanthropic fund manager.

"Just excitable, and congested, very congested," Jerry explained, clearly unfazed. "But a wonderful investor and Elizabeth thinks highly of him, especially because he's doing this free of charge. As he does for Swarthmore. So we are in good company."

Good company indeed — whores, slaves, whatever. It was all fine with me.

The point was Marlboro College had $12 million in the bank, and we were in the middle of a quiet campaign — a pre-campaign campaign — that was going to generate millions more. Never again would I or Rod, or Jerry, or Lil Farber or any of the longer serving trustees, or the faculty, or the staff, or the alumni, or the surrounding community, have to wonder whether the college was going to survive. A mode of thought had been displaced. What was once assumed to be inevitable was not, any longer.

I don't recall where we went after that meeting. Most likely Paul and I were off for a foundation visit, or meeting with a donor or, even better, a prospective donor. But as we strolled along, heading deeper into the city, I was suffused — there is no other word for it — with a feeling of contentment. The roar of Manhattan around me diminished to a muffled hum. Paul's long strides kept him half a pace ahead. It was a cool day and sunny and midtown looked magnificent. I could have walked forever, overwhelmed at all that had been accomplished over the past six or seven years, culminating for me in the meeting we'd just left, like huge vault doors securing the college's very existence.

Since the day I arrived in 1983 there was the sense Marlboro was in an endgame we could not wiggle out of. There had been talk of merger. The New England Association of Schools and Colleges, the other regulatory agency besides the federal government, was officially concerned whether we had the finances to go forward. Some of the most powerful board members insisted there was no more money, no more of their money. And if there were more students out there, we couldn't seem to find them. And if we found them, they had no money.

By the mid-1990s, when at last we felt we were making progress, the federal Department of Education, deeming Marlboro a risk to the Pell Grants they gave to students and the students paid to the college for tuition, compelled us to put $450,000 — real cash money — into an account until such time as the risk was mitigated. We begged and connived to borrow it from reluctant board members, tying up their money for years, restricting their giving capacity.

The college's then meager endowment provided only symbolic relief each year, offsetting the deficit to the effect of a single vole into a hungry coyote's maw. We hadn't balanced a budget since 1985.

At best we had miniscule raises for years, and the faculty were very outspoken about that. Our wages were so low it hardly mattered. Rod said he was the lowest-paid college president in the nation, except for a few nuns who did it for free.

Once, in an early dismal spring, we had only enough money in the bank for two paydays. One month. That was it.

But all that anxiety was gone now, as I kept pace behind my long-striding young president, and with our $12 million in the bank. The terrible struggle had been won. The future promised more. That's what it felt like, walking through the fields of opportunity that New York City was to us, then, and I'm thinking long, slow turnarounds are tough on people, and tough on institutions. Nothing seems to happen fast enough, yet you work at a desperate pace. You understand now that sustaining endowments, the big money, are not just given but also earned, and they come with a cost. They don't come from nothing. You have to stir up a lot of dust, take a lot of falls, a lot of falls. Put a lot of things in motion. Pay attention. Then in a moment, something breaks, something happens, something falls together perfectly in the unlikeliest way and, for a time at least, a length of time no one knows how long, you've got some room to maneuver, the path is widening, and you have earned a moment to stop. Just stop.

I'm thinking about all this, seeing one version of how it all came together, enjoying the sweet muted roar of street- level Manhattan. But at the same time, I knew, I could feel it and it didn't feel very good, that I was about done at Marlboro.

6

Going Once, Going Twice...

Beverly, Massachusetts, 23 miles north of Boston, and its two villages, Prides Crossing and Beverly Farms, grip the coves and harbors of Boston's North Shore, north of Swampscott and Marblehead, through Salem and over the Danvers River, below Magnolia-by-the-Sea and Gloucester. These are all Yankee towns, places with histories, places occupied, if you count Native Americans, for thousands of years. If you count just white Europeans you still come up with about 500 years. The Indian words and names are present in the area's geography — Cuttyhunk, Hyannis, Swampscott — and businesses, like Shawmut Bank. But European names ring almost as loudly today as back in the day: Lodge, Winthrop, Dodge, Cabot, Adams, Mather, and Hale. Yankees all, and, philanthropically speaking, all possessed of deep pockets and short arms, as they really do say, about themselves even, up and down the North Shore.

In the middle of this city of 40,000 is Montserrat College of Art, bordering the city's common and occupying a large three-story brick building, formerly a middle school, wherein are dozens of huge four-by-eight windows, ten-foot-wide stairwells, and twelve-foot-high ceilings.... You couldn't buy a better place for a professional college of art, especially for one dollar. That's what the college paid the City of Beverly, that and a commitment to help maintain the common, its stone paths, gardens and benches, the bandstand and pavilion.

At the top of the common stands the impressive brick edifice and 30-foot-wide steps of the Beverly Public Library, and in the other direction three short blocks of charming but unpretentious residential homes lead to the shore of Beverly Harbor, and the largest of many small beaches and shore-side parks maintained by the city. The pearl necklace of coastal residences, the mansions old and new, tasteful and not, the ones whose patios faced the sea and green lawns rolled down to the rocks and tides, are reserved for the very wealthy and there are many of them, difficult to see because they all had long, curving driveways, but grand and, to me, philanthropically intriguing when viewed from just offshore, from a kayak, for instance, while trolling for striped bass.

It is place, the physical, geological, ecological, geographical, natural, and human community in which a college exists and into or onto which it was born and where its roots were nourished that defines a college as much as its curriculum, its governance, its recorded history, its famous alumni and professors. Place is an alma mater's alma mater.

Marlboro College, founded in 1946, was the conception of its founder, Walter Hendricks, a professor at the University of Chicago who owned an old 19th-century hillside farm in southern Vermont, and had his eye on his neighbor's farm. In Berlitz, France, the debarkation point for thousands of American GIs waiting for transport home after WWII, Hendricks began teaching some of these younger men, teaching and dreaming about his college; how could he not, surrounded as he was by millions of potential students? GIs to fill the GI Bill.

The first students literally built the college. The lore is Hendricks enrolled students as quickly and as creatively as possible. Even then, as new colleges throughout the region were popping up like rocks in a frost heave, you had to show prospective students and parents the simple amenities of the institution. Hendricks built one dormitory room, nicely laid out. Everyone got to look at it. No one lived in it. Instead they were piled into rooms and attics among the abandoned farmhouses, some of the same rooms I lived in as a student, later worked in as a vice president.

Financing, always, was a specialty of President Hendricks. When one faculty member heard a local Vermont stoneworker reciting poetry as he worked, he persuaded him to enroll in the college. However, the new student, who went on to become one of Vermont's cherished poets, Bill Mundell, had no money. Maple syrup would do just as well, Hendricks decided, and Bill hitched up his East Dover oxen and paid his tuition.

Once enrolled, those students, with faculty and neighbors, converted the huge old three-level cow barn into classrooms and a library. Famously, and pictured in *LIFE* magazine, Robert Frost spoke at the first commencement in 1949.

When I transferred to Marlboro from the University of Denver, in January 1969, the GI builders and the younger students who joined them on that hillside were long dispersed, though the stories they left behind and recounted annually at boozy alumni parties became one history of the institution, as defining as any other. A handful of the original faculty were still active when I enrolled and for many years after I graduated, after I was employed, even, but just barely, after I departed 19 years later. Still today a couple teach on.

But regarding place, things had changed. By the time I joined the administration in 1983, perhaps much earlier, the college's seminal relationship to the surrounding hills and gullies, ponds and streams, and the immediate community of farmers and country homes had evolved to one of disengagement or remoteness from it. Maybe removedness is closer to what I mean. With such a classically focused curriculum, there was genuinely no academic reason for the college to engage deeply in the physicality of the countryside, other than for recreation and exploration.

From 1950-1951, when Adolf Busch, Rudolf Serkin, and Marcel Moyse established the soon to be world-famous Marlboro Music Festival, until this very day, the festival filled the short summers with music and people from away, and paid rent. With the college full on the rest of the year, there was not much time or incentive to develop a more intimate college to community relationship with the town and its people, who were, over the decades, more and more college-related people, then their sons and daughters, and their inheriting grandchildren. There's not much up there, besides the college, the festival, and the bloodlines of generations of college and festival people.

Marlboro College functions as its own self-contained community, where folks come and go and change constantly, yes, but once inside, for however long, that's where you were in your entirety, in this unique, intense, remote, concentrated academic environment humming with self-governance and cerebral as all get out. But other than pride of place, place never figured essentially in Marlboro's curriculum or culture.

Sterling College's origins and relationship to place are very different. Beginning as a boys' prep school in the mid-1950s, the school closed in the early 1970s, morphing to outdoor-related programs for a few years, then into a two-year associate degree college concentrating on agriculture and outdoor leadership. In 1998 Sterling was accredited as a four-year institution and today focuses on four academic areas: sustainable agriculture, conservation ecology, outdoor education and leadership, and environmental humanities.

Sterling's curriculum and emphasis on experiential learning made it academically dependent upon its surrounding community: its people, businesses, farms, watersheds, forests, rivers and streams, and its history, its ethics. Without that relationship, formed through all those cousins and in-laws who once worked at or worked on the college, and the farmers, loggers, game wardens, writers, poets, scientists, all the remarkable people hidden away up in the Northeast Kingdom, without all that, Sterling could not be what is has become. So at Sterling, place is central and alive, part of its very being.

Montserrat was established, that's the word used, in 1970 by eight, or possibly more, well-established Boston area artists who enjoyed teaching and thinking about art: it grew, haphazardly, I understand, as it moved from shelter to shelter in and around Beverly. In the mid-1980s, after working its way through the intricacies of the New England Association of Schools and Colleges (NEASC), Montserrat was accredited as a baccalaureate college, and became the newest of the 38 professional independent colleges of art in the nation.

I understood Marlboro's imposed individualism. And when I got to Sterling I understood the college willingly linking its curriculum to its community and physical environment. But at Montserrat I wasn't sure what I was looking at. Never in my experience had a surrounding community been so *closely* surrounding: so close you couldn't — I couldn't — distinguish how and how tightly Montserrat and Beverly and the North Shore were intertwined, although it was clear that intertwined they were. In its relationship to place, Montserrat was the youngest of the three, and its place was the most ancient, the longest inhabited, and, with the Atlantic pounding at its door, the most primeval.

As it turned out, Montserrat maintained a two-tiered relationship with the city of Beverly and the North Shore. One layer was being central to, and thus dependent upon, the artists and art lovers through adult education, summer programing, publications, lectures, and three public galleries where student shows and curated exhibits opened regularly. The artistic community up and down the North Shore was well established, reaching back to the late 1800s, so that artistic history was deep and highly respected generations before Montserrat's founders channeled as much of that as they could into their school, and their college. Today, Montserrat strengthens its credibility and status annually through the growth and success of the annual benefit art auction, where in 2004 we broke the $200,000 mark, but today the *Artrageous Auction* raises well over $300,000.

Montserrat's other tier, more like a prong, points directly at the Beverly and North Shore business and political community and the local, almost hyperactive, Chamber of Commerce. So Montserrat was artists, art teachers, art lovers, the Chamber of Commerce, politicians and Suits of every variety, and the fabulously wealthy whose mansions and cul-de-sacs and private ways occupied the very edges of the continent, just feet above the granite shore — all of it Montserrat's place and mine to explore for a short and wonderful time.

When you are hired into a new job, a vice president's position, for instance, you rarely get to know why it was you were employed over other candidates. But I was told why at Montserrat by a board member on the hiring committee. "You were the whole package," she said. And I was, I suppose. It was possible back then to know with some authority something about every aspect of fundraising, from annual funds to prospect research, from pooled income funds to charitable remainder trusts, from solicitation techniques to capital campaign design and execution, from grants and foundations to automatic fund transfers, and on and on. It was just my luck to be at Marlboro, taking up, and making contributions to, these practices as they were being developed at colleges and universities across the country. In 19 years, Marlboro went from manual typewriters and Addressograph machines, to Web-based communications via fiber optic cable and satellite technology. We went from an annual fund letter written by a retiring dean to a multiplatform advancement program managing numerous tightly identified constituencies, programs, and services. And, as an industry, we went from the begging bowl conception of how nonprofit fundraising was conducted, to the first, then the second, now the normal, billion-dollar campaign.

Among my direct responsibilities, however, was something I'd never experienced, the benefit fine art auction. Actually something of a staple at art institutions, Montserrat was on their 18th and it was presumed by everyone that it would set higher marks and earn more money than the 17th and its predecessors.

Being in charge of something you know nothing about and everyone around you knows all about is never an issue as long as you aren't so crazy to assume you really are in charge, and set about to prove it. I'd seen plenty of midcareer go-getters like myself who, finding themselves the boss of something they have zero experience with, insist on running things their way. The higher education industry is full of people like that.

The real boss of the auction, who worked for me, was the college's longtime director of community relations, Jo Lennox and her, that is, my, staff of four women. I was a few years older than Jo, but we had about the same number of years on the job and had developed an equal tolerance of and sensitivity to wealthy people. They were part of our nonprofit, mission-driven world and took sustenance from that world, as it attempted to take sustenance from them. So easily identified, but tricky, with those deep pockets to pin down.

The business community and the Chamber of Commerce, also my responsibility and Jo's labor, were more mysterious even than an auction that could generate a couple of hundred thousand dollars in a single evening. Marlboro town had no chamber, no business community. The nearest things even resembling them were in Brattleboro and had no impact on the college, 11 curvaceous miles up the mountain.

But for all the intrigue about place and how it fits an institution and the institution fits it, over time, over generations, Montserrat's problems and issues, strictly from the perspective of a vice president of institutional advancement, which is what I was, were straightforward: weak annual fundraising, no major gift program, no campaign experience, uneven public relations, almost no institutional research, a board that was playing — governing from the hip — and strategic planning heavily supplemented by the dreaming up of cool things. And debt. Of course. The slinking dog.

On the surface, the Montserrat board of trustees looked like most any board of a small or midsize college. There was a fair mix of male and female, of alumni, of lawyers, architects, real estate agents, retired businessmen and women turned artists, plain old wealthy people who worked or did not work, or who owned urban farms, or art collections, or sailboats, or businesses that didn't have to make money. Nothing unusual in any of this.

The governance structure was ordinary, their committee areas the normal. They met three times a year.

But, their paperwork, agendas, reports, meeting minutes, budgets, projections, and articulation of issues and information were a mess. And no wonder. The Montserrat board did not meet three times a year at a "trustees' weekend" as most of New England's college boards did and I assume still do. Instead, they met usually on a late afternoon on a weekday. They, we, assembled in a long, low, comfortable room above the art studios, a gallery, and the photography department. There was lunch, little ham sandwiches, chips, water, coffee. Meetings lasted about two hours, but occasionally concluded near the end of the business day.

And the committees? They met, in a sense, from the perspective of administrative staff support, all the time. There were six committees and each had to meet at least once and often more between board meetings, so each meeting had to be scheduled. Like the actual board meeting, committee meetings took place on weekdays during business hours. Because members served on two committee each, finding suitable times and dates for each meeting became the president's assistant's unforgiving and unrelenting task. For those of us producing those reports, agendas, and documents on the current workings of the college, the committee structure worked about as predictably as the coastline weather.

None of this is to say the Montserrat Board of Trustees couldn't party. Far from it. The annual auction was abundant proof of that. But without a weekend meeting schedule there was no way to deepen their collaborative interests and duties as trustees other than during actual meeting times. No cocktails and dinners, no bagged lunches out on the deck. The intensity of weekend-long board meetings puts new members and board veterans into governance and social situations that not only make for a better board simply through getting to know one another, but also makes them want to come back to the next meeting because they look forward to being with other members. It's interesting, and it should be intellectually satisfying. The Montserrat board missed all this.

There were other effects of this unusual methodology of governance. It meant that in order to participate effectively all trustees had to live or work locally. All of them were from the North Shore, half at least from Beverly and Manchester. Some were from right up the street. At the same time, Montserrat wanted to be seen as a national college, as opposed to local or even regional.

Once in a nominations committee meeting I suggested a prospective board member who happened to live in Lincoln, just to the west of Boston. The idea that this person would have a hard time attending committee meetings never came up in the ensuing, short, discussion. No, Lincoln itself was the problem. It wasn't where it needed to be, in this case, which was here. The committee members simply stared at each other, mumbling inconclusively about Lincoln, Lincoln? It was sort of like mentioning an off-topic subject in the middle of a serious meeting, like, "Can we pause and talk about hip joint replacement and what they're doing about it in Poland?" You'd get some pretty odd stares. That's what I got.

The longer-term result of this methodology was a strange version of provincialism. Imagine the irony of that, coming from 19 years in the provinces of mountainous, dirt-road Vermont, where you might expect to run into folks who hadn't left the county since they could remember.

The Montserrat board was not a bunch of local cronies determined to keep it that way. As much as anything, their meeting structure alone augmented their provincialism, unconsciously of course, in regard to their college, whose active world could be encircled by bicycle in a half morning's ride. In contrast, the Marlboro and Sterling boards sought out and included members from New York City (Marlboro many, Sterling two), Boston, and most New England states, and Washington DC, as well as the odd Michiganite or Floridian.

How frustrating to discover that a provincial board is like monocrop agriculture; everything looks normal, everything works, there will be no surprises. Whatever you want to call this contained urban province, the college and board worked it with considerable but uneven success over many years, complacently. There was no lack of devotion, just a strange and undeserved diminished level of institutional confidence, like a star high-school athlete who never left town.

———

At first, the Montserrat art auction struck me as a very risky way to make money. But I learned that with the right staff and with the right stuff, and a willingness to risk catastrophe, like an early April Atlantic-born storm on auction night, a really large, high-class auction not only brings in a ton of money, but it's an absolute kick to put together.

It's like a one-night stand of theater, with a circus running through, and tens of thousands of dollars hanging on the walls; the smooth-barking, cajoling auctioneer doing his stuff like a magic show, the whole production fueled by liquor and fine food, elegant dresses on the women and men in well-tailored suits and ties, the artists, usually less formally attired, standing out amidst the paying, bidding, art-loving patrons of the North Shore and Boston. And we, the staff, watching months of work sweep together in a single evening, working until the last frame had been wrapped and the last, tired group of staff and volunteers staggered home.

My first auction — it was Jo's of course — made $150,000, up $5,000 or $10,000 over the previous year. I was able to analyze the auction's cost, something apparently that had never been done before, and I came up with about $60,000 in wages and direct costs like advertising, the auction catalogue, the caterer, the liquor, the decorations and lights and easels and stands, and for art storage and security. The news was not well received by the president or the board because it indicated a profit margin out of sync with expenditures. For instance, an experienced fundraiser hijacked from another college would, back then, cost about the same $60,000 or a little more per year, but would in time generate considerably more than $90,000 dollars annually. So Jo, the president, and all the trustees who believed deeply in the auction were disturbed, even a little threatened, by the analysis.

I wasn't disturbed by the actual cost of the auction; if anything, it was disturbing that no one had bothered to total the costs before. But earned money should be only a part of a deeper fundraising program. I was thinking about the philanthropic potential of the auction, based on the general level of wealth along the shore of the North Shore, and on the other vital ingredient to major gift prospecting, money's elegant dance partner, status.

They were there in full dress, bidding on art, sure, but also watching who sat at which table during the live auction, and who bought what and for how much, and who was watching whom — that's what I saw and my staff saw as auction night rolled on into the evening. That's what we would report about and print pictures of in our new magazine,

PORTFOLIO, and that's what we would base a rejuvenated annual fund on, in what would be yet another short comprehensive campaign, just like the others, except with lots of great art.

For the length and breadth of the North Shore, the Montserrat auction was a public-relations boon. Appointed each year was an honorary chair of the auction, always some regionally well-known individual or couple of wealth or influence or great service. There were featured artists, and many levels of sponsorship, from $15,000 to $250. In 2003, the top sponsorship was $15,000, with only one taker, plus 13 prepaid corporate sponsors, and another group of 85 or 90 patrons, and the auction took in $150,000. It would do nothing but grow after that.

All this, year after year, each a little bigger and better than the last, adds up to a million-dollar public relations comfort blanket. Public relations is normally a cost item; at Montserrat it's a huge palate of new annual and capital fund prospects, and a bucketload of cash just in time for the summer drought and the June 30th end of the fiscal year. Good deal.

———

After what was described as a "borderline chaotic" board-run presidential search, Montserrat's new president had been on the job six months when he hired me, just in time to help with his inauguration, the highlight of which, besides the official installation of a new president, was the participation of artists Christo and Jeanne-Claude. We had to rent the largest space in Beverly to accommodate the crowd for their talk, at which Jeanne-Claude did most of the talking, with Christo adding a comment or two when the audience asked questions, which could have gone on for hours. Best inauguration I'd ever been to and it gave me confidence I'd made a good choice, coming to Montserrat.

Yes. But. I was learning the ropes, getting to know my staff, and hiring a new and a strikingly competent graphic designer, webmaster, and editor all wrapped into one woman, for an office of five. On the whole, while it lasted, it was the best staff I ever worked with. For the most part, too, we had all the pieces of a standard development and public relations office, by then more fashionably referred to as an

Advancement office, whence evolved the pretty magnificent title of Vice President for Institutional Advancement. The downside was in the college's chronic changes in leadership, which I was doomed to become part of. They, for a short time, we, could never fully employ all those elements at the same time, in the right order, with the same goals, for very long.

Meanwhile the president, like most new presidents, was overspending. Not that overspending isn't exciting: for instance, we designed new fancy signage that hung like giant band-aids on the big brick building, we built a wonderful new entrance plaza with flower pots and places to hang out, park bikes, eat lunch, smoke before class, replacing about the drabbest college entrance imaginable. These were just expensive peanuts compared to purchasing a string of three or four small, going-out-of-business stores — a shoe repair shop, an on-again off-again organic restaurant across the street from one of the college's Main Street galleries and studio spaces. I think that cost $600,000. They, the president and a handful of trustees, were planning to build a new student center on the site, with a formal gallery, public spaces, and student and faculty studios.

The chairman of the board was an excellent architect who knew zero about governance, and usually concentrated on his open laptop during committee meetings, where he played with design concepts for a new building, which were great. But still, after a year or more of this I was becoming suspicious. Where, exactly, was the money? The big project money?

On a programmatic level, it is wonderful when you arrive new at a college where the annual fund, which represents general overall fundraising, is underperforming, or better, doing really poorly. It's like working a magic trick, but it's not magic. The turnaround is quick. Impressive results in year one, and indicators of longer-term success the following year.

No complicated tools are needed because, almost inevitably, the problem you are solving stems from the college not asking for philanthropic support, or not asking the right way, or the right people, or on the right schedule. And having no plan, or no plan that's working.

The magic is in the asking, and the rules: communicate straightfor-wardly. Be nice about it. Call and say thank you. Get others to ask for you. Meet in person. Write good letters. Have informative, well-written publications with excellent photographs and illustrations on good paper. Know whom you are talking to. Have a plan about it.

Keep doing that and in a couple of years you will have more money and more people giving to the annual fund. You will have discovered major gift prospects — really, that's one big reason to work hard on an annual fund, to smoke out those capable of larger and larger gifts. You know already they are philanthropic: they gave to your re-energized annual fund.

After setting the annual fund on its course, you then start looking around to see if there's any programmatic potential for additional insti-tutional income, like Montserrat's three week pre-college program, which brings high-school art students to Beverly for three weeks in the summer for a college-level experience in the visual arts. It produces a good income. It also produces new students, something like 10 or 12 out of a summer attendance of 60. The program director was a mildly eccentric, energetic, then 35-year-old who wore silly ties and bright shirts and was demonstrably charismatic among students, supportive of his faculty, creative in his administration, and driven to let young people have the artistic experience of their young lives. He was also a disci-plined and determined enrollment manager. He wanted to expand the program and compete with other national art colleges doing similar programs, which was most of them. He wanted to work full-time, instead of half-time.

This was my kind of fellow. We run the numbers, look at the admis-sions figures and history, and conclude it takes about 10 more students to pay for an expansion to between 30 and 50 students. Let's go, I say. Plan it out. Let's work it.

The new graphic artist who edits and designs our new publications, the art-stuffed, oversized *PORTFOLIO* magazine and the new cata-logue, is also our webmaster, and she wants to work full-time and I des-perately want her to. A quick look at previous freelancer expenditures in her areas shows we'll save a lot of money and get a lot more, and better, product. We were right on budget, but she was underpaid and underemployed, and it needed fixing. A new title, let her work her own schedule, a little more money. Keep her, said Jo, or we'll all suffer.

We'd also written a successful $75,000 grant to the Davis Educational Foundation to begin the student internship program, staffed and housed, that the college desperately needed.

The president and I began to rub shoulders with folks who lived on the shore, right on the shore, and to reconnect with the disaffected, who always exist and are always worth trying to get to know and to bring back. It means something when the wife of an art collecting/art dealing billionaire expresses an interest in coming onto your board, after all.

And, hardly two years into the job, we were working the quiet phase of the three-year *35th Anniversary Campaign.*

Things were moving.

Then, apparently without notification, the deficit showed up. Overspending was part of that, lack of attention was another. The new president panicked. And that, after another eight months or so, was that.

<hr />

Deficits inflict a variety of punishments but also provide a number of opportunities; they make a board sit up and pay attention. They make presidents extraordinarily nervous. They give a president great latitude because everyone else becomes nervous. They provide an opportunity to get rid of deadwood, if you are so lucky to have some. They alarm your banker and your accrediting association. They provide an opportunity to take a look where the money is going. They concentrate the mind. They demand order, as opposed to disorder.

To get rid of one, you either work your way out of it, however long it takes but as quickly as possible, or you cut spending to match the real or projected overrun, in an attempt to slay the beast with a single, brutal action.

Montserrat's projected deficit was hefty, a couple of hundred thousand at least. The president chose to make extensive cuts to staff and programs and take care of the problem in one big move. The architecture firm hired to design the new building of galleries, studios, and the college's permanent collection on the yet to be torn-down $600,000 lot, was the first to go.

Then down went the idea of expanding the pre-college program, the program designed to make money and enroll first-year students. Down went any idea of salary adjustment, so off went my graphic artist and up went our Web management, design, and printing costs, all to be outsourced, I was told. The final cuts were to be across the board, uniformly applied instead of strategically, as I fruitlessly pointed out.

The president had decided, against the advice of five members of the senior staff, to fire a bunch of people, five, all in one day because he'd been told or had read that was the best way to do it, all the bleeding over in one day, he said. Well, that's how the bloodless brass of corporations takes care of things, and colleges like Middlebury, once, tossing out some 20 or more employees, locking them out of their offices and herding them in front of a few corporate hires to calm the hysteria. It never struck me as good practice.

But there you have it. I got away with letting one person go, a new hire just months on the job. I hated it, being, as I always had been and was doomed to forever be, an inept, reluctant let-goer, firer. At my professional level, I understand, it's a fault. At Montserrat's president's level, however, it was a rolling disaster. Firing the comptroller and having to hire her back within the week because he didn't notice there was no one on the staff with the skills to do the comptroller's job at half the wages, which was, apparently, his plan.

Everything seemed to stop. The college was in turmoil. The president confined himself to quarters. The board kept its collective head down, and allowed — encouraged — the president to hire a personal coach to help him manage what I had privately concluded was a case of near terminal micromanaging, or fear of the dog.

———

Even though our architect board chair didn't pay enough attention during committee meetings, which drove the president crazy, I liked him. About the last positive thing that happened in my short career at

Montserrat was his idea, and some of his money. He'd checked with the president, who was all for it

He had an eye for art and a feel for public relations and, like a lot of people, like me, like the president and the entire college community, regarded Christo and Jeanne-Claude among the most fascinating artists on the globe, so it was a big deal that, for two weeks and three weekends in February 2005, *The Gates, Central Park, New York, 1979-2005*, their long, long work in process, was going to open on February 12th and close on the 27th in Central Park. Close and disappear, dismantled, dispersed, not collectable, just like all their monumental art in all the huge places it has appeared around the world.

A month before *The Gates* was to open, the architect chairman and I took a train down to New York and headed for the Waldorf. We talked our way onto the upper floor, Central Park-facing rooms to see the grand view of the park, which from the Waldorf was terrible: tiny windows you almost had to climb up to see out of. No place for a party.

Out on the sidewalk, somewhat shocked, having assumed the Waldorf, with magnificent views of the park and its history and all, was the obvious hotel. We strolled west. Wandered into the lobby of the Helmsley. Rode up to the penthouse on the top floor with a rather cautious mid-manager — we didn't look the sort, I suppose. But up there we were practically hanging over the great expanse of the park, peering down 40 stories through floor-to-ceiling glass from a room 60 feet long, with one bed and three bathrooms. Yours for one Saturday night, $2,600.

We went back to the sidewalk. We've come all this way, said the chairman. It's a lot of money, I said. It could be foggy, he said. That would be a waste of the money, I said. I thought it would cost less than that, he said. We'd still have to pay for catering, that's another four or five hundred dollars, I said.

We walked up and down. Finally he said, "If the college will pick up half the tab, I'll pick up the other half, and half the catering — but I get the bed."

We had paused in front of the Helmsley lobby. It really is not my place to disappoint board chairs, so I said, "Deal." And we went in and put down the deposit.

Do you know *The Gates*? That was a party.

It was an installation of 7,503, 11-foot-high, five-to 18-foot-wide steel frames, each gate set across a pathway in Central Park. From each crossbar hung a wide, heavy, "saffron" (in Christo's notes, orange to the rest of us) cloth, which waved and furled high above between the saffron-painted posts. Seven thousand, five hundred-three of these giant gates, over 23 miles of the park's pathways. Sometimes there were 30 or 40 in a row, 10 feet apart, climbing a little hill, crossing a bridge, or stopping at an underpass and continuing on the other side. Sometimes just a dozen or less.

The day we were there was bright and cold, under 30 degrees, and just breezy enough to lift the curtains to billow and flap quietly above, or just gently move, undulate. It was art you walked though and under. As the sun set, the curtains glowed.

Like all of Christo and Jeanne-Claude's works, *The Gates* was a feat of engineering, as well as art, as well as a statement about environmentalism, because everything was to be recycled, every hole filled in, every bolt removed. And, too, as usual, it was a statement about money and art, a very unusual statement: Christo and Jeanne-Claude pay for everything themselves, by acting as their own agents and selling original pieces and prints depicting various stages of a project's conception and installation. No corporations. No grants. No museum sponsorships. No donations. No volunteers. No *The Gates* coffee mugs.

We invited everyone we knew to our penthouse, every Montserrat donor, alumni, and friend from Boston to New York. From 40 stories up *The Gates'* wide saffron cloths unfurled like elegant chamber music carried by beautifully crafted instruments, but separate, transcendent, weaving through the trees of the park, flowing like a saffron-colored tune. In the park, visitors strolled at an easy pace — there was no rush in the watching, listening how the folds in the fabric muted the city's pounding timpani down to human voices and the soft scuffing of shoes on tarmac.

We had catered platters of delicatessen cold cuts, salads, and cookies. Coffee. Beer. Water. All of which seemed to cost as much as the space. At times there were more than 40 people in that grand, heavily carpeted room, with a total count of maybe a hundred or more passing through, talking art, eating, then out they'd go in groups or couples to hike the pathways of the park. The skating rink was open, too, so I skated with Russell, my NYC-living son, a freelance digital animator who pined for Vermont but understood the restrictive economies of his particular art, which seemed to be you lived in New York or Los Angeles. No hockey sticks allowed, but still, to walk with him through the late afternoon park, our battered hockey skates over our shoulders, and to skate in Central Park with Christo whirling around us, The Gates snaking through the foreshortened countryside, and everyone, everyone in a good mood — it was New York, so that was about as strange and as wonderful a thing as the art, and because of the art.

Lulu, I, Jo, and other staffers stayed in the same hotel, the rooms in the back, on the lower floors. In the evening we joined an elegant dinner at a cavernous restaurant where Christo was rumored to appear, but he did not. Walking back through the park, under the shifting curtains in the cold breeze, between the path lights and the lights of the surrounding city, we were for a time alone inside the sculpture, weaving through its tunnels, climbing its gentle hills.

Early the next morning, before heading back to the North Shore, we took another walk through The Gates. And suddenly there he was, Christo himself, his big eyeglasses and scraggly hair and long-sleeved safari jacket, walking with long steps up a slope toward a section of gates. His photographer was with him, and Christo would point for him to shoot this, and now shoot that from this angle. They were moving quickly. Someone went over toward him and starting talking. Christo waved him off, without looking. "I'm working. I'm working," he called out and kept going without losing his stride.

———

By the time I resigned by letter, polite letter, but unequivocal, in June 2005, the college's fiscal and leadership problems had begun to filter through the North Shore community, and bits and pieces of support pulled away. The billionaire's board-bound wife, she pulled out. That hurt. By then the board was changing its leadership, and out went the architect, I imagine to his relief, and in came, well, a fellow who made our attention-challenged architect look like a savvy and practiced trustee.

My position as second in command put me in the squeeze: I could not speak negatively about the president's actions, or inactions, to board members, or staff, or faculty. That's part of the deal between a president and his or her senior staff, particularly the second in command. It's not in the contract, it's unspoken, but to me it was sacrosanct. In the industry it makes for trust, and it has to work even in conflict.

But that didn't stop people from talking to me. Lots of them. Too many. Thus the squeeze.

It was the going backward part I couldn't stand. It was the across-the-board budget slashing, the striking off of the first five heads that came within reach. Neither Rod Gander nor Paul LeBlanc would have tolerated such a scrambling retreat before an advancing deficit.

It could all be put back together, of course. A good portion of Jo's career had been putting it all back together. Marlboro was about 15 years of putting it back together, so I'd been there. But I couldn't understand it this time, with the leadership floundering, paralyzed, knocked down, and staying down.

I'd been spoiled by two presidents and a high-class board at Marlboro: we didn't always agree or even get along, but we were fighters, we always got back up.

Maybe some deep fatigue had set in, or it was some kind of post-traumatic stress from two decades at Marlboro that had weakened me, like a reoccurrence of malaria. Sisyphus, now with malaria, that's what it felt like. That's when I wrote the letter, and it was back to Vermont for Lulu and me.

There is a postscript to our urban adventure. Having bought a little in-town house at the peak of the market in 2003, when realtors were so busy they were writing contracts on the hoods of their cars, by late 2005, back in Vermont, we would have been smart to take the one offer of exactly what we paid for it, but we weren't that lucky, or smart.

Dumb, really, when it was discovered the little house needed an entire new roof. Dumb when we needed $17,000 to repair the sewage line. Dumb when we rented it to a chainsmoking, lite beer-drinking, quasi-employed couple, who lived like fleabitten coyotes in a dark cave. It took years and more money to finally sell the charming little cottage, at a huge loss that we welcomed, welcomed to be free of it.

I can't avoid thinking somehow the catastrophe of our urban bungalow was due justice, the cosmic sort, for having abandoned Montserrat and all those good people, in a time of need, of trouble. Maybe the president and I could have worked something out, worked through it. But my impatience would have ended that. It had to be my problem with authority figures. I couldn't deal with them anymore. Presidents.

⁓

When I come full circle, as I had in leaving Vermont and returning, I see there is something more to all this thinking about place and how place shapes colleges and colleges return the favor, when I think back on it from where I am today, as in, how did I get here to this place, literally right here, sitting, writing, I can discern an uneven pattern, a forested layout, of the places that helped shape me.

My father had a moving from place to place issue, which means either you have problems with the place you occupy, or simply a persistent and happy anticipation of the place you're going to next. He lived most of his childhood in Japan, in Kobe, where my grandfather was in the import/export business. He went to secondary school and high school in the Ojai Valley in California. In those schools he fell in love with the cowboy life, and my brother and sisters and I grew up with stories of him and his high school buddies packing deep into the High Sierras and battling rattlesnakes, catching golden trout by the basketful, doctoring horses on the trail, and generally living the most perfect life of freedom and adventure a young man could have.

Then, somehow, New Jersey and then college, Yale, where he became editor of the *Yale Science Magazine* mostly because it allowed him to have a telephone in his room, from where he could call my mother and keep watch on her, a practice she apparently approved of.

He went from Yale, to her, and then to *LIFE* magazine in 1941. He rose to editor. He had four children. Then executive editor. The last issue he edited was the Kennedy assassination issue. I was 13. He said it was a frantic week and he said he would walk through the typing pools where the women — they were all women — would be weeping at their desks and he's waving his arms yelling, "Type! Type!"

But what my father really wanted was to leave New York and our home in Connecticut and, each summer, get to Wyoming as fast as he could jam four kids and wife into a car and drive. Sometimes we split up and half of us got to go to Chicago by overnight train. But we always ended up at T-Cross Ranch, outside Dubois. It was owned by the Coxes, and Mr. Cox was so old he didn't ride anymore, or move about much. He'd been a WWI fighter pilot in the army. My Dad, when he was 14 or 15 years old worked on this ranch, so he knew Mr. Cox as a younger man and a boss, eventually a friend. When he could, Dad would get there early and spend a week wrangling, just as he did when he worked there summers. But that ranch worked on him, too, his whole life, and on us, and me, as a result.

I guess we children grew too large, or too old, to be hauled out west each summer, or Dad got too busy in New York, but eventually, my parents bought 126 acres and an old farmhouse in East Dover, Vermont. It cost $26,000 in 1963 and my father was so nervous about spending that kind of money he got up in the middle of the night and vomited. From then on, summers and winters, we'd pack up in one or two cars on weekends and drive the five hours to East Dover from Connecticut.

That's how I got to Vermont as a child. And it was how I got to Colorado, as a freshman at Denver University, at the last moment in August 1968, before I could be drafted. My older brother, Pete, was already serving in Vietnam — he was a helicopter crew chief — and I was strangely ambivalent about even applying to college, putting it off until Pete clearly indicated Vietnam was no place for his bother.

Denver, I guess, because I was tired of the endless New England stone walls and forests, which like a massive living fence seemed to enclose all the schools I'd been sent to, usually to little avail. I wasn't halfway through my first year at Denver before my father was flying out to meet me, and we'd drive up and down the Front Range looking at ranches for sale. He'd had some place in his mind since childhood, and he was determined to find it.

As I finish this circle, it turns out I have a similar problem with place, in that new places always seemed preferable to whatever place I am in, for however long. I suffered at the back of a private-school classroom all through primary school, then a new school for seventh grade, and another for eighth. Then, two high schools, one in Maine and one in New York. Then Denver, then finally, as a college junior, Marlboro College. For me, it was a pretty good solution, given my condition as an interested but selective and lazy student. But it may have set a pattern: before Lulu and I finally built our house in Marlboro and developed the flower farm, we'd moved 11 times in 9 years, or 9 times in 11 years.

Then 19 years in one place.

Then to Beverly. Then back. Then north to Craftsbury Common and Sterling.

It was more than just place, that first leave-taking after Marlboro; more than job fatigue provoked our flight to the North Shore. It had to be. After 19 years we picked up and just went. And barely two and a half years later we picked up and went again. After six years at Sterling, we moved to a little converted sugar house with a large pond that we'd bought three years into my presidency as a retreat from living in the president's house in the village. There I "retired" while we built an addition and landscaped. The retirement lasted hardly two years.

Something else had happened to move us not to Beverly but out of Marlboro. I think of it now as a reaction, a panicked moment run out in slow motion, where the next place had to be better than the current one. That there was stuff there in Marlboro from which we had to move away.

We were, Lulu and I, relatively early to breast cancer in May 2001.

The first in our neighborhood. After our immediate family's reaction to the news, which was stoic and supportive, we discovered Lulu's experience was even more deeply unsettling to others, somehow more threatening to them than to us. After the mastectomy, one woman asked me straight out, "Are you going to leave her? Are you going to leave her now?"

Another showed up at the door of the Marlboro house days after the surgery and burst into tears and noiseless sobs while I stood there at the doorstep. Lulu hauled herself out of bed, a light checkered blanket wrapped around her, brought the woman inside and sat her down and comforted her, settled her down, dried the tears, and eventually accepted the promise of — Lulu's choice — honey chicken or cabbage lasagna. That's what people did, bring food. That's what women did. Men, for the most part, avoided the subject. "How's she doin'?" was, gratefully, about the extent of it.

Then you live on with it. With no guarantees, a threat actually, like living with an invisible, manipulative bully in your house, unwanted but immune to eviction. While, over the years, in the neighborhood, other breasts were removed and women died. When we changed neighborhoods, to Beverly, then up to Sterling, we found the cancer already waiting, maiming and killing women, making orphans, testing men.

At first every three months, then every six months, year after year, Lulu went to Dartmouth Hospital, underwent a daylong series of tests and examinations, and then met with Dr. Garry Schwartz, a young oncologist, new to the East Coast. For a period of time he was in a wheelchair attending Lulu after tearing his Achilles tendon; during another stretch he was accompanied by a stern and thorough staff member as poor Dr. Schwartz struggled to conform to using electronic devices to record and document patient visits. He was impatient.

Then we'd drive home, wherever it was, and await his call, a day, sometimes two days, later. But he always called. And he always began with the words, "The tests," and, after the first year or two when various threats, indications, and unclear results propelled further unscheduled visits for more tests, the results were always good. We got used to it, only occasionally reminding ourselves, or worse being reminded, that women die of this disease at a regular but individually unpredictable pace.

Eventually, they look like AIDS patients — shrunken, sick for months, weakened, eventually resigned, then dead. It seems to take forever. But we'd forget all that, each time, until Dr. Schwartz was due to call with the test results.

I wonder sometimes. The way things had been going we were supposed to live out our lives in Marlboro, close to the college. Be part of that slow but ever-expanding community of former college people. But place is peril, too, and leaving one for another can be mere busy work to keep away from dying.

7

Search...and Destroy

If you need a job or are looking for a career change and think you'd like to be a college president you should take a breath, a deep one, and look in the mirror, a non-distorting one. You should ask yourself, why? You should check in with your ego — under control? You should measure the thickness of your skin — can it grow thicker? Are you comfortable speaking in public? Are you a good listener? Really? Do you have all the requisite human and business skills? Some of them? Any of them? Where did you get your PhD? No PhD? Do you cherish "down time"? Are you set in your ways about how stuff gets done? Are you at ease with young men and women of every ilk?

Imagine being a captain on a mid 19th-century oceangoing ship, a whaler, for instance, out of Nantucket. Once you are at sea the ship's owners, your bosses, are ashore and voiceless. Everyone on board works for you, just you, in what is now a little, heaving, wooden universe, the hierarchical structure of which is as evident as is the hand of God in the affairs of men and women.

You have leadership issues? No one is going to call you on them. You have some weird particulars, like, for instance, napping in the afternoon? People will tiptoe past you because they know the rules about napping do not apply to you. In fact, none of the rules apply to you.

A presidency is about power, a word rarely used in seminars and workshops and courses on management, or in descriptions of how college presidencies work, how they evolved, and how they stopped evolving. There are poorly spiced notions of executive management skills and quality leadership, even persuasiveness, but it is power we are talking about, the kind Captain Ahab exerted upon his doomed crew, but for one, of the Pequod, to do pretty much exactly what you want to do, however you want to do it, and behave however you wish, even if it sinks the boat.

Single-minded and dark as they were, Ahab possessed effective leadership/executive management skills, like "efficiency modeling" — in this case having a single clear goal, and demanding flawless teamwork 24/7, for years, without let up and without touching land.

Captain Ahab made effective use of motivational incentives, using drama, money, and manliness in nailing a gold coin to the mast for the first man to sight the white whale, during a team-building pump'um-up rally on the poop deck. Kill Moby Dick! Kill Moby Dick!

All that talent, all that technological expertise, all that sailing around oceans, all that effectiveness, and not a single goal achieved, a complete disaster. Ahab's is a deadly lesson in poor governance mixed with unfettered power that, though commonly available, went to the captain's head, that served his common madness. In the end, he didn't even kill the fish; the fish killed him.

So it's good that most college presidents are well within the range of normal: well intentioned and honest, ethical, and morally put together, likable and fully human. Thus the question is not whether you, the new president, can deal effectively with having so much power, but how long will you last before power begins to deal with you?

In any case, you are now ready to seek a college presidency, just by dint of having read the above paragraphs whatever your answers or deeper thoughts. You are ready just as you would be if you meditated on the Zen of the Presidency in a cold cave on some forlorn mountainside, or attended the Harvard Seminar for New Presidents three times in a row. You are ready because there is no proven, no ideal preparation or training for all that's going to come flying at you the second you take the helm. In a nautical sense, upon first sailing, you may not know north from south, bow from stern, or port from starboard, but relax. The ship can sail itself for a while. You'll catch on. You got this far. You are no amateur. You are new and everyone's pulling for you. Your odds of becoming a successful president have never been higher, and probably never will be.

＿＿＿

There are basically two ways colleges and university presidents are searched for, vetted, and hired, or not. Either a board of trustees employs one of the dozens of expensive consulting firms that specialize in presidential searches, or the trustees take on the task themselves. My direct experiences in presidential transitions are three: Rod Gander departing from Marlboro and Paul LeBlanc arriving; my candidacy and appointment at Sterling College; the search and hiring of my successor, Matthew Derr.

In each case, the board of trustees conducted these searches. And in each case, only one candidate was considered viable, almost from the start. In other words, in each case the college came close to having a failed search, had that one candidate declined there being no second choice. That's dismal for everyone — the incumbent president, the candidates, the board, and the institution as a whole. And it is a distinct and discouraging, and public, setback. However, considerably worse than a failed search is a board that chooses a candidate nevertheless, to fill the post out of desperation, rather than admit it's been a bungle and start over.

Ideally, all the effort a college's search committee puts into the months-long process culminates in three or four finalists, each of whom will be individually interviewed by every committee and constituency on campus, and will be required to make a speech or give a presentation, all during a 24-hour on-campus visit. And that, again ideally, will result in one final candidate and at least one other the board would favor unanimously.

＿＿＿

Marlboro's three presidential finalists for Rod's office each spent a day and a half on campus being politely grilled by every constituency —

faculty, students, staff, senior staff — but mostly they spent their time with board members, and would continue to do so for another couple of weeks as the board wrestled with their decision, their responsibility.

In this case, the one woman was the first to go, to be put aside. She was a dean at a prestigious liberal arts college, also in New England. Her resume was thorough. Her cover letter, of equal if not greater importance in an application, was brief and to the point in a sort of "this is what you get" attitude and thus refreshing. But as her day wore on she flagged, her honesty became too revealing in her frustration with her current position. And she was exhausted, too exhausted it seemed, to be reflective of Marlboro's situation and what she could do to help. In the words of one board member, she was running away from something as opposed to running toward something.

Paul Leblanc, on the other hand, all six-foot-four of him, smiling, friendly, fully engaged, already seemed to be running in circles around the place. He wasn't even 40 years old. He was, in a word, enthusiastic. Excited to be there. He laughed easily. He kept saying, "In my experience" which I wished he wouldn't, I remember thinking, because he had no experience. He brought cookies to the midafternoon interview with students, clearly stumping his competition.

The third candidate was very sophisticated and business suave, a Chicago lawyer to boot, and seemed to fit right in with the board leadership. Quiet, thoughtful, reserved, he seemed to take command of the interviewing situation and lead it wherever he wanted, smiling, nodding, agreeing.

I was leaning toward the tall, younger guy but I had no vote, of course. I did, however, have some influence with the board and had purposefully stayed off the search committee so I could help Rod finish up the 50th Anniversary Campaign, while meeting separately one-on-one with the candidates, something I had sought permission to do, of course.

The Chicago businessman/lawyer, meanwhile, invited Jerry and Elizabeth to fly out there for a meeting with him, no explanation but nicely expressed in a phone call, sounding as if the content was going to be more than worth the trouble. Who's running the show here? Jerry wondered. It's a testament to Marlboro's ability to attract and hold good people that they both, especially Elizabeth who was not even a trustee, agreed to go on such a mysterious trip.

The one-day trip turned out to be quite straightforward, Jerry said when he phoned Rod. The gentleman, as Jerry would have referred to him, had been working over the college's audits and was proposing a clear path out of the fiscal distress that had plagued us for a decade. He proposed that upon his appointment to the presidency, the trustees guarantee to pay off the annual deficit — make up the loss for the next five years, by which time Marlboro would be running in the black.

Was that brilliant, or what?

As one board member summed up it up: "What was he thinking? We may be rich but we're not stupid."

Jerry and Elizabeth were politely dismissive, and also put-off for having been dragged out to Chicago to discuss a bad idea that could have been dismissed much more easily over the phone. Rod was bewildered why someone of such apparent sophistication would do such a thing. I was happy because it took him out of the running, at least with Jerry and Elizabeth, and I was betting that was enough.

But we weren't done yet.

Lil Farber, the former board chair, presidential search committee member, clothier, and as near to a Jewish mother as I was ever privileged to have, had been unusually quiet after the Chicago episode. As far as I could learn, the search committee, too, was not happy, at least in part because they were feeling the sole-candidate pressure, the perception of now only one being left, and in this case he was the youngest, least experienced presidential candidate imaginable, with a résumé that had to reach back to high school days to have any heft to it. But he got this far largely on charm and smarts; everyone likes him better than the other two, almost everyone, at least. And he was last of some 50 applicants still on his feet.

Lil came into my office in Mather House, sneaked in is more like it, glancing back down the hall to check if anyone had seen her. She closed the door and sat in the red chair. And was silent. And pale.

"Lil," I said. "Are you all right?"

"I think we've made a terrible mistake," she said. "I think we need Rod back."

Wow. Now, what's my role here? I'd worked with Rod for 15 years day in and day out. Years ago we'd become friends, unacknowledged because presidents just don't have friends. But now my friend was done. He was cross-eyed with fatigue. Finally some real money was coming in, the budget was going to balance eventually, and Rod had sworn to leave at 65, at 15 years. He'd promised himself. Fifteen would be enough, if not too many, he believed. Even if he could have been persuaded to stay, if Lil's crisis had been substantial, maybe he would have out of a sense of service, but not for long and not particularly willingly, and not with great effectiveness.

I hesitated, and then looked her in the eye in such a way that it was difficult, I imagined, to distinguish dead seriousness from grim humor.

"No, Lil," I said. "Rod said it might come to this. He said if the search faltered even for a moment the entire board might lose its nerve and ask him to stay. You see, Lil, he was afraid he'd be too out of it by then, by this time, too done with the place to respond rationally. So, he told me if it ever happened I was to use my deer rifle and shoot him in the head . . . but I don't want to shoot him in the head . . . so you've got to let him go."

A long pause. . . . Then she begins to smile. Then she bursts out laughing — how Lil could laugh — and that was the end of that.

When you don't hire experts, you don't get expert advice. That's what a board of trustees should understand and acknowledge when choosing to conduct a presidential search on their own.

I could have used expert advice, for instance, about the actual, literal transfer of power; that is, exactly when does one president leave the president's office, the president's chair, and the president's secretary, and the new president sit down in his or her new president's chair and ask how the phone works?

How could I have avoided having the old president, Rod, still occupying his office as the new president, Paul, is trying to move in? The transition day arrived. Monday, July 8, 1996. Rod, I am saying, you have to get out of your office. The new guy is here. He's already moved into the president's house.

So Rod gathered up the last of his stuff and he and his typewriter moved upstairs to an empty space on the third floor of Mather House. The reason, he explained, was he hadn't completed the budget and considered the budget his budget, and it had to be completed and for that he needs his secretary, and comptroller, and so on.

While downstairs the new guy is asking, "What's the deal?" upstairs Rod was saying, "What's the big deal?

And I was saying a pox on them both, and why was keeping them apart my job?

That knot worked itself loose, as it should have, after another week or so and one day Rod wasn't there. He and his wife Isabelle were in their new place in Brattleboro, a tall Victorian overlooking the Connecticut River. Rod's retirement actually started in his office, while still president, when he began daydreaming of running for political office. Then he announced his intentions, to me at least and to Isabelle undoubtedly. Then he moved to Brattleboro and went whole hog, and ran a great race, bringing humor and humility and a fine-tuned political sense to a rather straight-laced constituency, and he won. Rod relished that job and spoke of little else for two years: the fights, the strategies, the good guys, and the bad guys. I hadn't seen him that engaged, that happy, for years, but then came cancer and treatment and a wasting away. He died in bed at night, after getting up and closing the window. I spoke last at his memorial service:

October 20, 2007

Dear Rod:
Instead of speaking at your memorial, I decided to write you a letter and then read it. In all our years of friendship, there are still things left unsaid. And I wanted to say them to you, instead of about you.

I know. I'm late.

Up at my little College in Craftsbury Common there's a very strange tradition. I described it to you a year ago when I hardly understood it myself. We thought it was sort of odd, but harmless. We weren't sure. Up there, at the conclusion of the weekly community meeting, which is mostly announcements, some complaints, some issues, are what is called "Appreciations."

They are just what they sound like. Someone stands up (that's not a requirement) and voices his or her appreciation for someone else, or to some collection of people, for something good, for some service, for helping out. I haven't been much of a practitioner. In fact, I've yet to offer up even one. For me, they do not come easily.

Appreciations are like hugs, Rod; and neither of us is big on hugs. But that's what this letter to you is, an Appreciation.

I appreciate, Rod, those years we worked together. I appreciate the faith you placed in me, and the trust you offered. I appreciate that when I screwed up your usual response was to find an example of some far classier screw up. Our own best seemed to always involve publications —

Remember our grim laughter when we looked at the commencement invitation one year and realized we'd invited 800 people to "Commenceemencement"? Remember when we produced a poster of the east coast, and left New Jersey off? A guy from Pennsylvania noticed it, that his state suddenly had a coast line.

I appreciate that you were my mentor. Most people don't even get one of those, and I had the best and I knew it at the time, I felt it. Do you know I am informed everyday now by our years of working together?

Everything I know about college finance, for instance, I learned from you. It was easy: First you decide you will not be crushed by the terrible march of negative num-

bers across the body of your college; then you get really, really good at subtraction and at keeping people comfortable with subtraction. Then, after a long struggle, you take up addition. And that's better.

I appreciate your unassailable talent as an editor and writer. At *Newsweek* you were the star editor to the star reporters (as I hear it) — but I had my own exclusive editor, the master himself, putting his pencil stub — his unique chicken-scratch - to my writing. At the top you would write, "Will, just some suggestions."

I appreciate your intolerance with pretension, hubris, the demeaning of human rights, racial bigotry, vicious gossip, sycophantry, cheating at cards or sports. I admired how you could suffer a fool, tolerate an incompetent, and not fuss over poorly prepared food. I appreciate, too, Rod, that you were not a collector of things, not a hobbyist. The material world didn't seem to do much for you. I believe you had only the vaguest notion that automobiles required motor oil, as well as gas, to run.

Your life at Marlboro was consumed by money. The terrible glacier pace with which it was obtained and the lightening speed of its disappearance. I appreciate that to you it was just money; that money didn't define you, and because it didn't define you, it didn't define the College, or any of us up there, back then.

When your salary was published in the Chronicle of Higher Education, the truth was revealed. "I'm the lowest paid president in the United States," you said. "Except for two nuns who do it for free."

Instead it was people, always people, as individuals and as groups, who seemed to drive you. Especially people who couldn't speak for themselves, or would not. And people . . . well, people like me . . . and I'll bet some of the young *Newsweek* reporters you mentored, and others, I'm sure I'm unaware of . . . people just quirky enough, just rebellious enough, just enough outside of normal, that without you were in danger of leading lesser lives, but on your wing covered territory they never imagined was for them.

I appreciate that, Rod, everyday.

I appreciate — it made me proud — at the end of your career at the College, "a rag of your former self" as you put it to me, you surprised everyone and instead of taking the relaxing walk down off the mountain, you turned around and climbed up it to the Vermont Senate. I appreciate your life of service, Rod, because in some mysterious way it reflects on those of us around you. It makes us better people.

Witness just this room. Hundreds of friends and family, with thousands of stories

— a life overflowing with stories, each one, Rod, carried along by a bit or more of you. I like to think that there are fifteen years worth of stories that weave a huge tapestry of your years at Marlboro College.

And stitched in there somewhere is our friendship. Because we were friends. And we are still friends. I appreciate that most of all.

In the president's office, the old typewriter was replaced with a computer and printer; the stacks of file drawers were moved to storage. The collection of six or seven rickety old chairs around a low octagonal table, where the senior staff had gathered once a week to chart the next week's course, Paul removed and left to the students, replaced by uniform and more comfortable chairs. The senior staff meeting was moved from Rod's Friday afternoons ("So they can more easily be canceled," he explained) to Paul's Tuesday mornings, and the transition was complete.

My own challenge in the transfer of power, 10 years later, 2006, when I arrived at Sterling, was to prod Jed Williamson, my predecessor, to remove his 10 years' worth of stuff from the president's house so Lulu and I had a place to move all our stuff, then being assembled from our homes in Marlboro and Beverly.

When my turn came to leave Sterling, to abandon my then-barren corner office overlooking the center of campus, there was an awkward procedural moment. Alarmingly, President Derr had called me the evening before, wanting to get straight the ceremonial aspects of the morning's official transition. Of which there were none. I felt I'd disappointed him.

"There is no ceremony, Matthew, I'm sorry," I said. "There aren't a lot of people around. And I can't go back in, I'm going trout fishing. Want to join me? You can go in late. The rules don't apply to you, you know."

What does all this mean? That for a board of trustees, on its own and working carefully, hooking and landing a new president is not all that difficult, when everything goes even moderately well.

I've never been sure the professionals have much of an edge over the home-grown search, except in releasing the institution from much of the actual work, credential checking, scheduling, consulting, and counseling that goes into a search. In addition, firms have considerably greater search resources than individual boards of trustees, however well connected or search savvy they may be. And finally, search firms usually know when a search has failed; boards of trustees alone are unlikely to call off a search, even if their first and second choices decline.

But consider the greater issue: The moment a new president is deposited on campus is actually the middle point, the slow tipping point in a presidential transition. Already as much as an entire year, the lame-duck year, the search-and-find year, has softened the institution's leadership, has affected the institution's business, slowed it down. Following this is a new president's first year, devoted to getting his or her feet on the ground. Statistically, too, a president's first year is also a year of overspending — new presidents slammed with urgent requests from important pieces of his or her instantly shaky empire. You want to make them happy. You think you need them. You do need them. Deficits are provoked.

Only those who land, usually with a thump, in the middle of a previously established deficit are spared the pressures to overspend. They have other problems.

In any case, such a clunky, drawn-out process of leadership change makes me question the whole industry, as if there's something I don't know about, where this system makes all the sense in the world and I'm the only one who doesn't see it.

———

The most prestigious program aimed at lessening the shock of becoming a new president is the Harvard Seminar for New Presidents, largely because of its name if not also its faculty and curriculum. The five-day intensive program is held once a year in mid-September at the Harvard Graduate School of Education in Cambridge. You are only allowed to attend once, and its $5,000 price tag is picked up by your new board of trustees.

My class was composed of 58 newly minted college and university presidents, 39 men and 19 women, almost all of whom had already been on the job for six or eight weeks. Every one of them, I felt, was more highly educated than I, more experienced in their academic fields than I who did not have an academic field, more confident, more mature, undoubtedly, and better dressed, except the handful of Jesuit presidents who wore cheap shirts and the same suit and tie every day. They and the two nuns were the only ones I was going to outrank on the pay scale. Everyone else in the seminar was making least $150,000, and many of them much more.

We presidents were separated by institutional profile; my group of eight, for instance, consisted of presidents from relatively small, independent liberal arts colleges. We formed one "discussion group" that would come together for various projects. Other groups were composed of public college presidents, large and midsize university presidents, and liberal arts college presidents. The nun and priest presidents were scattered among the liberal arts institutions.

The Harvard faculty were all fast speakers, so knowledgeable in their fields and precise in their presentations they impressed me to silence and caution. You don't want to be called out by one of these guys so you better do your homework, which everyone seemed to take seriously, especially the elaborate case statements and the spirited back and forth between professor and the tiered semicircle of new presidents. I, at first, did not take the reading assignments seriously at all. The most elaborate was an examination of a college's financial turnaround and the leadership decisions that propelled it. I got called out, or called in to the discussion, and barely escaped with my dignity and a commitment to read the next one with care, or at least read it, or skip the session.

Later we took on finance and human resources; another afternoon we listened to some fellow's elaborate analysis of leadership personality types where everyone was either a warrior or a wizard. I didn't get it.

Some evenings we attended short, less formal talks or presentations. There we learned, for instance, of one veteran president's formula for taking time off. She swore by "a day a week, a weekend a month, and a month per year." At Sterling I was to manage two weeks in the summer and scattered days off elsewhere, like a regular tradesman, which was often how I felt in my career, like a talented carpenter or plumber, a logger, or chef with his crew.

But I missed Paul LeBlanc's evening chat, presented at an earlier seminar, *"The President's House: Benefit or Time Bomb?"* This always newsworthy phenomenon, experienced personally by Paul and myself but only in its mildest, not newsworthy form, was really a serious topic that had some number of former presidents paid attention to they might no longer be former. Usually, they were the ones who sunk a half-million institutional dollars into plushy renovations of the president's house, before earning a single buck for the place.

The last day of the seminar the six discussion groups took the afternoon off to work on their presentations, that is, their theatrical presentations, their skits, to be presented that evening after dinner and lots of drinks. To me this was the strangest thing yet. All these presidents being shoved out the door of their own comfort zones; it struck me how these Harvard folks are endlessly entertaining themselves.

I had no choice but to get into it, brainstorming ideas, writing, editing, and rehearsing, if you could call it that. Our major challenge was we were supposed to be funny, and college presidents, I already knew, were usually funny-challenged in a serious way. This group didn't disappoint. And I learned that presidents are distinctly lousy actors, and have limited creative juices besides alcohol. Thank God for the wine.

In truth, it was fun. Or at least I had fun. All these tipsy presidents, one or two in tablecloth drag, belting out off- tune songs and fumbling their way through skits high schoolers could have written better. One or two were even unrecognizable as a skit, which is like a pun on stage, so it's not that hard.

A summary gathering over breakfast, the awarding of very nice Harvard Certificates of Completion, handshakes all around, and off we all went back to our new jobs having learned — having learned. The whole week was a thought provoking, stimulating, and occasionally intimidating mix of the profound and the silly, not unlike the life of a college president. That's what I learned.

━━━

I was also to learn much more about a presidential subject the Harvard instructors did not teach, did not even mention. It was all about me when I straightened up and took notice: that is, while the path to a college presidency is rarely easy, leaving a presidency can be frustrating, humiliating, and professionally difficult, when not downright perilous.

I understand why the seminar administration — mostly, that is, the ever-congenial, knowledgeable, and scary director Judith McLauglin — spends no time on the subject of presidential departures, whether they be congenial and affirming, or the other sort, the interminable, the messy, the tense, like a nuclear standoff. The last thing this group wants to hear is anything about the potentially bitter end of something so sweet that's just begun.

Here, for instance, is my Harvard discussion group and, parenthetically, the number of years our presidencies survived: Maine College of Art (3), Sheldon Jackson College (2), College of the Atlantic (4), Hampshire College (5), Warren Wilson College (4), Unity College (5), Sterling College (6), and Harvey Mudd College, where Dr. Maria Klawe is the only one of us left in a president's chair, and on her way, perhaps, to obtaining the classification of being a "longtime" president, which starts no sooner than at 10 years, I'd think.

So, of the eight in my group, seven are gone within six years. A random search through the participant directory of the Harvard Seminar (excluding public colleges) came up with 6 of 10 still holding their jobs in 2013. Combined: 18 presidents and seven years later 13 are gone, 5 holding on, less than 28 percent.

Smaller colleges appear to chew through presidents at a slightly accelerated rate, and the overall survival rate beyond seven years is only about 12 percent. I heard somewhere the average presidency lasts only four or five years. I wouldn't doubt it.

The length of a president's tenure is some combination of his or her character, the current dynamics of the institution, and the fates in general. One president in my Harvard group referred to faculty as having to be "potty trained" — no kidding. He also felt strongly that access to the president had to be "rare" and "special." So you have to wonder whether those strange ideas had anything to do with a shortened tenure. Another in my discussion group confessed his greatest worry was that he wouldn't be busy enough, that the job would not be enough for him. That wasn't the case, as I understand it, and he was a short-timer even in this group.

But you don't have to be run out on a rail in the dead of night to still have a lousy endgame, a crappy departure from a college presidency. Mine, in 2012, was smooth, informal, and it turns out rather idealistic. The experience was boosted by finding an ideal successor in Matthew Derr. Yet it was still a stressful time, as if my entire surrounding environment had been nudged off kilter, the light shining from an unfamiliar or impossible direction. The air somehow not as fulfilling. And I felt lucky.

Others, not so much. Between mid-September, when I conferred with Lulu and decided it was time to leave Sterling, and the mid-October press release announcing it, two other Vermont presidents were on their way out, knocked about by scandal or controversy, muffled in the case of Burlington College and painfully public at the University of Vermont. So when I, or the board of trustees actually, announced my resignation publically in a press release, one headline, in the Burlington Free Press was something like "ANOTHER Vermont President Resigns," very *Huffington Post*, like there was a specific disease killing us off. Still, I felt like I'd been caught running around with the wrong people, who weren't actually wrong about anything. They were presidents of colleges. It's not easy but there you are on the good side, mostly, of all things human: teaching, learning, community, on and on, for God's sake. Short of outright criminality or weighty ethical or moral transgressions, presidential reputations tarred at the last moment seem a raw deal to me. Unknowingly, the press stories about my leave-taking performed a valuable service for Burlington College, taking the heat off its president's sudden, trustee-mobbed resignation. (Of course, as noted toward the beginning of this memoir, Burlington College ultimately did not survive this transition. Its complete financial collapse occurred two presidents and five brutal years later.)

At the time, some reporter asked if I was getting a $350,000 deluxe parachute like the University of Vermont president was receiving, or even the $100,000 parachute the president of Burlington College was promised. I should have said I'd take a quarter of either; okay a tenth. But I was presidential, and said, laughingly, or so the reporter wrote, I didn't think that sort of thing was coming my way. I wonder now why I was laughing.

There are other examples. You hear about them periodically, the truly scandal ridden, the university presidents falling on their swords for sins too near to have ignored; the college president who comes pre-shell shocked and is out within a year or two, pre-contract.

You could conclude that, for places like the Harvard Seminar, it is less meaningful to talk about becoming a college president if you are not going to talk about the un-becoming of one. It's like summarizing life, but leaving off the death part.

Traditionally, presiding presidents are not allowed to participate to any important degree in the selection of his or her successor. While this is a good rule it's sometimes taken too far, too sternly, where the current president is practically shunned on the subject. A search, remember, can last for six months or more and I would argue natural curiosity should be satisfied. A board member might even learn something about being president from a president. Still, it's a good rule and frees up presidents to express concerns, encouragement, and opinions to the handful, sometimes the majority, of the search committee members who will privately discuss the search and the candidates with the sitting chief, despite the above.

What I first discovered in my lame-duck year was a depth and complexity to a condition I already believed no college president could ever look forward to; the expression itself is so inglorious, such a putdown after years of labor as to be nearly offensive, worse than a gold watch. I discovered lame-duckness is a team sport, with presidents actually on the reserves or serving as water boys. Somehow, I had put the effects of the condition on the individual duck, the outgoing president, whose power begins diminishing the second after the announcement of his retirement is made. It's the notion that the resigned are, really and truly, resigned, having weakened of energy, of will, of ideas, and will continue weakening until the day a replacement shows up.

Lame-duckness radiates around presidents, true, but it emanates from the people around them, from the institution itself, like radon in the basement. You see its effect on major donors who might have otherwise increased their giving, but who upon reflection hold back, waiting to see what the new president is like. Who can blame them? They might really dislike the person and save themselves tens of thousands of dollars.

The same goes for the faculty, who are already a semi-autonomous and occasionally hostile state within the institution's borders. Suddenly, it is no longer you who will intervene with the comptroller and find the money for a teacher's project, a field trip, a new piece of equipment. No longer will they submit long proposals articulating the reasons your plans should be changed to more reflect their plans. No longer do you give out the raises and sign the paychecks. So you no longer see as much of them.

Even senior staff, a president's own imperial guard, handpicked and faithful to a fault, can be near terminally affected. Who can blame them? The president experiences a gentle turning away from such staffers and vice presidents. "Why should I worry about what this guy thinks? He's gone in ten, nine, eight, seven months, so I'm not hanging my hat on any big decisions, any changes above small and inconsequential ones." They can't help it.

The board, too, begins to sag. They don't want anything much coming their way from a president who is on his way out. "Don't spend any money!" the rather hysterical board chair at Sterling shouted over the phone at me, and took considerable calming down, and references about how signing paychecks was not spending money but fulfilling an agreement about paying employees. "That's not what I meant!" Indeed, but I understood, reluctantly now, the nature of the resigned beast.

So lame-duckness spreads until, and finally, finally the day arrives. One president fades to nothing, the new president steps into the spotlight. And the second yearlong half of institutional lame-duckness commences as the new president gets down to work learning a new way of viewing reality, and what it is really like in that chair.

All this, to me, is nuts.

I don't believe there is a successful business leader in this country, perhaps on the entire globe, who would understand how any of this works rationally. In "normal" cases, a college president's resignation comes a year before his departure. During that year the president is paid his full wages and enjoys the perks of office little hindered by former responsibilities. He or she is, in fact, discouraged from too actively pursuing those former responsibilities. Finally, during that year the president can contemplate the size and shape of the cash-filled parachute being negotiated. Meanwhile there is an overall weakening, a slacking off, on the part of the entire partially leaderless organization for that year.

This happens with the full knowledge that once new presidents finally begin, they are worth perhaps 40 percent of the salary, signing checks, making decisions forced upon the office, while spending the rest of the time learning about their new institution and, usually, how to be a president; that is, learning how to meet the expectations put upon presidents. With no institutional memory and often no experience in institutional finance, new presidents almost always overspend, on good things sometimes; other times on things that get them in trouble — new furnishings for the president's house, new furnishings for the president's office. It's a fact, too, that new presidents have less trust in their boards than older, more experienced presidents. So that can't help.

Look at the entire institutionally imposed, one-to-two-year period during which the office of the president is operating at half speed as an opportunity for the institution itself to wander off a bit, the staff laying back, the faculty plotting how to get everything. Do you know or can you imagine how difficult and time consuming it is to push an ocean liner back to the channel with a three-horse outboard on a six-foot dinghy? It's something like that.

I think the good folks at the Harvard Graduate School of Education should put their heads together with the human killer-aps over at the Harvard Business School and see if they can't come up with a better way to change out presidents, before anyone else clues into this and the industry is further tarnished.

⌒

Returning from the Harvard Seminar, I hardly remember the drive back to northern Vermont through the New England summer afternoon. My mind replayed the seminar in bits and pieces, skipping like a needle on an old LP record, a jumble of ideas one moment, fear the next, then joy for having survived at all. If anything became certain it was, however much knowledge I had gained, there was still a net increase in my ignorance and worry around almost every single aspect of being Sterling College's president.

After dinner alone in the president's house — Lulu was in Florida tending to her 83-year-old mother — I put in a call to Paul LeBlanc, who was then two years into his new job as president of Southern New Hampshire University, an independent university in Manchester, after seven years at Marlboro. Over the next decade Paul, his entrepreneurial genes kicking in and an entire small university in his oversized paws, would transform what had been a rather placid, homey sort of place into a dynamo of online education and training, out-footing the for-profits, and providing his university with the sort of fiscal security ordinarily achieved only by endowed money, accumulated over many years. If it isn't unique in higher education — literally earning your own endowment, sans donors — then it's very rare.

As one of the most positive, upbeat men in the entire world, Paul sounded good after my Harvard experience, which he had endured in his first year at Marlboro. He became friends with Judy McLaughlin, the senior lecturer and director of the seminar, who had seen rank upon rank of newly minted but untested presidents stumble in and five days later march out to their individual fates. We spoke for 45 minutes on a range of presidential subjects — his giving up tennis for squash because the university had courts, me still coming to grips with abandoning my old-man hockey team in Brattleboro, which was a young middle-age-man hockey team when I joined. We talked about his board and what little I knew about mine. And we talked about Jerry Aron and Elizabeth and that whole bunch of stalwarts still there at Marlboro, doing exactly what they should be doing.

It was good to catch up with Paul. It was very good and I didn't know why until I realized that only Lulu and Rod, who was still alive, and Paul could understand how I felt at that moment, what I was facing. But we didn't talk about it specifically. That wouldn't have helped.

Our talk was also a confirmation of what I and my newbie colleagues at the seminar had been hearing from other presidents who had been brought in to scare and entertain us, and from seminar staff, and even from the few Harvard faculty we were exposed to: that being a college president is one of the most rewarding, difficult, challenging, lonely, horribly public, frustrating, but somehow ultimately satisfying jobs in the known universe. And I believed them. We all did. And it was the truth. *Veritas!* Thus spake Harvard.

8

The Dog Is Back. Kill the Dog

The first thing of substance I learned about the Sterling College trustees came at the midpoint in the presidential search, when the search committee had whittled down their pool of 20 or so candidates to 3 finalists. It was the October board meeting and I'd been invited to show up and meet the assembled members, just a preliminary introduction, I was told, very informal.

So I drove the three hours from Marlboro, jacket and tie, and arrived just as the meeting was reconvening after lunch. The curved ceilinged Trustee Room, dominated by a huge alumni-constructed meeting table and a dozen or more captain's chairs, was directly across the foyer from the president's second floor office. Jackson Kytle, the vice chair of the board and chair of the search committee, met me in the hallway and in we went. It was very brief. The chairs were filled, the room overly warm as Jackson made the introductions. In less than five minutes they thanked me for coming all this way. I thanked all of them, and Jackson and I departed to the foyer where the current president, Jed Williamson, was waiting. In his office behind him were two senior-type trustees, by the look of them. They waved me in, sat me down, and Jackson disappeared.

"Well," said Jed, sitting at his desk, "What did you think of our trustees?"

"Arrgh," I thought. Rogue question.

I said, "It looks like a good board. I've met about half from the search committee."

"But any issues? Anything you see or hear?" the elder of the two trustees asked.

"Like any board," I said, "this one has its own culture, its own problems and issues. . . ." I could have gone on to generalize, but was interrupted.

"Like what?" The fellow asks.

I had to come up with something, and I had read the list of board members and their biographies, so the issue was sitting right there like a giant egg balanced on the president's sideboard.

So I said. "Well, you have 21 people on the board but only 4 women."

Then right in front of me three men, one president and two trustees, are counting on their fingers. One, two, three, four.

A moment of silence. They are looking at me as though I had something to add.

Jed the president bailed us out. "It's true," he concluded, "hard to believe, though. They seem to do all the work."

At that moment Jackson Kytle returned and took me off to another meeting, also very brief.

"Learn anything?" he asked, smiling, on our way down the stairs.

"Learn anything?" Lulu asked, hours later.

"Only that I'm still in the running, and they don't have enough women on the board."

"All the way up there for that?"

In fact, that short stopover demonstrated to me how little I did know about Sterling at the moment, and how little I cared about that fact. My task was to persevere through the search process and to focus entirely on beating out the competition, about whom I knew nothing. If required, I would have driven the three hours to Craftsbury Common every day for a week for a five-minute meeting. My only job, having no employment at the moment, was to be offered the job. Then would I worry about the details.

One could easily understand Sterling as a younger, smaller, poorer, more northerly, and less academically rigorous version of Marlboro College. It's not inaccurate, except to note that in a curricular sense, Sterling is of an entirely different order than Marlboro, and that such an understanding would be wildly off the mark.

Marlboro is a model of Oxford University's tutorial-based education, imagined by its founder, Walter Hendricks. Marlboro was or attempted to be all about traditional academics where clear writing was held equal to motherhood and a sense of the divine; in fact, high-quality writing was the base metal of Marlboro's academic requirements. When I was a student and throughout my years as an employee, Marlboro seniors and most juniors had their own small offices or studios, and each had a tutor, a faculty member who regularly controlled their academic existence, and thus often their personal lives. Or at least it felt that way. The Marlboro course of self-designed study, an individualized two-year project called the Plan of Concentration, concluded in a three-hour oral exam conducted by an outside examiner. If you didn't get an "A" it felt like failure.

Sterling's academic genes derive from its physical place — as if the old houses and shops, fields and woods of half the common had always been there waiting to evolve into a school. At Sterling, academics were about agriculture and axes, environmental justice and activism, outdoor education and the environmental humanities. Sterling was seat time versus real time, its commitment to "experiential academics" (a tagline we created) was as real as Marlboro's obsession with graceful prose.

Sterling depended every day upon its immediate community, natural and human, to support and to equip its curriculum. Marlboro, because its curriculum didn't need it, had little interaction with its physical place, or its immediate community and all that it contained.

Remembering that both colleges tuck comfortably together under the protective umbrella of the liberal arts, which was the more dynamic, or radical, approach? That's unanswerable from my perspective. Amidst all the commonalities, they are different as night and day, east and west.

⸺

I've kept journals for many years, in many kinds of notebooks, lined journals, and annotated annual calendars, but more recently on my desktop. It's an erratic process for me. The physical journals and calendars take up little shelf space, and none of them are completely filled in. My electronic journals are stored somewhere, I'm sure, and I should probably print them out and file them next to the others.

But the journal of my first year as president of Sterling was different. I wrote three or four times a week, usually in the early mornings, beginning about a month before moving to Craftsbury and into the president's large, breezy, ill-heated, early 20th-century house. My little desk in a front room looked through the broad, covered porch to the expanse of the common, in one direction, and into the post office parking lot in another.

On journal keeping, one piece of advice from a friend of Rod's, the New York-based writer Tom Matthews, stuck with me. "You should write every day if possible," he said. "You can get going by writing about the best thing that happened the day before. And never go look to see what you wrote the day before. Don't look back."

That's what I did, plowed ahead. But why? I can only think for the same reasons one keeps a journal on a trip, or an adventure, or during a terrible time, a war, an illness, a dying. To solidify the experience. To make it retrievable. And to be able to articulate it — to whom? To myself, at that moment, as a way of holding onto my own voice amidst the cacophony of voices that define a presidency. And writing was privacy, the only place where I could achieve solitude, a dose I seemed to need every day or two.

When that first year ended, July 4, 2007, I stopped writing almost every day. Then every week. It was over. Whatever it was that filled me so consistently over the year had drained away and at the keyboard at first light, my hands suddenly heavy, my mind wandering. Eventually, I bought a little writing journal, in case something had to be expressed, or expunged. It sits on the shelf with the others. I never went back.

August 6, 2006
From my First Year Journal:

My day whips by in minutes:

It could all just be a huge pile-up of boxes stuffed with ongoing projects, problems to be assigned a priority, assignments due, strategies afloat, decisions working their way into reality; one issue or problem per box and one box per person, boxes carrying the voices of advice, the voices of need, of concern, of maneuvering — each to a box. The boxes are made of mesh, by the way. And what is inside easily reaches out and tangles and mingles with the contents of the other boxes. I'm the only one outside a box. And everyone inside a box is watching my every move, and is capable of turning to anyone else and discussing and analyzing what they see in a language I do not understand.

The idea seems to be to keep the boxes moving, spending enough time pulling them apart or putting them together — or leaving them altogether alone — so there is some order, so nothing is dropped, so I can see the whole little universe of boxes at one time, and thus know at the very least that everything is safe, stuff is getting done, and the outlines of the greater firmament are slowly taking form.

The stuff I actually have to do and the places I have to be in physically, combined with the incessant need to mentally track all the players and pieces in their boxes, all that makes for a job not like anything I've done before.

It's why I pace the porch, and smoke little cigars, again.

───

As I began my presidency the state of the Sterling board of trustees would have made a great case study for the folks at the Association of Governing Boards, AGB (you may remember them and their quest for order and perfection). They would have had to act quickly, however, because a large handful of Sterling board members had already informed me they were on their way out, as soon as the new guy got his feet under him, or sooner. This included the chair (now down to three women), the vice chair Jackson Kytle, the treasurer, and another member I never actually met who resigned by phone. Phone message, actually.

These departures were not unexpected, just unwelcomed. The fact is, when presidents transition, so do board members for their own and various reasons. The chair and the vice chair had pretty good excuses, having served many years, on many committees, and coming from afar. Now that they'd brought in a new president, they felt their part was done. But the treasurer was a different matter, and what I did about him wasn't particularly presidential: I drove out to his home in the countryside and begged him to stay on for at least another year. I also urged him to maintain his annual fund gifts because he was, at that moment, the college's largest donor, and although I could understand his reluctance to retain occupancy of that unique spot, there was no one to take his place. I'd yet to learn the brutal reality, but I was suspicious, and of all the board members, I knew he knew the fiscal reality of Sterling in the summer of 2006.

Needing some measure of board stability I was prepared to argue, but he didn't let me, agreeing instead to stay the course. He was the first best thing that happened. From tales I'd heard, I knew he was the first best thing for Jed Williamson, too, at a time just 10 years ago when Sterling was, unbelievably, financially even worse off.

Others were not to be persuaded to stay beyond their upcoming term, most for their own good reasons; others I couldn't help thinking was because they feared for the future.

———

August 21, 2006
From my First Year Journal:

Well, a whole different voice spoke today and it said just seven words, "Take a look at this projected deficit!" Delivered by a visibly shaken (but hardly subdued) Vice President Ned Houston. And there it was, crude, preliminary numbers, a $130,000 deficit after annual giving of $215,000, money that needs to be raised in the next 10 months. If this is correct, it's only August and we're already $345,000 in the hole. Great.

The next step is sitting the right players down and figuring out exactly where the increases are over last year. Somehow, a perfect storm of financial crosswinds have landed exactly on our square; what are the pieces? Increases in heating oil and health insurance, added to overspending in the becalmed sea between presidents? A freshman class even poorer than the last freshman class? Hiring too many full-time faculty? It doesn't add up. Something's out of whack.

I've been told over and over that Sterling deficits have been minor things, attributable to specific one-time actions, like the 2003 takeover of the Center for Northern Studies, which I will get to in a moment, but that alone wouldn't have been enough.

I was also informed that there hasn't been a "real" (meaning large) deficit at Sterling for seven or eight years, Indicating there had been "small" deficits, perhaps $25,000 or even $50,000, which can be paid off in a good year without much damage. But that is not the case, or no longer the case. I haven't been here two months and what a mess. I was looking forward to starting off clean, with a balanced budget.

I should have known better.

I feel like I am in the scene in the movie Men in Black, *where there is always an evil intergalactic invasion force of blood-sucking aliens hovering above Earth bent on its immediate and total destruction using an undeniably vicious and destructive death ray. What's your problem? Why would you not be ready?*

One thing I did not want to do was explore too deeply the source or, more likely sources, of the deficit. I was afraid they might lead directly to individuals or groups and blame would be assigned, and that would just make everything that had to be done more difficult. I preferred to concentrate on the soon-to-depart comptroller, whose bookkeeping methodologies, I was learning, lacked analytical capacity, so solid numbers were difficult to obtain.

At least two problems stood out, one more dramatically and painfully than the other. A few years before my arrival the college had "absorbed" another, smaller, academic institution in Wolcott, Vermont, the next town west of Craftsbury. You can call what happened to the Center for Northern Studies an association, a partnership, or a merger — it was called all of these, though the legal documentation made clear that Sterling now owned the Center. It was a takeover, with both sides willing participants.

The Center was not a credit-bearing institution, and thus had no independent academic certifications. However, since its founding in 1971 to about 2000 it had been on the receiving end of a remarkable funnel transporting full-pay students from Middlebury College. Once at the Center, a rambling, rustic building of classrooms, labs, and library, heated by wood and gas, on the edge of the boreal Bear Swamp, students studied for a semester or a couple of years with a distinguished but disorganized body of circumpolar scholars and adventurers, then returned to Middlebury to graduate.

However, Middlebury's interest in the center had faded all the way to nothing shortly before my arrival. Consequently, the center ran out of money, and, lacking any administrative talent to build themselves back up with new programs, came to Sterling with their hands out and the Sterling board said yes, and thus assumed the center's by-then ramshackle building and wooded 10 acres six dirt road miles from campus, and the salaries for three or four employees. Ownership also included the 300-acre swamp, part of that sustaining curricular community, filled with all the plants and animals Sterling faculty and students love to incorporate into their studies.

It's such a long, disjointed, and dispiriting story, but not my story, at least not originally. It's a story where no one agrees with anyone else on any of the dozens upon dozens of turning points, educational, financial, cultural, each one encrusted with bitterness and suspicion. Welcome to academe, welcome to mergers, welcome to lost missions, resentment and blame.

To me, who would be wrestling with the Center's death throes almost until the day I left in 2012, the hardest part was absorbing the blame as essentially the sole perpetrator of an institution's sad demise. By my final year, we knew we had to sell the building. The center's founder had retired and spent his time watching the growing crisis and disparaging the college's efforts at resuscitation. The academic program was already much changed, and was being conducted at Sterling. Even the faculty had eventually abandoned the Center for the most basic reason: they could not transport a class out to the Center and back in anything less than three class periods, confounding the academic schedule, a machine with more moving parts and thicker heat shields than the space shuttle.

It was easier for Sterling's trustees, those in the leadership who had voted for the takeover in the first place, to say to me, you take care of it now, we've done our part. The founders and alumni of the Center were, according to their own editorials, completely without blame for the demise of their own institution, and chose to concentrate their outrage and anger in scathing private letters (so well written), public forums, and detailed petitions delivered to the board and to me. There was even a website, where I was castigated dawn to dusk as the man who took their lifelong achievement and shut it down like an old mom and pop store.

Where was I?

Yes, the deficit. The goddamn dog.

So, it was clear that some significant portion of Sterling's projected 2006 deficit, more than half, was caused by the takeover of a weakened institution with no income, housed in a homemade, out-of-code, almost unheatable structure six miles from campus.

Other factors were also complicit: some unexpected salary and compensation issues added tens of thousands of dollars. Impending student/faculty international travel commitments would account for tens of thousands more. Beyond those was an even more disturbing set of line-item numbers affecting the deficit. The instructional budget had increased $147,000 over the previous year, and health insurance by $40,000. Other budget increases in the business and development offices and the kitchen/dining service totaled $225,000.

At that moment, the often nearly invisible details hardly mattered. The dog was back, as though it had followed me north from Marlboro. But it could not have because that dog was dead and buried under, by then, a $26 million endowment.

What doomed the Center from the moment they signed the transfer of assets? What provoked Sterling into legally adopting an institution that had run its course? What is the lesson?

The background details were already obscured, the decision-making process distorted and lost. I couldn't find anyone on the board who had been for the idea when it was first proposed. The most outspoken were the three center trustees who transferred their trusteeship to Sterling, expressly to advocate for the center. There's a lesson. It's akin to independent colleges whose faculty is unionized. They are inherently tricky to manage because two different missions are at work in the same small space. Similar, I would suspect, to having board members whose primary mission is to protect and advocate for a particular entity within an institution.

A more interesting lesson may have to do with the idea that no one, really, likes a merger between two nonprofit institutions. The idea seemed sound. One side (the center, in this case) saw salvation, relief from fiscal pressure, and life renewed. The other side (Sterling) saw opportunity: we get all this, and we didn't have to lift a finger. In this case, both sides spun stories to themselves which they liked, but in fact Sterling didn't have enough money or expertise and the center's attitude at being under the college's sway turned and was, well, unhelpful.

Finally, there is the reality that if the host institution were to suffer a serious financial setback and needed, in Harvard's phrase, to "retrench," who would be first on the chopping block? Well, in this case, the center was last on the chopping block and somehow, remarkably, when informed of the impending sale of the building after six years of struggle, conflict, and the abandonment of the center itself, the news surprised as well as outraged them.

Friday, September 29, 2006
From my First Year Journal:

It's a rainy morning, and Sunday is forecast to be rainy as well, but Saturday —
tomorrow, The Day — is supposed to be chilly but sunny, so I'll take it. It is a

relief, edged by dread, to finally arrive at this day — my first board meeting, my first meeting with the Center for Northern Studies (CNS) advisory council, and my first and undoubtedly last presidential inauguration. Nothing left to do. More than a month ago, I realized I had to put almost all my efforts into this single weekend. Sterling has never put on such a big party, not nearly. And although the board meeting looks like those of the past, I've made proposals that will radically alter the way the board meets in the future. And I put it all in a board book, another innovation they've never experienced and the one which, by its sheer demonstration of organization and forthrightness, compels the members to uncritical trust in me and thus to vote for the meeting changes. Or not, of course.

This will also be the first time the board will be brought up to date about the ongoing operational deficits Sterling has suffered for the past three years, and the projected deficit for this year. The culture of the place does not account for this revelation, at any level. I've already started calming the faculty and staff over the issue. I told them, regarding the board, that there is nothing like a healthy deficit to make them sit up straight and pay attention. But still, it very well may throw a wrench into the weekend's works.

My speech is written. Only Lulu has heard it; she's heard it probably a dozen times in its various configurations. The other speaker, Bill McKibben, has confirmed and his citation is written. All the other pieces, the tents, food from the kitchen and fancier food from the caterer, the wine stacked in our little pantry, the beer on the porch, the wrapped plates and glassware, the lists and name tags, the schedules and seating orders, the stage, the elusive lectern, the groups of students ready to set up and take down chairs, the tour guides, the ushers, the party tonight at Bob Shelton's, the new board chairman whose house hangs over the west side of the common, the party Saturday night here at North House, the delegates from other colleges and universities, my sisters, my son and daughter and our grandchildren, babies, and friends and colleagues from Marlboro and Montserrat, the ironed tablecloths hanging from the banister, Barbara Morrow the development director and Micki Martin my assistant are in charge and I'm almost helpless to affect anything at all once we get going. Which is right about now.

Monday, October 02, 2006
Yesterday was pretty much a recovery day. I didn't get much done today, either. I cannot report on the weekend. It's already ripped through my mind a hundred

times, except for my speech, which I don't remember. But it all went well. Every bit of it. They laughed. They cried. They were persuaded.

I'm also a little surprised, although obviously I shouldn't be, that September is gone. Looking back over these notes — I don't actually have to look back — I can put this month down as one of the most difficult and exciting months of my life. I know it's ridiculous, but sometimes I feel a little like James Cook or some other 18th-century explorer sailing about in an unknown world. You come upon nothing so strange that it is unrecognizable or alien: plants are plants, animals are animals, people are people, and the weather that surrounds them is the same as weather everyplace, yet everything seems new and undiscovered. I travel miles every night and all day long and every day the closing horizon reveals some unexpected combination of the familiar that renders it new and wholly unfamiliar. And it is you — me — who has to explain it, or recognize it for what it is or is not, and sail around it or through it and, most important, bring everyone along. Some follow in ignorance, others skeptically, others critically, and a very few with so much enthusiasm and interest you can hardly hold them back. What a great job.

How many members of the Sterling board understood the financial condition of their college the summer I was hired remains a mystery to me. By the October board meeting, in fact just hours before the inauguration, everyone understood because I documented for them the starkest single measure of Sterling's fiscal health, the now $550,000 projected loss on an operating budget of $3.2 million. They had never seen such a huge animal.

If Sterling were a company making widgets, such a projection would slam shut the doors, stop the production line, and call for a declaration of bankruptcy. Fortunately, that's not how nonprofits work. For us there is another bottom line under the bottom line, and what it does is add in the money given to the college (also referred to having been "raised" by the college) in annual fund donations (called "gifts") and bequests, grants, and such like. Those monies then mitigate the projected deficit; ideally they eliminate it.

Colleges and most nonprofits maintain a certain level of annual fundraising success that can be counted on with some confidence, and that increases over time with new ideas, new people, persistence and, or, good luck. Call it anticipated income. However, when you are raising about $150,000 annually, there is no point in anticipating a $550,000 annual fund just because you need it. You will only disappoint.

In my first budget, over which I had only nominal control, I was projecting Sterling could raise $225,000. That was a leap, more than had been raised in the past, and a glaring $240,000 shy of closing the projected gap.

This spurred declarations from all around the trustees' table.

"It's not enough!"

"We should and need to raise the whole $550,000!"

"It's in the budget, and that needs to be cut."

"You, Mr. President, need to find who are the bench-sitters and get rid of them. The deadwood. There is always deadwood."

"It is imperative we balance this budget. That's all there is to it."

"Clean house and start fresh."

If the hairs on my head were tiny red flags, all of them would have jumped up, unfurled, and started waving frantically at this discussion about what certain Sterling board members imagined was the path to fiscal solvency. Theirs was the equivalent of a medieval physician bleeding a sick and anemic child, then contemplating a dish of bat organs to figure out why she wasn't getting better.

But it was all so much worse than that.

The deficit of my first year (my second year, my third year) caused the deep wear on the Porch of Worry, but it was not the only threat to Sterling. It was merely representative of others, which were just as bad and just as immediate.

I made a list, but not a list of clean columns of numbers ending in red. This was a different sort of list that shaped itself in fits and starts, growing almost hidden, but not for long, amidst the intense routine of every day. It grew in complexity and length until I began to wonder whether there was enough muscle left on Sterling's bones to fight back.

A summary of the larger items on that list:

The Physical Plant: Generally, the place was falling apart, in many places practically crumbling, from one end of campus to the other. In higher education this is often caused by "deferred maintenance." Budgets are sometimes balanced on deferred maintenance, in that if you don't fix things, they won't cost you. If you don't fix a lot of big things like whole buildings and septic systems, kitchens and foundations, leaking roofs, you will save a lot of money. Rod Gander employed a wonderful and sometimes effective leadership tool in the expression, "ignore it and maybe it will go away." Useful, but it does not ever apply to the deferred casualties of ignored maintenance. Even Sterling's barns and farm equipment, which were academic structures and equipment, were almost indistinguishable from the rundown, hardscrabble farmyards of the long-failing Vermont family farms ones sees too frequently along highways and byways of the state.

Information Technology: Sterling's curricular and administrative electronic infrastructure resembled something out of the early 1990s, when our students were small children. There was no T-1 line linking the college to the outside world. Sterling had "computer labs," cubicles where students could work on a hard-wired machine, just like first grade. Wireless had yet to reach most of Vermont's Northeast Kingdom, so the college and the entire community constituted a cellphone-free zone that stretched for miles in every direction. Academically, administratively, not good. Regarding what students want and expect, very much not good.

Salaries: Sterling's faculty were woefully underpaid compared with their peers, compared with public school teachers, compared with skilled laborers in almost any trade. Other than recognizing low wages, no one, not the board or the faculty themselves, understood the longer-term institutional danger that underpaying faculty represents.

Curriculum: Sterling curriculum too closely resembled the two-year curriculum from which it had been only recently developed. Half the courses were preset and required, narrowing student choice and satisfaction. There was only one path to graduation, laid out in diagrams and matrices of exquisite precision and faculty control of every step. It was, in my opinion, a curriculum developed by faculty

Marlboro College

Marlboro, circa 1947-1948. *This photograph appeared in* LIFE *magazine in July, 1948. One of dozens of "GI Colleges," start-up institutions poised to take advantage of the GI Bill after WWII, Marlboro grew rapidly through the 1950s, steadied itself at 175 students in the 70s, slipped precariously in the 80s and early 90s, then grew during Paul LeBlanc's years to over 300. Today Marlboro is smaller again, and growing.* Photograph courtesy of Marlboro College.

Rod Gander early in his 15-year career at Marlboro. *Rod's sense of irony wrapped around his sense of humor helped ward off nearly insurmountable fiscal problems. The photo of a smashed-up typewriter was a departing gift from his New York journalist friends, who thought he was crazy moving to Vermont at 50 years old, and at the top of his* Newsweek *career.* Photograph courtesy of Marlboro College.

Marlboro College, cont.

Author and Rod Gander — mid-90s. *Taken by a professional photographer, this photograph was part of a broad attempt to get useable pictures of President Gander. Though never used, it appeared on my desk with the caption, "Development Director Will Wootton and President Rod Gander try to determine how big a trout they have to catch to offset the bottle of Dewers in the drawer."* Photograph courtesy of Marlboro College.

Elizabeth McCormack and Jerry Aron. *Elizabeth's deep ties to the New York and Chicago philanthropic communities and Jerry's role as presidential confidante and board member, combined with their long-term dedication to Marlboro, made for an unstoppable duo. Their significance to Marlboro's success is unmeasurable to this day because it is still in effect. Jerry died in July 2004; Elizabeth is retired.* Photograph courtesy of Marlboro College.

Marlboro College, cont.

Trustee Lil Farber. *A determined philanthropist, the IRS repeatedly audited Lil because she gave away so much money. A true companion for Rod, when she became the first woman board chair at Marlboro. Paul LeBlanc's youth and speed, however, practically disoriented her. "I'm a person that if the vase at the end of the hallway is two inches out of place, I'm upset and fix it. Now, Paul is absolutely turning my college around in circles! I can hardly stay standing up!"* Photograph courtesy of Marlboro College.

Paul LeBlanc. *Marlboro's third president in 1996, at just 37 years old. Paul arrived with a Ph.D. in English and little relative experience; he rode his motorcycle to his inauguration — apt symbolism. After being knocked down (inevitable for a college president), no one got up faster, or with such positive resolve and good humor. Today, his innovations and success in non-profit on-line educa-tion at Southern New Hampshire University refute the for-profit diploma mills.* Photograph courtesy of Marlboro College.

Montserrat College of Art

Hardie Building. *Formerly a public school with huge windows and high ceilings, Hardie was perfect for the young art college, accredited in the mid-80s, in Beverly, Massachusetts. The trustees paid $1 for the massive building in early 1991. The unusual signage we designed in 2004 is gone today, and Montserrat has expanded to about 400 students.* Photograph by Elizabeth Thomsen.

Gallery at Montserrat. *With student art studios clustered around town and three managed galleries, Montserrat was intense and always interesting, a classic demonstration of the power of experiential learning. Asked what a professional college of art actually did for its students, one faculty member explained, "We turn play into work."* Photograph courtesy of Monserrat College of Art.

Craftsbury Common. *Charted in 1781, this village of nearly 1,200 is 25 miles from the Canadian border. The large fenced Common (to the right) and steepled United Church of Craftsbury (upper right) are a five-minute walk from Sterling's white clapboard buildings, indistinguishable from private houses. Along the road, you'll pass Craftsbury Academy, the local middle and high school, North House, formerly the president's residence, and the cemetery (lower left).* Photograph courtesy of Sterling College. Photograph courtesy of Sterling College.

View of the common. *Many of Vermont's 237 towns and villages have a "common," or public space at its center. Once a place to graze cattle or sheep, commons became places around which to situate a church and houses. Craftsbury's is unusual in having retained much of its original size and in remaining uncluttered.* Photograph by Steve Wright.

President's house. *Built in the late 1800s and renovated many times since, North House, despite its structural and functional handicaps and liabilities, was in better repair than many of Sterling's structures when I arrived. The porch faces the Common directly west, and provides beautiful sunsets and often views of dramatic, quickly approaching storm fronts.* Photograph by Steve Wright.

President's Porch of Worry. *The porch at the rear of the President's House. The attachment on the right is part of the College's maintenance garage, which itself is attached to the Craftsbury Common Post Office.* Photograph by Steve Wright.

Sterling College. *Founded in 1954 as a preparatory school for boys, Sterling School operated for 20 years before a years-long transition to an agriculture and outdoor-focused Associates Degree college, accredited in 1985. President Jed Williamson (1996-2007) took the College through the long process of becoming an accredited four-year institution, graduating its first Baccalaureate class in 2000.* Photograph by Merrill Leffler.

Sterling student at the reins with draft horses. *A frequent sight around the village and college is a student in the Draft Horse Management class practicing her skills. Note the instructor close behind.* Photograph courtesy of Sterling College.

Sterling College, cont.

Hamilton and Jefferson residences. *That wild monkeys wouldn't have lived in these dormitories may exaggerate their condition in 2006, but even hardy can-do Sterling students had their limits. A combination of federal, foundation, and private money for rehabilitation came together in a whirlwind of luck and circumstance, and just in time. (Note the book cover mural on the side of Jefferson House.)* Photograph by Steve Wright.

Ned Houston. *After the protracted process of purchasing the Inn on the Common, the Sterling Trustees renamed the new residence Houston House, in honor of Ned, the college's longest serving administrator and faculty member, who arrived in Sterling in 1976. No president could have wished for a better backup.* Photograph courtesy of Sterling College.

Willy Ryan's barns. February 15, 2007. *A nighttime storm delivering two feet of wet snow collapsed dozens of milking parlors and cow sheds in northern Vermont, including at the Ryan Farm in Craftsbury. Dozens of Sterling students and staff joined in to free trapped animals. Someone had covered this downed cow with a blanket, barely visible amidst the wreckage of the barn.* Photograph by June Pichel Cook and courtesy of the *Hardwick Gazette.*

The aftermath. *At least ten cows died in the collapsed barns. Some of the upper barn's poles remain standing, as firefighters and volunteers finish up the rescue effort.* Photograph by June Pichel Cook and courtesy of the *Hardwick Gazette.*

Sterling College, cont.

Two presidential views. *Look at the confidence and poise emanating from a new college president, in 2006 answering reporter Tena Starr's questions for an article in the Barton* Chronicle. *Six years later, the author is alone in the middle of a dirt road in the middle of a winter storm, six miles from Sterling, and feeling pretty good about it.* Photograph (left) by Tena Starr and courtesy of the Barton *Chronicle* and (right) Lulu Wootton.

Lulu and me. *In 2008, after my first Expedition, a Sterling College tradition where all new students (after introductory skills and teamwork training) take a three-night, four-day 25-mile winter camping hike along the hills and mountains of the Northeast Kingdom. No tents. No stoves. This one consisted of temperatures 20°F below to 5° above, and three feet of snow in blizzard conditions. Perfect conditions for learning in the opinion of the faculty.* Photograph courtesy of Sterling College.

Family

Wootton family portrait. *Left to right: Linda Reyes and Russell Wootton, their sons Lincoln and Holden; Will and Lulu Wootton; Fred Bethel and Clara Wootton, their daughter Cecelia and son Taurin.* Photograph by Steve Wright.

My mother at Singing River Ranch. *My mother occasionally drove a two-wheel horse buggy, or rode side saddle (as pictured here), both practices my father believed to be inherently dangerous. Similarly, when she prepared wild mushrooms for guests, he'd say he'd go warm up the ranch car to be ready to drive the inevitable victims to the hospital, 60 miles away. Over the years we lost only one guest, and found that one well before sunset.* Photograph courtesy of Will Wootton.

My father commuting from Connecticut to New York and* LIFE *magazine (1961). *White shirt, skinny tie, jacket, and briefcase, he rode these trains for over twenty years, rarely visited the bar car, and was nearly always the first off on the home-bound run. It was an exciting and rewarding career in which he flourished, becoming an Executive Editor in 1961. But my father also longed for a different life, and by the early 70s was roaming the Rockies from Montana to New Mexico, looking for something he could only find on a ranch in the high West.* Photograph by Alfred Eisenstadt.

My father and I heading towards the mountains. *This photograph was taken when Singing River Ranch was in full operation, my father riding Sonny (right) and I, Jasper. We're in the high meadows above the ranch, heading towards the National Forest. I'd ridden all those barb-wire fences up there many times, and led small groups of riders through much of this countryside.* Photograph courtesy of Will Wootton.

for faculty. Alarmingly, there was a severe problem of student attrition in the junior year and, uniquely, in the senior year, where in every other college in the nation attrition shrinks to near zero.

Student Housing: As things were, there was not enough of it, so growth from 100 students to 125, which was critical, was also impossible. Way worse, however, the two largest student residences, Hamilton and Jefferson, would finally become completely unlivable in just three years with mold, ice, irregular heat, and bathrooms monkeys would not use.

Dining Services: The college kitchen looked like something that was assembled from used and overused equipment. Everything — shelving, flooring, cabinetry, the not-very-cool walk-in cooler, the stoves and ovens, the work counters, the Hobart dishwasher — was bent and dented with age and fatigue. The exhaust fans and grease management system were a fire waiting to happen. Hygiene practice and stations I could not contemplate.

Transportation: Sterling's fleet of three or four 10-passenger vans should have been pushed off a cliff, for safety's sake.

Thinking about governance and the board of trustees, their responsibilities and challenges, the consistency and quality of their own leadership, it's not remarkable that this dark Pandora's box, chock-full of potential disasters, had not been peeked into by any of them. No wonder, really. They operated moment-by-moment, crisis-by-crisis. And now it was my board, entirely.

And I knew, because I'd been there before, that to shut down budget-slashing, people-firing imitations of any actual strategy, I had to come up with a better way, or a different way. Like a sharp knock on the head, or a twist in the gut, that moment I experienced the jump — the jolt — from being a candidate for a president's job to being a president. There were no options to follow; there was no one to follow. So this is what it feels like, in the empty zone between a president and everyone else, I thought. And then I realized with my first board meeting over, I had to go get inaugurated and make the worry official.

———

Saturday, November 25, 2006
From my First Year Journal:

Now a weekend, when I'm not supposed to work, but the temptation to get to my office is, at seven in the morning, already upon me. The least I could do is get over there and straighten the place up. There is nothing to do in North House. That's one of the insidious tricks of presidential housing. For the first time in about 30 years I have nothing to take care of, our house and farm is three hours south. I've no shop to keep in order. No lineup of minor projects, things to fix, stuff to secure for the winter, or even get ready for next spring. No lawns to mow, trees to trim. No carpentry projects; that affects me the most. Just presidential work. I'm relieved of everything else, which is completely distorting, at times disorientating, especially when I think of all the projects little and big waiting to be done down in Marlboro. These past two days, for instance, were especially nice for stone wall building. My Marlboro wall is hardly half done and it may be years — or never — before I get back to it. But there is always plenty of Sterling College work to be done. It builds up in the back of my head even while the front of me meets and greets and functions in all the normal ways.

December 16, 2006

I have survived six months on the job, and there has to be some meaning in that. I just can't figure out what meaning beyond the fact itself.

I could search for it. I could count the hundred or more people we've met, and separate them into categories, like the multiple realities of string theory, except this string is all looped out and everyone is everywhere and it's all a jumble of, for instance, senior staff, faculty, and regular staff, residents of the common, residents of the Kingdom, longtime Vermonters, transplants, those who represent agriculture, those who represent outdoorsmanship, outright academics, half academics, academics who concentrate on the far north, current trustees, former trustees, those who work outside, those who work inside, those who like trout fishing and those who don't or have given up, those with aggressive personal agendas, those without, those who are "on my side," those who are neutral, those who are not on my side, advocates of change, opponents of change, angry people, passive-aggressive people, just downright nice people, people building tiny empires, those who've given up building anything, students, former students, wannabe students, and their parents; liberals, conservatives, wealthy, poor, those living off the grid, vegans, meat eaters and those in between; people with a sense of humor and those who shed humor like a duck sheds water, people quick to anger, people reluctant to speak out, people who apologize and those who don't; content people, deeply frustrated people; people who think they'd be a better Sterling president, and those who wouldn't want to be president under any circumstances; people boring as pebbles, and people so interesting you could listen for hours; people of multiple talents, people seemingly without talent at all; people with mysterious backgrounds, compassionate people, dismissive people, people who love animals more than humans, people who serve, and people who do not.

We would not have met any of these people if a year and a half ago I had not become so frustrated watching Montserrat College of Art fumble and hesitate, then charge off, then pull back. The college was chewing itself, like the dog that followed it. I quit Montserrat well before I'd even looked at the help wanted pages, and had I not found the advertisement for the only job open at Sterling, the presidency, and decided, I'm not sure how, to throw in my hat and somehow — I guess I could go back and read about it — succeed in actually landing the job and now, well, tomorrow, I will have survived six months in what must be one of the most unusual and misunderstood professions anywhere in the galaxy.

9

Depression Is Preferred

Sterling's dire situation in 2006 was as obvious as a car wreck, with pieces of fenders and mirrors scattered across the road, a tire blown out, a headlamp dangling by its wires. I came across just such an accident at five one April morning down from the common on Rt. 14, where I was headed to the Black River to fish for trout.

A woman in a red bathrobe had just emerged from her house where they sell eggs at three dollars a dozen and she was trying to comfort or calm a hysterical young woman, who apparently had just emerged from the car. "Oh my God," she was shouting over and over, walking around the wreck, unbelieving, frantic, but helpless to do anything but yell "Oh my God," and "I'm in so much TROUBLE," over and over.

I asked her a few times whether she was alone in the car, if there was a passenger, but got no response; it was as if she could not see me or the woman helping. She kept up high volume "Oh my Gods" without pause.

I went down the lower bank and searched along the edges of a cornfield but found no blood or bodies. Back at the car, nothing had changed much. "I'm in so much trouble. This is so terrible. Oh my God."

She seemed to slow down a bit, and breathe. Then she focused on the front end of the car that looked like it had been attacked by a gang of chainsaws and sledgehammers. She became aware of another level of reality and wailed, "Oh my God...it's so...it's so...it's so...*obvious!*"

Exactly how I felt. I asked the helping woman's permission to go fishing and she said someone else would be along soon enough.

The first thing many new presidents do is embark on an institutional self-study, where everyone gets together at the president's direction and works through all sorts of issues and systems. The new president is trying to understand all the pieces and people as quickly as he can, to see whether they fit together, which they do not, of course, and never did. These studies can be rammed through in a day or two, or the new president can hire people practiced in conducting these studies, in which case they can take weeks. The result is usually a series of moves on the president's part: framing and prioritizing the problems and opportunities he or she sees, and institutionalizing that vision, giving a clear direction in which to lead everyone. Fair enough. There is always a bit of grandiosity in these plans. A new direction, something bold, something dramatic, even moderately risky, something everyone can get their heads around.

At Sterling, in 2006, there was no time for any of that, for studying what was so blatantly evident.

Just to make room to breathe, which included needing to increase the college's ability for short-term borrowing, we refinanced with the college's bank, Union Bank, and its longtime president Ken Gibbons, with whom I would meet repeatedly over the ensuing years, and who would, after his retirement in 2012, join the board of trustees. We increased our line of credit from $50,000 to $200,000. Our collateral was the entire campus of a dozen buildings, the farm, and about 140 acres. Ken Gibbons thought it had been over-appraised, but he didn't balk. That's the kind of banker he was. On top of everything on campus, we threw in the endowment of almost $900,000, of which $650,000 was untouchable, and the rest available to spend, but less so now, being part of the collateral.

With finances in order, if not in balance, we needed a plan that would take Sterling from a frightening level of debt to a level resembling solvency, and which would stand up to multiple audiences, from trustees, to parents of students, to the students themselves, and faculty and staff, and our neighbors, likely foundations, the media. Whatever plan we devised, I knew that just beyond its borders the solemn, probing, data-obsessed folks at the New England Association of Schools and Colleges (NEASC, again) were going to be waiting, and inquiring. Under their control already was Sterling's just finalized accreditation as a four-year college, as a college at all. They saw our books, our budgets, our bottom line, and all of these confirmed the association's suspicion about small colleges: that they are ephemera, not academically, not that at all, but financially. They knew that the fiscal equivalent of a couple of heavy rainstorms could wash away a tiny college in a single a moment. And that would reflect poorly on NEASC and the higher education industry in general.

With NEASC there is no choice but cooperation: without accreditation there would be no federal aid for our students, particularly Pell Grants, worth, back then, as much as $2,600 per student (about $3,000 today), per semester, if, that is, your family's income was under something like $25,000. Nationally, 7.6 million students receive Pell Grants. At Sterling, over 60 percent of students received some level of Pell support, and everybody received a discount off the sticker price. Almost everybody. There were the few, the precious few, capable of paying Sterling's posted tuition and fees of about $20,000. I remember four of them in one year. Four percent of our 100.

To me and probably to most everyone who works or teaches at small and midsize colleges, the higher percentage of Pell-eligible students in your institution, the higher your status, and the greater the worth of your institution, but it doesn't work that way, curiously. In fact, the opposite appears closer to the truth: the wealthier and already status-bedecked institutions have proportionately far fewer Pell students than most small and midsize colleges: Harvard, 18 percent; Brown 17, Stanford 16, Dartmouth 14. Figures that speak their own story.

Tuesday, January 09, 2007
From my First Year Journal:

When you create a plan [the elements of which follow this journal entry] to work your college out of annual deficits, and share it broadly for comment, what happens is some folks — members of the board and faculty, senior staff, former board members, even a few students — begin listing reasons your plan won't work. At least won't for them. They take it apart, not comprehensively, but bit by bit: how we tried this, how we don't have enough data, how it would be better to wait a year before implementing that, how the results are uncertain. According to these advisors, I'm left with a something between nothing and very little. Some who don't object outright just turn slightly away — do what you want, you're the boss. Which is to say, "I'm with you, but not so much that if this plan tanks, or you tank, I'm still with you."

The other part is, of course, I have no idea when my plan will have a measurable effect, even though time — the lack of it — is an essential reality of our situation.

We now have seven initiatives packed into a three-year timeframe, and the notion that all the goals will be accomplished in full and on time is speculative, to choose a word. It would require success in grant writing and major gifts, new staff, increased income through admissions, incredible good luck, and a sustained determination on the part of the board and college as a whole.

So you would think, then, given the stakes, I'd have cartloads of critical analysis coming my way; that someone — anyone — board member, faculty member, child off the street, would take the time to go over the entire plan and its assumptions and speculations and offer some constructive criticism. No. Other than picking it apart selectively, the plan has been accepted by the trustees as it stands. It's like a just-born colt, standing on shaky legs, blinking in the sunlight, not sure at all how to put one foot in front of another. Yet everyone stands around admiring what a fine animal it is. That horse will carry us into the future. Yes, sir. Good looking. Good job.

———

The Sustainable Sterling Plan, as we called it, had another critical requirement: it had to be easily and quickly transformed into a multiyear fundraising campaign, with a set of goals and objectives that upon attainment Sterling would achieve the level of fiscal security it needed and deserved. As argued, at least.

Nothing happens fast enough and it took a full year to pull together all the pieces in order to announce the campaign with as much hope and flourish as possible, in the fall of 2010. We used simple grey file folders printed on the front with:

Sustainable Sterling
A Four-Year, $2.3 Million Campaign, 2009-2012

It came with a handsome package of potent materials, case statements, and economic impact studies, all which required actual reading, the imposition of which bothers fundraising advisors and consultants. Their fear is if you require people to read anything of depth, you'll lose their attention and your campaign will flounder right at the start.

How does the marketing industry get away with such chin-flapping ideas? Just because they, as an industry, can't string together a couple of sentences worth reading, or write an explanation worth contemplating, or make a metaphor that hits home, doesn't mean the rest of us have to behave that way. These professionals write *few* when they mean *less* and *less* when they mean *few*. They write *podium* when they mean *lectern*. People fall to the rocks *below*.

Among the reading materials were the Institutional Initiatives, followed by the reasoning supporting each that I won't burden anyone to read here, where a simple note will help fill in the context. But notice that the Institutional Initiatives are the same institutional weaknesses I discussed earlier but wonderfully transmogrified into goals for raising money and hopes.

1. Increase the full-time student body from the current 100 to 125. This means the college needs more students because it is going broke, but it doesn't mean the college can house, teach, or otherwise retain more students any better than it retains its current numbers. So like all goals, it represents the shiny peak of an otherwise submerged mountain of trouble.

2. Construct a new 20-24 bed student residence. We had no place to house more students if we could attract them, so a new residence — an eco-dorm — is a critical goal. It would be cool and energize the college, boost morale. Meanwhile the twin dorms, Hamilton and Jefferson, were self-destructing at a frightening pace and soon we'd lose those beds unless, until, impossibly, the twins could be patched back together.

3. Complete the development and implementation of the Continuous Semester system, establishing Sterling as a genuine year-round college. This was significant, to me. Even as a student at Marlboro I never understood why we all got thrown off campus in the summer so the Marlboro Music Festival could take over. Twenty years later, as a senior staff member, I proposed the idea seriously. Even with the festival on campus, we could run year-round programs in dramaturgy and all things theater, film, and writing. What could be better? And the money. The money, I said. Ten summer semester students paid more than the entire festival!

Have you ever seen a bird shot out of the sky? Talk about transmogrification. That was my proposal back then, plummeting lifeless to the rocks below.

4. Strengthen the liberal arts, especially in the first and second years, through new curricula in writing and communications, and in traditional and visual arts. There was a problem in the first and particularly second years: too many students quit, they dropped out, transferred to another college, or returned home to find employment. Of those who stayed, too many couldn't write a college-level academic paper. Some who got to their senior year still couldn't write. The answer was to institutionalize the pursuit of clear writing and to increase student advising by about tenfold. I had a foundation in mind and thought we'd give it a try, or, two, as it turned out.

5. Expand Sterling's academic capabilities by creating new classroom, presentation, and public lecture spaces, and a new visual and traditional arts studio. Essentially a bust, this all worked out in some ways: we managed to cobble together some arts studio and teaching space by moving the college bookstore to the comptroller's office, which was her idea. New classroom and presentation space did materialize, but in ways unimagined at the time.

6. Conduct a broad-based, multiyear fundraising campaign to provide the sustaining resources and time to achieve the initiatives. This is straightforward enough, I'd say. We need money and time to get from where we are to where we have to get to.

What's weird about this? If it was all obvious in the beginning, what took so long? This guy's been on the job for three years and just now is getting something together? Doesn't sound very impressive.

Actually, it was under two and a half years. And, you see, multiyear campaigns always begin on the quiet, at home, with the board and a few others, working over goals and initiatives one-on-one with the people you hope will become engaged and will give money in support of the goals and initiatives they helped to create. So, by the time a campaign is announced the first year has already passed, your "leadership" gifts and multiyear pledges are in, and have helped define the size and direction of the campaign. It's low-balled, of course. Which is why campaigns never fail, they sometimes just don't succeed spectacularly.

Year 1, 2008, the quiet first year of the campaign, did remarkably well, garnering $728,000. Of that, $359,000 was unrestricted pay-off-part-of-the-deficit money, and $20,000 was restricted in various ways. The kicker, $350,000, was earmarked to help build that brand new student residence, which I am still getting to.

———

In fall 2009, however, my original three-year contract was coming to an end. The board chose a comprehensive presdiential review process, including a survey of the collective opinion of the faculty, staff, and students. They adopted a self-review style wherein the reviewee is asked a number of questions in writing, and is expected to answer them convincingly. I was asked. I wrote.

Tuesday, September 15, 2009

To: Dave Stoner
From: Will Wootton
Re: A performance review
To me any self-evaluation, especially one created from the strange penultimate pinnacle of a college presidency, with the board above and the surrounding community below, is rightly suspect. Why, for instance, would anyone want to know a president's opinion of himself when it's the opinions of the College community, on one side, and the board of trustees, on the other, that actually count?

I am an unfair judge, and incapable of describing how the College community as a whole rates me as a president or a person. I have not been run out of town; I do not generally receive notes of praise or thanks. I believe I have most people's respect on campus, and I have equal respect for them. But I have no way of measuring any of this, no way of evaluating it.

Leadership, however, can be measured to a high degree, sort of. The tactical effectiveness of a president engaged in institutional change — the shaping of a high-performance team, the finding of resources, the generating and fostering of ideas, the applied persuasion, and engagement in the unending details and conundrums of daily administration — is one good measure of leadership. Until or unless, that is, the strategic idea behind those changes ultimately doesn't work. However many good ideas are worked, initiatives taken, problems solved, advances secured, and however many people will be able to claim success in the end, there can be only one person responsible for failure — the president. That would be a measure of the quality of his strategic leadership.

That's where I'm caught at this moment, beginning the fourth year as Sterling's president. It's in the no-man's land between the tactical and the strategic.

I think I've managed to lead the college, faculty, staff, and the board through, or into, actually, a series of sometimes difficult changes, all essentially tactical. These can be misinterpreted as "accomplishments," but only as compared to the fumbled, boggled, mishandled, or abandoned efforts of which I have an equal number. I think "changes" better reflects the institutional or collective impact of "accomplishments."

These changes include:
* Recognizing and correcting serious problems in the college's faculty-led cur-

riculum that were, in my opinion and with some evidence, strangling academic advancement;

* *Forcing, if you will, dramatic changes in student advising in order to attack a threateningly high attrition rate;*
* *Creating, early on, the Sustainable Sterling plan, essentially an articulation of initiatives and ideas designed to lead Sterling away from the perilous edge upon which it exists;*
* *Conceiving and articulating, and now beginning to implement the "continuous semester" year-round college;*
* *Designing, testing, and now launching a $2.3 million fundraising campaign;*
* *Persuading, against all odds, the Vermont State Legislature to give us $350,000, thus giving reality to building a much-needed residence.*

But the strategic goal, if it is obtainable, is still in the future, around a corner whose sweep I cannot yet see. In the simplest form that goal is to bring the College to a balanced operating budget: With more complexity, it is to bring the College to a genuinely sustainable level of economic security that provides for its mission and maintains its progressive ethos and practice as an institution of higher education.

Thinking back to the letter of application I wrote, now almost four years ago, I remember hesitating over using an expression that I was a firm believer in, the cliché plan the work, then work the plan. I hesitated only because I resist the usefulness of clichés, just as I try to avoid using war analogies and terminology, like "tactics" and "strategies." But sometimes these things are just too compact and simplified to resist.

I note this pocket-sized operating methodology only because in a review where the board is looking for something (anything!) upon which to hang a cogent opinion of my performance it might serve as a hint at how I frame my day-to-day professional life. Really successfully working a plan, however, requires the operator to stay anywhere from six months to a couple of years ahead of everyone — the board, faculty, staff, and in some ways the industry of higher education. I'm most comfortable in the three- to six-month range. At Sterling, I believe I'm averaging a lead-distance of somewhere between 10 minutes and a month.

One result of that is the amount of time I need to devote to operational management and coordination. But more interesting, as much time on my part and oth-

ers is devoted to improving and maintaining the various changes we've provoked. It does no good, it is damaging, to create and implement an entire student advising system on top of a dramatically restructured curriculum then fail "to work" that successful change aggressively. And that work absorbs time. The same holds true for initiatives and new programs in institutional development — publications, web sites, and media initiatives. Our somewhat surprising opportunity to build a new residence is really, at this moment, only an opportunity: Ned Houston and Steve Smith will spend a tremendous amount of time on this over the next year; we are also still $200,000 short. More time. And, of course, it is true for the Sustainable Sterling Campaign. We've squeezed out a very successful first year and now the job is to continually build, not ride, that momentum. More time yet.

The cost, if you will, of successful initiatives cannot be matched with increases in staffing, thus forward momentum is slowed. In our case, it is a momentum of ideas interrupted by opportunity. In the next few years choosing which ideas to engage and which opportunities to exploit will be an increasingly difficult task if we are not to compromise the advances we have achieved and are now building into the fabric of the College.

In an attempt to help give the performance review committee a more quantifiable methodology, from my own perspective as the reviewed, I can offer only some questions that might lead to a sort of rating system, if that's what is sought. Here's my list, but there is room for plenty more:

- *Has the president been successful, or at least made good progress on, the basic rubric of underfunded colleges: fundraising, admissions, and retention?*
- *Has the College's (local, regional, national) recognition and reputation advanced?*
- *Has the president successfully managed the operating budget?*
- *Has the fiscal profile of the College improved, remained static, or become even more marginal?*
- *Do the president's personal and professional relationships with faculty and staff foster a spirit of cooperation, shared responsibility, and a sense of institutional pride and security?*
- *Has the president developed, or helped to develop, a more effective, focused, informed, and near-manageable board of trustees?*

- *Has the president suffered defeats, postponements, disappointments, frustra-tions, and irreconcilable differences, and, if so, how do these setbacks affect his leadership?*
- *Is the president prepared — is there enough left of him at this point — for another term of service?*

Timing is everything in a campaign. You are bringing to life a new little planetary system where each body revolves around your college in its own particular orbit, coming closer, flinging itself off into space, only to return later in entirely different company. Out there are stars, and vast empty spaces, and pockets of humanity everywhere, but just not every-where for you, necessarily. But no matter, with the right alignment, at the perfect moment, you push your campaign into the light, fully formed, and good things begin to pile up, one upon the other, because your plan is working and you timed it well.

Timed it perfectly for October 2009, when the money-sucking maw of the Great Recession was wide open, inhaling whole communities, whole industries, ugly, quick, unrelenting, and unforgiving. We, our little campaign, had stepped into the light, opened our eyes, spread our arms, and discovered our toes dangling on the very edge of a ragged precipice; stretching out to our right and to our left other colleges, small businesses, service organizations, farmers, old people, college students, all of us peering into the abyss, wondering, teetering there.

Like most colleges fortunate to have an endowment at all, Sterling's took flight immediately and wasn't seen for three years, when it reap-peared scrawny but alive.

All around us, it seemed, farms were selling their milking herds and going out of business, carpenters were looking for painting jobs, loggers were idle, school budgets frozen, unemployment climbing. It was all too real in Craftsbury Common, when time ran out and the innkeeper of the regionally famous Inn on the Common packed up and left town, leaving Union Bank, our bank, and its president Ken Gibbons as the new and very reluctant owner.

The Inn on the Common, whose west-facing gardens and pavilion and stone enclosures gently dropped downhill and merged with the college's barns and chickens, and cows and drafts horses, all as bucolic as it gets when the sun sets behind far-off Camel's Hump, lighting up the receding ridgelines like a sea of gold-tipped waves stilled for the moment alone.

Too bad the current owners, the bankrupt ones, had done 10 years previously what 50 percent of Vermont inn buyers traditionally do: bought high, real high in this case. It's as regular as sugaring season. The first buyer buys low, works hard, and builds a place up to its destination status, like an Inn on the Common. They sell high. The next inn-dreaming people can't match the performance; they had no idea what they were getting into. They sell low. The new owners buy low and the cycle begins again.

But the inn closed and was put on the block. At the same time just down the hill in Craftsbury Village, the Historic Craftsbury General Store, the larger and somewhat more upscale of two country stores, went broke, leaving a lot of local investors embarrassed, poorer, and uncharacteristically pissed off.

Nonprofits everywhere around us were frozen, as if in fear, or amazement, watching their annual funds drying up around the edges and shrinking like a pond during a prolonged drought. Giving away money just wasn't making sense any more, and maybe never would again. That's what people were thinking.

Sterling had no choice but to push on with its campaign. Too much was at stake; too much had already been invested. And really, when you think about it, what better time is there to go out and raise money than a time when you are prepared to do just that, even when money was disappearing? Think instead if you had been sitting back pretty, counting on the boom-time philanthropic bling that had been piling up for years. And then, bang, it's over and gone. For once, Sterling was ahead of the game, by mere hours perhaps, but ahead. In this case, that's about as positive a spin as could be spun.

On the Porch of Worry, however, pacing back and forth, I felt like we'd been punched in the face. Along with everybody else. Already, as we'd worked to put the campaign together over the previous year things just weren't working out. Nothing, for a while, seemed to be breaking our way. For instance:

The Vermont-based Freeman Foundation, which for a decade had been giving Sterling $60,000 a year in student support pulled it all, the president informing me that, "Nothing goes on forever." I successfully begged for another year. Thanks for that.

A former Sterling board chairman, a Boston businessman and entrepreneur who had given the college hundreds of thousands of dollars to renovate Mager Hall, central to the campus, had pledged $100,000 to get the campaign off to a good start. One afternoon he suffered a stroke, and his wife was already suffering from cancer. Their philanthropy now went to hospitals and their minds focused not on Sterling but on recovery. Who could blame them?

Two other efforts, both attempts to link my former Marlboro connections to my current Sterling crisis, died quick, relatively painless, deaths.

At the Endeavor Foundation, Julie Kidd's doorkeeper responded to my letter addressed to her boss with a shiver and a chill and one of those, "Our priorities do not include a place like Sterling," epitaphs. On the phone she said, "Do we understand what we are talking about here?" And I said, "You mean I should never call again?" She muttered a "thank you" I think, and hung up. I will never believe Ms. Kidd read that letter.

The Kohlberg doorkeeper was a sweetheart, honestly, and said they'd keep a watch on Sterling, which meant nothing and never materialized, though it was comforting to hear, comparatively.

The full-on reality of the still descending recession had a sickening impact on my mind. Everything I had faced at the college, like that list of threats and weaknesses, like the disappearance of expected philanthropic income, like the still wobbly curriculum, and like residential spaces now about the ugliest problem we could not do much about, all of it felt worse, it all darkened down as though now we had to fight back from this shadow world, this world from which we could hardly be heard, and from where we could barely see to fight back.

And it was personal. Sterling had 50 employees in jobs they counted on in a territory where steady employment can be tenuous in good times. They were dedicated, tough, generally uncomplaining, and of consistent good humor. The idea that somehow through what was coming the college would actually fail and all these people would lose their jobs, the town its college, was the most frightening thing for me to think about. I'd experienced recessions at Marlboro, but this didn't feel at all like those; and its official name — The Great Recession — sounded more like a sleazy sideshow hawker's call to come into the tent and see for yourself, see *The Great Recession*.

I prefer depression.

I admit, too, it was all motivating for me, this darkening world, this sudden worsening, this doubling down. Under such strain your mind either gets sharper or it cracks into little pieces that start floating around aimlessly; either way, it changes. And over a period of time, a journey of some miles on the porch and of the consumption of many, many little cigars, I thought about survival, what it was, and what it meant.

Survival is a thing you manage. By definition it is short-lived, in that you survive or you do not. If you survive, it doesn't matter much what shape you're in at the end of it. You have succeeded in surviving; life really can't do anything now but get better.

But maybe not. If Sterling survived this recession and emerged alive but so weak it couldn't even stand up, we'd die anyway. That would be even more depressing. No one in our business was going to wait, nor would students and their parents: if you fell too far behind, even right there with whispers of daylight in sight at the end of the tunnel, you'd be trampled anyway. I was sure of that.

Survival is not regarded as a strategy, like "retrenching" at Harvard, or "value-engineering" on the part of architects to increase their billable hours. But on the Porch of Worry, under the circumstances, you decide survival is, in fact, a strategy, and one worth pursuing. Work at it long enough and survival as an idea bends and folds and stretches time, and time is what you need. Survival, like meditation, reveals nuance you never noticed before, when life was just crude and desperate.

Once I'd determined I'd use survival as a strategic way forward, as an operating methodology, the panicky urge to always place the mangy dog of deficit front and center slipped sideways to a more comfortable place among the pile of other, suddenly equally important things. An intimate threat now felt like a stitch in my side, or a pebble in my shoe, instead of shooting pains in my head.

Those red warning flags were waving together now in celebration that my brain had created a way to think about the narrow path ahead. Even the campaign goals came into focus, the shifting resources, such as they were, beginning to align themselves.

If the college could emerge from the recession dirt poor but out of debt and wholly put together, even shined up, the endowment coming back, the curriculum barreling along, and room to grow provided, then at the end of the tunnel we'd have the strength to rejoin the race. Survival as a strategy, a good-enough idea, but I absolutely wasn't going to talk about it out loud; I was not going to share it or explain it. I wasn't that crazy.

10

My Father's Problem

After introducing Rod Gander on the Amtrak platform that miserable night over 20 years before, I wrote that during almost three decades in higher education I had to lead a human life, as well, but went on to tell little of that life, in contrast to the institutional one. This was working fine until I was presented with a literary delta of choices by my friend John Elder, who, earlier, had set me on the path of memoir. It turns out I'm confined only by a subject's relevance to the circumnavigation of the landscape of my excursion: so it is too much. I can't take it all in, let alone carry it all. In addition, there are areas I see but I am blind to. There are storerooms of stuff of no concern, or no concern here. And there are stories that tumble about with other stories. Thus I am swept along, with limited, or unpredictable control over steerage.

When I think about it this way, which channels in this elaborate delta are open to me and where each might lead, I am forced to choose almost randomly, and set off to see what's around the bend. Thus....

Although today I am a father of two and a grandfather of four, and have a 96-year-old mother, Marie Core Duffy, who has forgotten nothing, and an intact family of three siblings and many nephews and nieces, it is my late father I measure myself against, not measure, really, but stand next to and compare the similarities and the differences between us. Of everyone, he's the most mysterious in my mind. I wish

I'd known him better. He would have been fascinated with my life as a college president. We would have had great phone conversations. I wish I could listen to his stories all again. I wish he were still alive so I could fill in some of the gaps.

I am soon enough caught in this gentle current and willingly, although it's getting darker, push on.

Tuesday, July 4, 2006
From my First Year Journal:

The bitter news that will mark this 4th of July, my second day as president, is that I broke my fly rod. The tip, in the rear door of the car, crushed, at the end of a long afternoon driving around the Northeast Kingdom fishing small streams for trout.

It's a bad sign. I don't seem to handle high intensity emotionally negative incidents like I used to, if I ever did. I have no room for this now. But instead, I spent hours in a dark, headshaking, desolate, foul mood. Consuming myself. It's a fly rod, for God's sake. It's an opportunity to buy another. Lots of people own half a dozen rods. But I've fished streams from Colorado to Maine to Florida to Vermont with this little seven-foot Orvis my brother-in-law gave me 35 years ago. It made its bones at Singing River Ranch, my father's dream, that ranch. Nine thousand feet up in the southern, front range Rockies. For years I fished on three miles of two creeks, the Huerfano and the South Huerfano, for rainbows and brook trout that never saw a hatchery and that were as wary and as hungry as any wild trout anywhere in the world. I packed the rod high into the Rockies, fishing up the ice-cold blue headwaters of the Huerfano into the upper valley right under the near glacier hanging, summer and winter, under Mt. Blanca's peak, the trout getting smaller and smaller as the mountain grew above me. And, horseless, I'd thrash my way a mile into the brush to reach beaver ponds where I could stand on one of a series of dams — the local beavers' history written in ponds and dams, ponds and dams, active and defunct, ascending the meadows. Without alerting them, I could position myself above them and whip flies — even with this little rod — 60 maybe 70 feet out over the pond where the fat lazy succulent pond trout — 15, 16, 17 inches — swam in circles, wary, but com-

pulsive at the perfectly laid fly six inches — light as dust — from their snout. Then what a commotion!

And on the South Huerfano, a whole different scene — locked in a narrow valley, hidden under a tangle of elk brush, alder, downed aspen — trout paradise. That's where a seven-foot rod was at its best, as I duck-walked along low and narrow animal paths — deer, bear, coyote — to reach the most inaccessible places. My right arm would get sore on the Huerfano, at the ponds and at places along the creek where I could wind up and cast upstream. Yes, upstream. I alternated up and down, that's how cautious the bigger fish were. Sometimes I'd take half an hour to approach a certain pool, only in the last seconds before casting a dry fly spooking the fish, and they'd dart around like crazy and shoot into their hiding holes and I'd be left there admiring the creek. Sometimes I'd try waiting them out but I never succeeded, I'd always get impatient and move on. On the South Huerfano sometimes I'd have to crawl into position and release the fly arm-length by arm-length, feeding it down stream, watching it float under the overhanging foliage, seeing it disappear and then Bang! But very difficult to land — I was using barbless flies then and with such restricted use of the rod the fish had the advantage.

Given the afternoon off from ranch duties or heading out at dawn or skipping dinner, only hunger and fatigue drove me back in. Colorado and elsewhere provided a thousand opportunities to break that rod. I'd tumbled down rocky banks with it, forced it ahead of me as I blindly crashed through the Vermont streamside pucker brush pursued by angry paper wasps I transgressed upon. I'd toss it over piles of logs and fallen evergreens and then catch up with it on the other side. I'd fallen in the stream and yanked the rod out even as I was being enveloped in the swift, cold water.

Then, maybe 10 years ago, I'd pretty much given up trout fishing in Vermont, and Colorado was a long-ago sweet memory of youth and mountains and horses and wild fish. I enjoyed fishing on South Pond in Marlboro, standing up in the canoe 30 feet from shore and placing the fly here and there along the deep parts of the swampy shoreline, catching fat fish put there by the State of Vermont. But stream fishing in southern Vermont had deteriorated because of roadwork runoff and overfishing and a lack of catch and release rules. So the rod sat in the mud-room, or in my office; my collection of reels and line and boxes of flies in a cardboard box in the workshop.

But up here in the Northeast Kingdom there seemed to be potential. The Black River almost encircles Craftsbury Common, running quickly and roughly from the north on the common's eastern flank into Craftsbury proper, then swinging around to the swamps and cornfields and heading directly north destined for Lake Memphremagog 15 miles away at Newport. Then there is the Wildbranch west of Craftsbury that one drives along to get to get to Rt. 15 and Morrisville. And, of course, there are the innumerable creeks and streams that sometimes hold great fish, not large, but hesitant and quick. So I retrieved my rod. Dug out my line and flies. Oiled my oversized Pfluger Medalist, and then took the big step, buying my first license in years. What an empowering action that was, the freedom it represented, not to go fishing really, but to go. Into the woods, to the creeks and streams, down the embankments, through the pucker brush, through the weather to where again only hunger and fatigue remind you to stop.

Then, like a soldier who survives combat but is struck and killed by a bicycle in Central Park, or like a faithful and obedient old dog that is run over and killed or drowns or freezes and dies because of a single inattentive moment on its master's part, my rod met an end it didn't deserve.

<hr/>

My father, Philip Henry Wootton, died in 2001 from a combination of Alzheimer's and Parkinson's, age 83, at the last of my parents' southern Connecticut homes. Visiting only every three to four months at best, to me the dementia came upon him suddenly. I knew it was happening, but being in Vermont I wasn't exposed to the weekly or monthly changes in his condition. So when I got there, and recognized it on my own, I immediately felt the almost physical shift that occurs when one unshakeable reality — an entire filial relationship — suddenly is no longer and can never be again, and has been replaced with another, unknown and probably unknowable, seamlessly and irrevocably in the same body, the same man.

All the things I wanted from him, wanted to ask, wanted to know, wanted to understand, I'd waited too long. I'd been too far away, or he had.

Except for my being thoroughly dyslexic, a condition undiagnosed until early adulthood, and which in effect made me appear convincingly stupid as a child, my young life was as close to ideal as I can imagine. With a father who rarely sat still and an artistic mother way too clever to ever be left behind in much of anything — cooking, riding, trout fishing, history, literature, the Bible, the visual arts — and being most definitely the chief operations officer, while my father served as chief excursion and equipment manager, boat buyer, horse rider, trail hiker, lawn mower, shop master, cowboy with an office and secretary in Manhattan, and a way of jumping off the commuter train as it hissed to a stop so his wife in the station wagon with a couple of kids in the back could be first out of the parking lot, get home, knock down a cocktail, have dinner, retire to his home office and, presumably, plan out the next weekend, the next move.

I never saw my parents argue. They must have. I saw them disagree, and once at the ranch I heard raised voices from their office/bedroom in the main cabin. It sounded like an argument, but I couldn't hear clearly. Still, I immediately found my older sister and reported the phenomenon. Can you imagine growing up and not being exposed to your parents arguing? My high-school girlfriend had to teach me how to fight, how to argue. It was a bitterly experiential education where the advantages were all hers, slicing and dicing this ignorant, hockey-playing, slow-reading, apparently aimless and soon to be ex-boyfriend. Of course, Lulu honed my skills over the next 40 years by deftly employing her overstuffed portfolio of technique and experience. "I think we are equals now," I informed her once. "I don't want to argue about it," she said, informatively.

I don't remember the first book I read, I don't remember any books I read up until I read the first book that influenced me. It was Dalton Trumbo's *Johnny Got His Gun*. That was in eighth grade. I hadn't been a good student at all. My mother sent me to tutors in math, writing, spelling, reading, paying attention, not being lazy. It was no use. After flunking second grade, my educational life was a persistent humiliation. I sat in the back of all the classrooms, whether they were alphabetically organized or not. When we weren't under our desks waiting to be incinerated by a communist nuclear blast, once a week we got to sit on top of them during spelling bees. When you missed a word you had to sit in your chair, and the last one remaining on his or her desk won the spelling bee. It was often Lucy Winslow, my sometimes alphabetically compelled partner. I never made it past the first word. Ever. Once I received a test back with the grade 88 in red pencil with an exclamation point. I was excited and amazed. How did I know all that stuff? But it was Lucy Winslow's and I had to exchange it for my 48. "Willie," she said. "You keep trying and some day you'll pass one of these tests."

Fifth grade, I guess, I hardly recall those blurry, interminable school days when I couldn't really read and numbers seemed to drift off the page, chased away by the battle tanks and fighter airplanes teachers let me draw because, well, I couldn't read and numbers seem to have no effect on me at all.

Idleness provoked pre-adolescent love, or falling in love, always with unreachable girls, like Christie Nichols.

I was also in love with Lucy Winslow. And I was in love with Annis Gilbert. There were others. I kept them all to myself, of course, because I was smart enough to know that being stupid — I mean, it was obvious what I could do in the classroom and what they could do — also meant being unloved and deservingly so.

My mother, my brother, my sisters all still live within striking distance of one another in Connecticut, and they (but not so much my mother) still run into grade-school chums, in fact sometimes they marry into them, as Connie, my older sister did, into the family of Christie Nichols. Connie married Nick Nichols. So Christie Nichols often attends Connie and Nick's annual Christmas Eve party, which I almost never do because being from rural Vermont you always have an excuse to stay away from Connecticut, which I think of as a near continent-size suburb of New York City, Yale included.

But Lulu and I did recently attend. And Christie was in attendance with her husband. I hadn't seen her in a decade or longer, and then at one of these family gatherings where there were polite hellos amidst the crowd. Connie and Nick's was a grand party, my ancient mother and her younger ancient sister huddled in oversized chairs sipping white wine, nieces and nephews, cousins and in-laws. Young couples, new boyfriends and new girlfriends. Sons and daughters, brothers and sisters, and a busy undercurrent of small children sweeping through the elders like wave-washed currents in a tidal pool.

Christie spoke with Lulu about errant children, one of which I believe she possessed, but she and I didn't say hello until she was on her way out, bundling up in the hallway.

"I never seem to catch up with you," I said, meaninglessly.

She said something about the back of the classroom, about our classmates. I wasn't listening. I was trying to think of something else to say, something like chat, which I don't do especially well, but instead said, "I'm sure you know, I was in love with you." And instead of putting this ridiculous attempt at chatting into context, that I was in love with all the pretty, smart girls, I said nothing.

Christie laughed and looked at me a little strangely. "And you," she said. "You were the last person in the whole world anyone ever thought would be a college president."

That's dyslexia for you. The affliction that keeps on afflicting.

———

While my mother fretted about my schooling, my father ignored all that in his third child. Growing up, my older brother's proclivity for causing havoc while being highly productive — a savant nearly — in model-making, engine rebuilding, hotrod building, sculpture, machining, road-bike and dirt-bike building, and running away from school, racking up cars, and generally causing parental distress, all of it took attention away from my older sister and me. Our considerably younger sister, on the other hand, was most definitely my father's and mother's favorite. Somehow, as older brothers and sister we were copacetic with that, that she was our parents' favorite, and it seemed only natural the youngest deserved that distinction.

Even sibling rivalry, however, suffers with non-arguing parents. Today, as genuinely older adults, the Wootton siblings still don't fight, don't argue with each other. It's as if when we are together (admittedly infrequently on my part) our egos are left hanging in the mudroom, to be donned upon exiting, while peace reigns inside. At the same time, my mother and her ancient younger sister can quarrel like drunken hens.

August 1968, I arrived at the University of Denver, with just a backpack. The boxes I'd shipped — clothes, a typewriter, my laundry — had been stolen from the university post office. They'd found the empty boxes, I was told. I was at Denver because it was a place someone like me, who had done nothing about applying to college, could be accepted in mid-July with the briefest of applications. And if I weren't in college, I would be joining my brother in Vietnam, a place he thought particularly dangerous for someone like his younger, ditzy-headed brother. So, Denver, and eventually a favorable draft lottery number.

I lasted at the university until halfway through my sophomore year, then transferred to Marlboro College in January 1970. Free from high school and able to choose, I took wonderful courses at DU: human geography, two studio art courses, a philosophy class entitled "The Problem with Evil"; I even talked my way into a junior-level class on American humor, barely survived, and never did anything like that again. Finally, an English class reading *The Brothers Karamazov*, where for the first and really only time, I attended academic lectures delivered via clip-on microphones in very large, tiered lecture halls with hundreds of other students. I thought it was all great.

Hockey, too, was great. I played two winters on the same ice as the 1968 and 1969 Denver University NCAA champions. Their team leader and captain, Keith Magnuson (who went on to play with the Chicago Blackhawks) was my club team's coach, along with a couple of his teammates as assistants. Scrimmaging one afternoon I stole the puck from him (he was looking away) spun around and scored on an All-American goalie who was warming up with us, thus deking two All-Americans in about five seconds. I ragged on Magnuson. "You're not as fast as I thought," I said. "For a carrot-topped Canuck, pretty sloppy play all around," I said, and paid for it moments later with a mildly violent demonstration of open ice checking, my hard landing softened by Magnuson partially catching me on the way down, after having been bounced off the boards. "Did you call me a Canuck?" Coach Magnuson said — I was on my back, he was standing over me, grinning. My teammates merely watched. "No," I said. "A Canadian. Sir." This was my only close brush with NHL stardom, so it's cherished.

Great teachers and great hockey at my very much less than All-American level of the game, so why leave? Because I had to declare a major. I hadn't filled out the form and was called in by the dean, some dean. He was passively annoyed.

"I'll complete the form for you," he said, unclipping a pen from his breast pocket. "What have you chosen, English? This is the English Department."

"I'd like to combine English," I said. "Mostly poetry. With art, sculpture."

"Art is another department. They cannot be combined."

I won't go on with this story. But back in Vermont over Thanksgiving I visited Marlboro, which was only 10 miles the back way from our house in East Dover. My transcript was complete. I was interviewed by the faculty member in charge of admissions that semester, Dick Judd. He explained to me how independent academic work at Marlboro was conducted. It was confusing. I asked, "Can I do a Plan that combines writing and sculpture?"

"Of course you can," he said, his famous eyebrows, like slumbering black caterpillars clinging to his forehead, making the slightest wrinkle in confirmation.

In January 1970, I transferred back east to hills and forests and stone walls.

Within two years my father purchased the ranch and for the next five years or so my life was pleasantly interrupted with driving between Colorado and Vermont, summers to fall out there, winters and springs in New England. Twice in the early 1970s I had to be at the ranch in winter, once alone from February to May, when other people started to show up, and once with Lulu, from March into the summer.

In between I cooked. I labored. I lived with friends in apartments and run-down houses. One summer I rebelled and told my father I was heading to Alaska to try fishing instead of helping out at the ranch. I bought a ragged old Chevy Apache panel truck, fitted it out with a plank bed, a stove, a food box, a rack for two rods, and another box for clothes. I taped screening to the sliding side windows and drove alone, my second time up there, the first just after high school.

Things didn't work out too well. I missed a job on a fishing boat. Was rejected for one as a cook in a logging camp. I spent one day hauling up king crab pots for $25 and all the king crab I could eat. I hiked. Fished. Watched bald eagles wade in the shallows with sea gulls. Caught shrimp off the Homer pier in the brief hour of midnight darkness. From 11 till 3 every day in a diner on little hill in Homer people like me could eat all the pancakes, margarine, and fake maple syrup they wanted for $2.00. Staples for wandering young men. I didn't eat another pancake for 20 years.

After a month, I put in a collect call to the ranch and learned from my sister that the foreman had cracked a vertebra and was down for the season, and if Dad knew I was calling he'd want me back down there as fast as possible. Put him on, I said. I'm starving.

And a couple of days later I'm in the Rockies. Everything is familiar. The horses. Suzy the Austrian Shepherd. The milkhouse and Frank's cows. Frank Sanders was the foreman; about as close to a real cowboy as you could find. He had a wife and boy, about seven. He was tall and lanky and had been a medic in the army in Germany, instead of Vietnam. Just lucky.

He'd fallen off the horse trailer and slammed his back into something, nipping a bone. He didn't look all that hurt, but I spent the rest of the summer hauling pig scraps out to his pigs, feeding his cows, cleaning up the milk house. He did manage the chicken house, collecting the eggs and carrying them over to the kitchen. So things were pretty sweet for Frank, except he couldn't ride. Not at all. Couldn't wrangle. Which put it all on me and one hired hand, a tall, good-humored Californian who'd attended my father's old school, Thatcher, and maintained all the traits and physical mannerisms of a young cowboy with a good education. He could rope a little, and was good with horses except he seemed to fall off a lot. Almost frequently. We'd be riding along some trail at a fast trot, something would happen, his horse would shy or stumble and Chip would be on the ground, reins in hand, straightening his big felt cowboy hat and brushing off his pants, taking it all as a matter of course.

I was 24 years old in 1973, unmarried, with a Marlboro degree in writing and sculpture, and everything I owned, including my saddle, my typewriter, a small cast-iron wood stove, and a straight-backed chair, fit neatly in my rusty VW Squareback. At the ranch, my job revolved around the saddle horses for the guests, and the horses we used for leading trail rides, wrangling, and other work, the irrigation ditches for the hay fields, for instance, and getting the bailed hay into the barns. My responsibility was to take riders, some experienced, some appallingly unqualified for the high mountains, on morning or all-day rides into the mountains, and return them safely to the ranch. It was a small operation really, with room for about 20 guests and a staff of 10 or so, including my mother who ran the kitchen and everything else outside the corrals and barns and machinery. My sisters Connie and Liz and our cousins composed the domestic staff, so to speak, and a variety of young men and women over the years filled in as carpenters, wranglers, kitchen workers, and general laborers.

Each evening, just before supper, we'd open a series of metal gates and our horses would leave the corrals and head off for the night into 2,000 acres of creeks and little valleys, humping foothills, steep-sided arroyos, and dense forests and bogs. We'd kept back our wrangling horses, of course, and fed and watered them in the corral next to the tack room and the little porch and rail everyone sat on or leaned against in mornings, as the horses were saddled for the day's rides.

Wrangling means getting up before sunrise and pulling on yesterday's jeans, shirt, and boots, then a warm riding jacket, gloves, hat, chaps in cold or bad weather, and walking across a wooden bridge over the Huerfano Creek to the corrals. Sometimes Chip would have already bridled our horses. Occasionally he used Sargent, my father's favorite. And occasionally he overslept. We didn't say much. We saddled up and rode out in the coming dawn, leaving the gates open behind us. By the time we were in the open, meadows in one direction and rocky climbs in the other, the sun was up over the plains and full upon the high mountain ridgeline that dominated the valley. One of us would head down to the South Huerfano, the other up to the higher meadow, and maybe down the other side.

The idea was to find the horses, who would be in three to six smaller groupings, each with its own leader, and each leader with his own personality and evasive or cooperative reaction to wranglers. Horses will only wander as far as the feed in the pastures, along the watercourses, patched into the aspen forests. The dryer the year, the less feed, the further they searched for grass and the deeper the wranglers have to go to find them and push them home. Usually we stayed together until one horse group was seen, another often would be nearby, and we'd have a fair idea where to go next. We'd split up, and push horses to a more central spot and then home. It could take an hour or three, once four. And no breakfast or coffee until every animal was in.

I used four or five horses for wrangling and trail riding, but I kept exclusive use of two. Jasper was a gigantic black and white paint, with a muscled neck and flaring nostrils. He came with the ranch. He'd been abused. Roped. Whipped. Because of his size and strength and, for whoever it was who did that, his refusal to be trained even if broken.

So Jasper was just kept with the herd, unridden, too much to bother with. In the corral, to keep away from anything human, he'd dart around behind the other horses, wild-eyed and snorting; he had to be the last horse caught, when you could corner him and approach him talking softly, hand outstretched. Get that hand on him really gently, and slowly slip a length of rope over his neck, and you had him, 1,500 pounds of quivering nerves and muscles held by a piece of string. He spun when you mounted. Once in the saddle, the slightest movement — removing your hat, for instance — and he'd jerk to one side or throw himself forward as though poked from behind. Worst of all, he didn't ground tie, meaning you couldn't dismount and simply drop the reins and walk away to fix a post and scoop a drink from the creek, then go pick them up whenever you were ready. Jasper walked if he could, and there'd be no catching him on foot.

But after months of riding him he got to know me pretty well. When a horse fly landed on his forehead as we rode along, and there were no trailside bushes upon which to rub his head and shoo the thing off, I could take my four-foot leather quirt, bring it up over my shoulder, take a careful aim, lean forward and bring it down with a moderate smack on Jasper's broad nose and occasionally on the fly, which he appreciated. So there evolved something like trust. And I could take off my hat without causing a major ruckus.

Still, Jasper was a wonderful ride. Huge and nimble. Completely responsive, if a little excitable. Tireless. And although he appeared frightened of everything, it turned out he just startled easily. As a wrangling horse, Jasper was like blasting around in a souped-up, re-enforced, four-wheel-drive, rock-ready Cadillac convertible.

The other horse was Alvin. He was probably 12 years old or so. Midsize. Brown sorrel. Nothing distinguished about him. Born in the high mountains, in the thin air above 9,000 feet, along the rocky trails and pitted prairie lands at the very top of the high plains. Even on the very worst trails, cluttered with rocks and boulders, Alvin rarely stumbled.

I never actually did this because it's a stupid thing to do, but with Alvin I could have wrapped the reins around the saddle horn and wrangled that way. When I thought we'd best cut off a bunch of horses by scrambling down this steep hillside and through the brush down there, Alvin would see the plan, and a touch of my hand on his neck and some pressure with a leg and down we'd go.

Heading toward a pod of saddle horses reluctant to leave their pasture, down one of those steep, rock-covered hillsides, populated with 10-foot-high brush and pinion pine, eight mule deer were heading uphill toward Alvin and me, and crosswise, two large coyotes were about to intersect the converging groups — the deer, the saddle horses, and Alvin and me. In a situation like that on horseback, all kinds of bad things can happen. Young Chip would have been on the ground in an instant. Jasper would have stomped and snorted and flung himself around, clattering stones and backing into trees.

Alvin. He did what I was about to do. Stopped dead still and watched as the deer missed the coyotes and the coyotes, heading home in the early morning, seemed bent on just passing by, without trouble. And the horses below gazed up and, because Alvin was positioned correctly, started slowly walking home by themselves, seeing the game was up for that morning.

Another time just as the sun was coming up Alvin and I were down on the South Huerfano searching for one or another group of horses. I found a place to cross the creek and in we waded and immediately Alvin was belly deep and sinking.

Quicksand is the strangest stuff. Green, just like the firm bank of the creek it merges with, and not exactly wet or dry and just slightly corned, like soft but granular snow. Within moments the tops of my boots were endangered and I could feel Alvin was beginning to react with consternation, but without much effect, confined as he was by the quicksand and a 50-pound saddle and me on his back.

What else could I do? I took my sheath knife from my saddle, hoisted myself up and stepped onto dry turf not two feet from us. Then I turned around and lay down and fixed to cut off my saddle — save that at least — but at that moment Alvin gave a couple of heaves and pulled himself out. The quicksand slipped off him like it was oiled, a clean, green mud that left no trace on his hide.

Another time, and this is the last story I'll tell about Alvin, we were wrangling north of the ranch, above the hay field, down along Deer Creek. Wrangling is mostly done at a walk or a fast trot. You don't gallop horses across the hills and dales and into the corral. You walk them in, urge them. They know what you want, but if you rush them it's just not worth the results. They can scatter. One or two horses can break off and run and you have to track them down and bring them back, leaving the other wrangler alone with a pack of 30 horses suddenly reluctant to leave their pasture for a day's labor.

But along Deer Creek there are stretches of grass and a couple of ditches, an irrigation ditch and then a wider, deeper runoff ditch. It was a place to let loose, and Alvin anticipated this eagerly; he'd be saying, "Here we are, man. Let's go!" I'd ease the reins and knee him forward with a soft verbal "Let's go then!" He knew what we were after, to jump those ditches, to come up to them just perfectly, a team effort, and at the edge bolt over, fly over, then pound up the trail to find the horses. So we're flying across the flats, the ditches ahead, and the next thing is I'm hanging onto Alvin's neck for dear life, under his neck actually, and he's stumbling forward and my boots are dragging where his steel-shoed hooves are scrambling for grip. I can't hold on. He's still moving forward. I drop and Alvin stops immediately before trampling me. I'm on the ground, on my back, reins in hand; Alvin towers over me and I'm staring at his forelegs. He lowers his head and gives me a sniff. From where I am lying, his head is the size of a boulder and his soft dark chin comes within inches of my face. I scratch his chin and push the giant head away.

Nothing is broken. There's a scrape of mud and grass on his chest, and I notice as I pull myself up my right shoulder is muddy and streaked with grass, like we hit the ground together. How I ended up hanging under Alvin's neck with my boots dragging between his hooves I have no idea, but there's no way to get there except straight over the top.

We walked back and found the hole he'd stepped in, barely noticeable, where a little tributary to the Huerfano had penetrated the bank without disturbing the surface. Huerfano is Spanish for orphan. Out on the plains, 60 miles eastward, is a geologic feature standing all by itself, a volcanic pipe eroded to a single conical hump. It's referred to as the Huerfano, and was a guidepost for travelers.

It was as soft a landing as one could hope for. Alvin and I stood around looking at the hole for a minute, then I got back on and we headed over the ditches and up the trail at a walk, looking for horses to bring in.

———

My father was at last in his element as owner of a small dude ranch and a small herd of cattle (my mother's herd, really), at the end of the road in a magnificent mountain valley in the high West. Finally he had enough horses to keep him happy, and enough land practically to himself to feel, I guess, he'd reached a place where his soul was so perfectly occupied as to suppress the anxieties that tormented him. Not the anxieties of a father of four. Not those accompanying his final leave-taking from *LIFE* magazine and heading off on his own — the magazine was floundering anyway. No, these were anxieties — things of the soul —

that had tormented him his whole life. That he never spoke about, that he almost didn't know about, and hinted at only to my mother, and then vaguely, and rarely.

It's lore. Family lore, bits of which we knew as children but had no idea of their significance. Here it is:

My father, nearsighted since childhood and now with trim turtle-shell frames, dark hair, a confident smile; he's six feet tall and in good shape, in his second or third year at Yale. But things aren't going well. The academic work isn't particularly difficult for him. Geology and writing seemed to be what he concentrated on. He had a great girl-friend, my mother — there's a wonderful photograph of her, leaning up against my father's elegant (but we knew unreliable) Ford, her long hair full, her smile easy, she's looking straight at the camera, she's thin and stylish, a regular prewar flapper. So what's his problem?

He goes and sees a psychiatrist. They talk. My father talks. He tells him about growing up in Japan; he doesn't know why, maybe the doctor asked him. They talk about Dad being an only child. They talk about Thatcher School in California, and horses. They talk about a Western kid with an unusual background at Yale. They talk more about his being an only child.

I guess the rules were different back then but, the story goes, the psychiatrist telephones my grandparents in New Jersey and he says, "I'm working with your son up here at Yale, who is having some psychological issues (Would he say something like that?) and I have a very specific question for you, if you don't mind."

They are parents, what are they going to say?

"Your son says he grew up in Japan. Is that correct?"

"Yes."

"This is my question: He says he is an only child. Is that correct?"

There must have been a long pause....

———

Cooking in restaurants, I discovered almost immediately after graduating from Marlboro in 1972, had three advantages over other non-ranch jobs I'd had: you could always find a job, you were indoors, and you were fed. For all the fun, romance, and adventure of working in the Rockies, the ranch was marginal employment, full-time work in half the time over a four-month season, and some cash when needed.

My first restaurant was Natalie's, an Italian place in Cambridge, Massachusetts, where I lived around the corner with my old college roommate and various women at various times. I worked about 80 hours a week, washing dishes, making pizzas and salads, doing prep work, listening to the three brothers who owned the place, they and their cousins. Vinnie was the head cook, and the only sane brother. The oldest, boss brother, drove a fat black car, and was always in a violent, angry hurry but had all day to hang around and try to boss Vinnie. Then he'd storm off. To where I never discovered. The middle brother was doltish and pleasant, one of the weekend cooks, who was constantly burning himself and dropping sizzling pans.

The last task I did every night was open a dozen number 10 cans of plum tomatoes, run the fruit through a hand strainer to remove the seeds, and line up the refilled cans on the counter next to the eight-burner stove. I took the huge 10-gallon saucepot and put it on the stove. Then I went to the cleaning closet and took the wooden, sturdy, home-built two-step platform and placed it securely against the stove, in front of the pot. Onions, carrots, peppers, a hunk of salt pork, parsley, garlic, dried spices. Vinnie boxed up the ingredients and left them on the counter. He took a large wooden paddle off its hook and left it on the counter. Then we closed the place, usually between 10:30 and 11:00.

Back in the kitchen 12 hours later, the pot was on the stove, warm and bubbling slowly, the deep red sauce filling the tiny kitchen with the first pungent fragrance of the long day ahead. The 12 cans had been rinsed and placed neatly back in their cardboard boxes to be discarded. The counter was clean, the vegetable scraps in a white plastic bucket. The two-step platform was back in the closet. I never saw her, but all this prep was about the boys' mother, who I was told was well under five feet tall, and who arrived every morning at six and made the sauce, without which, everyone knew, life would be nothing and there'd be no restaurant.

After five months of this, when the routine became routine, I called

Vinnie and quit, which to him meant we negotiated day by day when I would come in, and that system got me down to 40 or 50 hours a week, so it felt like a vacation.

Other restaurants provided more training. I learned that when cooks quit or get fired — something which happens with the frequency of, say, weather — dishwashers became cooks, and cooks become chefs; the difference, according to Hans of the Silver Skates? Chefs pay attention to food. Cooks just heat it up or cool it down.

I ended up back in Marlboro, at the Skates, with Hans and Victor and Hans's sister Fifine, who managed the dining room. It lasted, on and off, for a few years. When Lulu and I married in 1976, the reception was at the Skates. Two years later, our son Russell took his first rolling steps in the bar, clutching two spoons above his head. Soon after that, we pulled up and moved to Somerville, Massachusetts, and I started graduate school in journalism at Boston University.

And that opportunity was thanks to a conversation with my father, and a result of his buying the house and 126 acres in East Dover, Vermont, in the early 1960s. To help Lulu and me and our new son survive our first genuine urban experience, he sold timber off the land, about $6,000 worth. I wonder, though, if it wasn't also a result or reflection of my father's problem, his willingness to afford his third child a chance to break away, to move, to engage, to jump ship, to experience, and then to see what came of it. Our second attempt at urban living was more than 20 years in the future, at Montserrat on the North Shore. My father was dead by then.

———

I can only imagine that pause on the other end of the line, when my grandparents were asked whether it was true my father was an only child. Because he was not. And he didn't know. My grandparents never told him he'd had a younger brother when he was hardly three years old himself. And that brother had died, we believed as children, violently, in front of my father, the three-year-old.

My father grew up in Kobe, Japan, which is about 325 miles south of Tokyo and, as a district opened to foreign trade in 1851, one of the areas where foreigners lived a life of relative, as in hugely contrasting, wealth and privilege. We learned as children, for instance, that in those days there were three ways foreigners ascended Mt. Fuji. They could hike up. They could be carried up in a litter hoisted by four or six men. Or — this is the one we were fascinated with and practiced — you could have a laborer, a servant, a poorly paid native, or your brother or sister put hands against the small of your back and gently push you up the trail.

My grandparent's car, a huge Packard I believe, had a button you could push that sent an electric shock through the automobile's metal body, instantly casting off any of the crowded lowlife attempting to lean against or sit on the automobile. The Japanese driver, of course, was the one who would push the button.

Besides drivers, in attendance were maids, cooks, and gardeners. In my father and his parents, there was also a deep respect for Kobe and the Japanese who surrounded their lives. Throughout his life my father was impatient with people who judged, who thought they understood, but who knew nothing about the Orient, and the Japanese.

We have old films, very old, that even decades ago when we watched them had to be constantly patched back together with clear tape as the film cracked apart every foot or so, of birthday parties on a lawn with my child father running around, or sitting in a tiny peddle car. The surrounding guests are a mix of Americans and Japanese, but they are hard to see because the camera focuses on the only child.

We know that at just a few minutes before noon on Saturday, September 1, 1923 my grandmother, a young woman, wife, and mother, was three rungs up on a step ladder hanging curtains in the living room in Kobe, when the ladder started rocking and she looked down to my five-year-old father who was supposed to be steadying the ladder and admonished him, "Philip, hold that ladder still. Stop playing...."

But it wasn't him and it didn't stop.

It was instead the Great Yokohama and Tokyo Earthquake and it shook the earth for 4 to 10 minutes while 140,000 people died and thousands were injured and made homeless. Not so much in Kobe but in the large cities.

Somehow as children we linked this story to the whispered story of my father's younger brother. Whenever the story was retold, among so many other stories with no similar effect, I imagined the child dying in the earthquake. Which doesn't make sense, since my father was five at the time and would have remembered. Maybe I thought this as a child because I had nothing else to fill in the gaps and mysteries.

My younger sister, with whom my mother lives in Connecticut, visited Taiwan in the early 1990s, and on her return trip flew to Tokyo and took a train to Kobe. Using information from my grandfather's archives (he was a great filer: after his death we found a file titled, "flea found in cellar, 1938," and at the bottom of the old manila folder was the filed flea), Liz located the well-kept Westerners-only cemetery, one of six in the city, and took a photograph of the stone. It said: "Baby Wootton, July 7, 1921." We learned he was just a few weeks old when he died, our uncle without a name.

More than 20 years after that, when my father sought the counsel of a Yale physiatrist for a condition he didn't understand, it all must have come out. We've no idea how it came out with his parents, whether there was a showdown, or, more likely, something closer to a depressing discussion my grandparents wanted never to happen. They never spoke about their child's death to their son, but who, even at three years old, had to have been aware his mother was pregnant, aware the baby had been born, and aware the baby disappeared, apparently unacknowledged. Then it was over and forgotten until it wasn't.

For my father as a young man, with the reality of the deception coming upon him, one can only guess what such knowledge carried to him and imposed upon him. There was continued silence on his part, although late in life he did tell Liz his brother died because of "Japan," meaning the Orient, meaning the abysmal level of medical and hygiene knowledge and practice at that time, in that part of the world. Whatever mechanism the survivor's syndrome employed had cleansed his conscious mind entirely — but temporarily — of any direct knowledge of the death of his brother and replaced it with an inner misery that never went away, that did not fully dissipate even with knowledge, or understanding, or time.

Instead, I think, he developed a well-organized compulsiveness to move from place to place looking, feeling his way, for a place where everyone could be assembled, where everyone was safe and accounted for.

Buckminster Fuller used to come to my father's office at *LIFE* and they'd use bits of tape to patch together Fuller's new invention, the geodesic dome. My father knew Gordon Parks, the photographer, and they'd go to lunch and talk about picture taking. Along with other journalists, I'm sure, Dad was invited on a two-night voyage aboard the navy's first nuclear powered submarine, the Nautilus. He turned it down as too risky, too experimental. To his sputtering, incredulous third child who couldn't seem to let it go, he said, "It's not just you. I have other children, you know." He also spent time at Cape Canaveral, later Kennedy, and with the first seven astronauts. He thought of Gus Grissom as a particular friend.

My father could boil water because he drank tea, rarely of the bagged type and never with milk or sugar. Beyond that, I don't even recall him even toasting a slice of bread. But he loved good food: for example lunch, as an editor of Life in New York City, was often a gastronomical way stop on the road to a story, like the group of Russians who fed the Life editors mounds of caviar and glasses of champagne ("Did you do the story?" I asked. "No," he said. "It must have died at some other lunch."). He knew my mother was a superior cook and baker, and regretted when they had to go to someone else's dinner party, rather than having them over, with Mom doing all the cooking. He liked restaurants and sought them out. He frequented the Silver Skates, when he and my mother were at the house in East Dover. And he liked owner/chef Hans Imboden, although he didn't understand exactly how crazy Hans was.

I went out to the East Dover house one day in 1977 and had a sit-down with him. I said I wanted either to start a restaurant or go to graduate school in journalism.

We talked about restaurants and their alarmingly high failure rate, but that's not what bothered him. I said Hans would be involved, especially in the menu making. There was a sweet old house in Brattleboro that could be converted without too much expense. Hans and I had gone to see it.

Dad liked the idea. I could tell. His own life was not exactly packed full of well-considered decisions — he'd had plenty of offers after leaving *LIFE*. Major magazines and startups that wanted to become major magazines, in New York and Washington, DC. He flirted, but turned them all down so he could keep going out West.

"How much does it cost to start a restaurant?" he asked.

"About $60,000, what Hans and I figured," I said.

"And how much to go to graduate school?"

"It depends where I'm accepted. Boston, with a year's housing, about $7,000."

I must not have handled it right because he immediately slapped his hands on his knees, a familiar gesture of finality, and announced with a big grin, "Congratulations. You're going to graduate school."

About 10 years later, my parents sold the working half of Singing River Ranch, the main cabin and surrounding smaller cabins, and the barns and corrals, foreman's house and bunkhouse, hayfields, and about 700 of the 2,000 acres. They built another place across the dirt road on the South Huerfano, two cabins, and cleaned out the barn over there and built a tack room and riding corral. They settled into something like retirement, shuffling back and forth between the smaller but complete ranch and their "current" house in Connecticut (there had been at least three recent moves: to a condo, then a house with a pond, then a house with the long lawn and tall evergreens).

Eventually, Singing River, the high mountains, got to be too much. My father's mild heart attack was the first warning; inability to keep up maintenance on the ranch was another. In 1995 the new ranch sold, the two other large lots having already been bought. And that was it for Colorado, my parent's lives — all our lives in a way — suddenly constrained to a suburban house in New Canaan, as my father's illness came on.

What was it in him to move from place to place? To quit *LIFE* where he could have gone on for another decade, to turn down cool jobs, to buy a dramatic but rundown family ranch 9,300 feet up in the Rockies and turn it into a quasi-successful venture? Was it to absorb the hyper-activity which itself deflected his survivor's syndrome? Did he just like dabbling in real estate? In some ways the ranch was a reliving of his teenage California days at Ojai Valley and Thatcher schools, where he and friends took their horses and pack animals deep into the Sierras with a sort of freedom almost unimaginable today. His stories from those adventures, of rattlesnakes and switchbacks, forest fires and trout fishing, storms and flooded creeks, of great horses — they were the cookies and cakes of our childhood, anticipating a family life where Western culture, which in this case began in the Southwest and con-cluded on the eastern shore of Japan, was thematic and decorative in art, literature, furniture, travel, and friends.

When my father slapped his knees and sent me — us, Lulu and two-year-old Russell, and a large, spirited retriever of mixed parenthood, Emily — to graduate school in Boston, he expected nothing back. Nor did he expect anything of it, in the sense of a career necessarily. He did-n't make deals like that. What few talents I had, cooking, wrangling, I guess that was about it, he was perfectly happy with, if he thought about them at all. Instead he was excited about the opportunity for change, for expansion, for learning new stuff, for seeing where an idea, just an idea, would go, once given a shove. Where it all went, like his own life, was merely a matter of immediacy, and that seemed to be the point.

My journalism career lasted about two years after the one-year Boston University MS program. Besides a six-month stint on the *Burlington Free Press*, I spent one year in Chinatown and another one freelancing around town, sometimes for the *Boston Herald*, and mostly for the *Real Paper* and the *Boston Phoenix*, both long defunct. Then, with Russell and a one-and-a-half-year-old daughter, Clara, and the same dog, we packed up and moved to Amenia, NY, where in a prep school setting we taught dyslexic boys and I coached sports and decided however much fun I was having it was Vermont I had my eye on. After two years, I returned to Marlboro College and met Rod Gander and started my 19 years of service, beginning as editor of the alumni magazine, *Potash Hill*, and director of alumni. Then, but with a new large black dog of mixed parentage, Anna, we moved to Montserrat College of Art, and from there eventually back to Vermont, then to Sterling College, where after a while Anna died and has yet to be replaced.

11

Pennsylvania's Coastline

Marketing and public relations are two pieces of the small college management puzzle essential for day-to-day operations and for survival itself. No kidding. Without them no one would even know you even exist. So if you count on people knowing at a minimum that your college (or school, food bank, daycare center) does exist, you have little choice but to engage wholly in these sometimes-maligned practices.

There's a difference. Public Relations, usually capitalized and abbreviated to PR, refers to the type and management of the information you put out to the public, as well as the management, as best you can, of what the public puts out about you. PR operations do not directly seek payment or contributions.

Marketing is all about seeking payment or contributions. And it is ethically more elastic, let's say, than PR. When marketing exaggerates, promises, attempts to frighten, warn, or even shame you into purchasing something, well, that's expected, and that's "just marketing."

However, if in trying to manage what others think of your college you write a series of ham-handed press releases, for example, that are bloated and misleading in a "just marketing" sort of way, that's not going to work. You are going to look like you don't know what you're doing.

There was a time not too long ago when the very word marketing, used, for instance at a Marlboro faculty meeting by, well, me, was received with immediate suspicion and distaste. It was the early 1980s and the faculty didn't think their college needed to join that ethically blurry realm of hucksters and scammers. We didn't need anything more than our annual catalogue and maybe some sort of brochure or little booklet or something to send to prospective students who write and want to apply, or visit. Marketing was a for-profit thing, unpleasant and essentially needless. It tricked you into exaggerating about yourself just because someone wants to know something about you.

Today, of course, these same sorts of professors are publishing their own books and marketing them like, like *business entrepreneurs*, two more words the liberal arts wrestled with for decades before acknowledging, then accepting them individually and even coupled.

When I arrived at Sterling its reputation locally wasn't in the cellar but it was beat up, kind of ragged, a 6 out of 10, say. This was despite, or maybe because of, the fact that over the decades of Sterling's existence in various educational shapes pretty much everyone in the region, or his cousin, or her nephews or nieces, brothers or sisters, mothers, fathers, or any in-law current or former, had worked at the college, full-time or part-time, for anywhere from a week to an entire career. Everyone else was a neighbor or otherwise simply a presumed expert on Sterling's history and current operations. All, apparently, had the right to express what Ross Morgan, a forester, faculty member, and good friend explained to me was an "opinion of fact" about Sterling College.

It takes a real PR program to mitigate that sort of widespread but non-lethal problem. As a new president, however, all I had was my face. My chin, specifically.

With the help of a local trustee and his wife we set up a half dozen get-to-know-the-new-president coffee hours where I'd give a little intro-ductory talk about being the new president, then ask for their impres-sions of Sterling. Their honest impressions. This is where my face came in to play, because from the first of these coffee klatches from hell to the last, I basically took it on the chin for an hour or more, until the food and coffee ran out.

I listened to old tales and new, with no reason to doubt anything because the truth doesn't weigh much against what people believe, and

I didn't know the truth in any case. There was rampant drug use on campus; any stolen vehicle was stolen by a drunk Sterling student; the college wants to grow until it owns the common; Sterling alumni hang around too long, they're not dependable workers; the place has serious problems, and on and on.

I admit I enjoyed these encounters, and they were effective, for the most part, because we weren't inviting just anyone to come and complain. This was public relations, not purposeful self-abuse. The preferred group included disaffected major donors, disaffected potential major donors, nearby people of means or influence (often quite separate in Vermont) who knew Sterling well through hearsay and rumor, and one or two people who liked Sterling and would pipe up in defense, occasionally helpful. So, you have to figure they came because they were interested even if disgruntled, and wanted something from Sterling and the new president. The new president wanted something from them because they had means, status in the community, or some other useful connection for the college. It's all about keeping up with one another. Visiting more often. Finding common ground.

But it's slow going, that sort of PR. One friend at a time.

So the question is, how do you affect a whole community? How do you shift a big piece of a community's knowledge and attitude from hostile, or dismissive, or simply not caring, to paying attention and seeing good where they thought there wasn't much of anything?

In my singular experience, first you need an act of nature, act of God if you prefer. Then you need someone like Willy Ryan, a dairy farmer down from the common, who was deeply and loudly involved in village affairs, and came with the whole Ryan family, which with the Martins, Darlings, Rowells, Uries, and Andersons, accounted for some 40 percent of the local population, or it seemed that way, maybe it was more. Willy was single-minded, hyperactive, and exasperating, I'd heard. A big man, with a head the size of a small barrel and rough-cut hands that could wrap around it. I'd been told repeatedly he had no particular love of the college — that seemed to be well established, if not understood.

I'd only met him once at some meeting in the town library, which he pretty much took over with a voice like a thunderstorm in a gymnasium. Afterward, I introduced myself. You can't just assume what you've heard or even what you've just witnessed as the whole truth to a person. So I said hello and we shook hands and I said who I was and we should sit and talk sometime, over coffee.

Willy Ryan replied immediately and so loudly I thought I'd fall over backward, that he had no particular love of the college.

So you need someone loud and popular who doesn't like you and whom everyone knows doesn't like you. Then, in this case, you need a terrific blizzard and tons of cow shit.

———

February 15, 2007 6:15 am
From my First Year Journal:

A storm worthy of the name: very cold, windy, and piles of snow, a dry but heavy snow that whipped about like ice crystals before a hurricane. Mitch "I'm on a roll" Hunt, our farm manager, plowed twice yesterday and I took over after dinner, barely making it through the long driveway to the lower dorms and getting stuck once. Lulu came with me and we dug for 15 minutes and freed the truck. The college truck is too light for this heavy work, the banks now falling in as the plow passes, so we're hardly keeping the lanes open. I imagine he's going to show up any moment — Mitch has indefatigable energy. Otherwise I'll go out and see if there's anything left of our efforts. It's zero. Only six inches of the posts and half the upper rail of the fence around the common are visible, meaning about three feet of snow has fallen and blown.

7:15 am
Things are in pretty good shape. Mitch must have plowed around 4 am, so I just cleaned up a bit, helping one faculty member dig out cars, and pushing back banks. The student parking lot is untouched, so I don't know how we'll take care of that. I do hope someone comes to work today, as opposed to yesterday when hardly anyone showed up, including Micki Martin my secretary who lives just down the road. Still, such a storm raises everyone's spirits around here so the mood on campus is very positive.

4:00 pm

The parking lot at the Center for Northern Studies was not yet plowed and there was a student stuck over there, I learned immediately upon entering my office this morning. Gwyn Harris the admissions director was still digging out, she phoned. Barbara the development director was digging out, she emailed. Micki called and said she'd be in soon, but as of that moment she hasn't made the two-mile trip. So it went for an hour, with me as command central. Then, about 9:30 Perry Thomas the dean called and the pace picked up right away.

She was calling from down in the village: two cow barns at the Ryan farm on Gilot Road had collapsed in the night, killing or trapping 30 or 40 cows. Members of the Craftsbury road crew and volunteer fire department were on their way, and we should help. Within 10 minutes I'd located every shovel on campus, decided not to use the college vans as too dangerous in the snow and ice, sent off Mitch to see how dangerous things were going to be when we got there, assembled various students who happened to be up and around — they were searching for transportation and shovels — and headed off in five or six cars and trucks, including ours that Lulu had just cleared of snow with the help of two students who happened to be passing by. They jumped in, too.

The Ryan farm is a typical northern Vermont dairy farm, with a house, out-buildings, a large red barn for hay and calves and machinery, a trailer or two for farmhands, and a metal-roofed milking parlor where the cows are milked and fed and can stay indoors in such weather as we have today. We parked at the end of the drive and, carrying our shovels, marched up the hill. Already some 30 people, half in fire department turnout gear and the other half neighbors and college students, were shoveling snow from the collapsed roof. No one knew how many cows were trapped under it. One lone Holstein sat forlornly nearby, seemingly dazed and covered with an old blanket. There was no room for anyone else on the roof, so we lined up and waited to spell them. Then we learned there was a second collapsed barn, farther up the hill, with 20 or 30 cows, so Lulu and I and a handful of students head up there, where the same scene was taking place.

There were chains reaching out to the front loader, which was attempting to lift up the roof on the taller part of the barn, while we all shoveled snow off the fully collapsed shed portion. A recent Sterling graduate whose name I never caught and I positioned ourselves near a hole, basically assisting two firefighters who'd found a way into the barn and located some cows. Beside us, people were bending up sheets of steel roofing, passing a chainsaw back and forth; they slowly enlarged the hole in front of us until two filthy, frightened, weakened cows, yet still gigantic, were able to scramble out to the muted cheers of the shovelers. More cows were emerging from the other end of the barn where another dozen firemen and volunteers had been working directly under the taut chain extending from the front loader to the suspended, busted up roof, but we couldn't see that far and were concerned only with our own little area. Once out of the hole, the two cows hit the metal roof and slipped, crashing down on their chests, and struggled their way off it to the drive, where others herded them gently to a pen that Mitch had set up and spread hay in. Within a few minutes these two shaken cows were munching away in a field of hay and snow.

The third cow in line, however, was even more stressed and weakened and seriously balked once her head and forequarters were out. Her right foreleg was buckled under her, and the idea was if we could straighten the leg, she could rise up and fight her way out of the hole. Two firemen, who had been down in the hole, actually in the interior of the barn under a partially collapsed section, were at her rear. On her head was Louise Calderwood, a former assistant secretary for agriculture in Vermont, who teaches a course at the college and who I just met at dinner yesterday. I was assigned to wrap a cord around the foreleg and pull, which I did, taking off my mittens and lowering myself right on her, forcing the length of green bailing cord behind her knee, pushing her with my shoulder to no effect. I was soaked to the elbows in cow shit, which this poor creature had been lying in for hours. My hands looked like they'd been dyed brown. The odor was, of course, of highly concentrated cow shit, not wafting over a field or emanating pleasantly from a barnyard, but packed into my skin and smeared over my jacket. Later, of course, everyone around the hole was commenting on the pungency of the experience; even the firemen, whose gear regularly reeks of smoke and oil and all kinds of crap, found the concentrate notable.

The cord idea straightened the leg with much pulling, but she was still too weak to pull herself out. So next we maneuvered her back into the hole and were working on the idea of connecting up with the people at the other end of the barn where two of our other cows were forced out that way. But she turned and suddenly reemerged in the hole and this time heaved herself forward and out, effortlessly almost.

Then we had to deal with the fallen roof we were all standing on that had been cleared of snow. No one was sure what lay underneath. So the firemen, who always respond with enthusiasm in situations of rescue, started pushing and pulling and ripping the metal roofing, turning up the roofing beneath us. Shovels, crowbars, and a chain saw were applied; the chainsaw — too close to too many people — ripped through the rafters and straight through the corrugated roofing. We pealed back the steel and right away revealed our first dead cow. Then another, wounded beyond saving. Then three more dead, but here was one smaller animal saved between two larger dead cows; this one pretty much jumped right up and walked out. Then another dead one.

By 11 I was done. My feet and hands were frozen. Lulu, who had shoveled and hauled hay bales, and thrown lumber and had worked harder than I, was also tuckered out. And I had to get back to the college and sign paychecks or no one was going to get paid. I smelled awful, powerful, and even changing clothes and showering didn't do it. Finally, before an art opening this afternoon, I had to shower again and scrub madly to stop people from having too much fun noticing that certain country odor about me.

Later the wounded cows were shot. The students shoveled off the remaining roofs so the surviving herd would have a safe place for the night. Seeing five students climb into the bucket of a front loader and be deposited on a snow-covered shed roof, next to an already collapsed shed roof, in order to clean it off, with the possibility of that roof going down and someone being hurt — well, as a safely officer I well may have objected and as a college president, I may well have objected. But I didn't and everything turned out okay.

A month after the big storm the college received about the most appreciative letter of thanks I've ever read, directed to the students who poured down to the Ryan farm and put 30 shovels to work, tirelessly, until the job was finished in the midafternoon. There was a check enclosed, a first-time contribution. Even better was the public relations leap. All Willy Ryan had to do was speak well of the college to one person at one end of the common and everybody at the other end would hear it as well. We had indeed made a new and influential friend, through service of the most unusual kind.

Colleges, all of them, require a highly specialized marketing program whose singular and obsessive target, the college-bound student, is an audience of millions of barely post-adolescent people of indeterminate sex and unknown academic talent who will someday run everything, but that from a college's point of view are an audience that reemerges every year, herd-like, new and fully energized, whose alliances and passions could be the complete antithesis of the alliances and passions of the previous herd. The only certainty is they arrive with a hunger for food, sex, pot, beer, love, and academic challenge and achievement away from home.

As a director of admissions, it is your job to locate a certain number of these individuals who, ideally, fit a profile, a matrix you have created that describes the perfect student for your college, academically, socially, and financially. Then you must be persuasive enough so those students become applicants willingly paying a modest application fee for the honor of applying to your college, where, if they are allowed in, they will pay your salary and the salaries of everyone around you. At the end of four years of this, if they persevere, they will still owe you or the federal government, on average in the nation, about $22,000. This they will pay off in monthly installments over decades while your alumni office methodically asks them to contribute to their alma mater, which, sometimes in surprising numbers, they do. What a business.

At most small and midsize undergraduate colleges, tuition and fees account for about 95 percent of income. College presidents are aware of this, pathologically aware when admissions numbers are down. Yet there are board members who will insist the admissions office is spending too much money trying to recruit students. Thus, it happens that marketing and public relations are often the first places cut to ribbons by presidents under pressure from trustees, who ideally serve to make wise decisions, but many seem incapable of doing so when it comes to marketing. Instead, they see bags of cash disappearing with little to show for it. Somehow they do not see the 95 percent of income.

Almost inevitably some large proportion of money spent on recruitment will end up in the pockets of the for-profit service and consulting industry that feeds off higher education at every level, around every corner. It is housed far away, in a snappy set of offices in some city near a good airport, from whence well suited road warriors depart every Monday bound for colleges and universities across the nation, armed with technology- and salesmen-based solutions for your admissions programs.

In fact, there is nothing these folks won't do for you and your admissions efforts, but mostly they counsel and advise in order to sell systems for searching out and communicating with a few hundred or an infinite number of prospective students, using a veritable host of psychological and propagandist tools to inform, ensnare, encourage, make welcome, excite, or otherwise propel the prospective student to a seat in your classroom. The whole array of consultants and software and training aimed at imposing order on the chaos of your floundering efforts will cost you minimally $250,000 over two years. The upper limit of cost is beyond any horizon I've ever glimpsed.

However, if you wish or because you have no money, you can run your own admissions marketing and public relations shop: be your own in-house Suit. Designing magazines, writing about finance and fund-raising, interviewing faculty and alumni, stealing ideas from around the nation, beating deadlines by hours or minutes — it is where you gain control over your operations. As an operating method we employed a spiky version of Paul LeBlanc's already perfected practice of just-in-time planning, which makes for a fast-paced and nimble office.

At Marlboro in 1984 we were on the cusp of the Internet age. But who knew? Practice still more closely resembled that of the 1920s. We had telephones and the post office. As a college employee living in a college-owned and genuinely ratty house, when I wanted to make a non-local call, to my mother, for instance, I'd dial 0 and say, "Marge could you call my mother?" And Marge might say, "She called you earlier but Judy was on the line. Here you go." Regional newspapers were our printers. Do you even know what a stand-alone Addressograph machine was? Somehow lucky, I was issued one of the college's two electric typewriters.

By the early 1990s, however, at Marlboro we were well practiced and relatively well equipped as an in-house publications and marketing team, producing besides the catalogue, the alumni magazine, a development newsletter, all the admissions pieces, response brochures, event posters — all that stuff. And it was all cleverly integrated with fundraising and public relations; integrated in the sense it was the same six or seven people doing everything.

We used local outside designers in helping conceive and create template designs for the catalogue and the alumni magazine, then brought everything back inside to our publications staff and handled it from there. Until the next time we needed help as the needs expanded.

Still, it's a legitimate question, which works better: in-house or consultant-driven? I'm biased, being extremely consultant-wary. I've seen college operations where the leadership's idea of leadership is the coordination of half a dozen consulting firms and a handful of freelance writers, photographers, and designers. There will be swings in quality, as the marketers and designers come and go. They are always going to be expensive.

The in-house marketing program is authentic, that's for sure, but with a really obvious downside when things go wrong, and things go wrong regularly and it is always your fault. When that's not costly, it can be humiliating, when not funny.

But it happens. Case in point: we'd created one of those poster/maps of the Northeast, from south of New York City to the top of Vermont and through Maine, with a big green star where Marlboro was located, as if it were in the very center of everything, the way all such maps are designed. It had been used for a couple of years, and the original was hanging in the admissions office waiting room where you couldn't miss it. But plenty of people did, until some sharp-eyed parent, from Philadelphia it so happened, pointed out to the admissions director that Pennsylvania didn't have a coastline. That's New Jersey. But it says Pennsylvania.

The director came and told Rod and me, to which Rod responded, "So what happened to New Jersey?"

"I dunno," he said. "Maybe they just gave up and turned the whole state over as a suburb of Philadelphia."

"What did the parent say?" Rod asked.

"He said he couldn't believe we had the thing hanging there for two years."

"What did you say?"

"I said it was a test poster, and they were the only family to pass. The only one."

"Good answer!" said Rod.

Most of this banter was aimed obliquely at me, whose ultimate responsibility it was to make sure such embarrassing things did not happen. You've got to be philosophical about it: embrace the irony, like when we invited 600 parents to Commencemecent right there on the invitation.

On the back cover of the Sterling magazine, *Common Voice*, the word "environmontal" appeared, as in "Sterling is an experiential-based environmontal college...." Unfortunately, the former president was on campus when the discovery was made. He and others argued we should mail a note to the entire readership explaining ourselves and asking pardon, I guess, for bad proofreading. Terrible advice. No one notices. Those who do are forgiving. If they are not, they don't have enough to do. Just try not to let it happen too often, especially on front or back cover.

Being on our own, we experimented with all sorts of marketing ideas, including 20-second radio ads aimed at the University of Massachusetts Amherst area with its billions of students. The ads were of no measurable effect, unlike a regular Marlboro graduate-school program spot on Vermont Public Radio, funded by a friend of the college, which did very well with the listenership age 50 and above, none of whom seemed to want to sign up. We tried quarter-page ads in those Boston area alternative papers I once wrote for, the *Real Paper* and the *Phoenix*. That ended quickly: sitting atop our Phoenix ad, which was all sincerity and earnestness, was an ad for nude sunset harbor cruises featuring two naked rather big-butted people, sunset-watching at the ship's rail, cocktails in hand.

"Moons over Marlboro!" Rod declared. "That will bring them in."

***

I'll look at two examples of consultant-driven admissions marketing programs, the first ludicrous, the second cautionary.

In the late-1980s, we experimented with having a marketing firm propose an admissions publication program for Marlboro, and we interviewed two firms, chose one, and went through the standard three-day orientation where the marketers run around campus trying to understand your programs, history, and culture and charge you a bundle for their getting up to speed. Then they retreat. Silence ensues. You are waiting for the marketers to mock-up stuff, get their sloganeering down, and their rationale if they have one, for the program they are about to propose.

The big day arrives. The marketer's headman or -woman shows up prepared to sell, with a PowerPoint presentation and literature designs, the whole package except the anticipated bill. In this case we are gathered in the admissions waiting room when these folks from Boston begin.

And this is what happened: after just three or four sentences, and the little curtain lifted away from the display board, my ears turned off — I couldn't hear — because what I saw and had heard my brain had instantaneously and completely dismissed from my mind, replaced with stunned amusement and disbelief. I dared not look over to Rod, or anyone, but refocused on the presentation.

Sure enough, this was a marketing campaign for Marlboro built around the word and concept *IMAGINE*. As in, we were earnestly informed by the head guy, "*IMAGINE* a small Vermont college where Robert Frost gave the first commencement address." And, "*IMAGINE* just you and the teacher, one-on-one," and "It takes Your Imagination to find yourself at Marlboro College!"

Well, you can imagine how fast we got out of that room. That took a month and $5,000 already? After the poor sops left, we all sat around making up *IMAGINE* scenarios we'd like to see: "*IMAGINE* a college that serves canned mushroom soup every day for a month." "*IMAGINE* if all the dorm rooms at Marlboro were actually heated." "*IMAGINE* a college unburdened by the corrupting influence of money, power, and hope... but with a heated library." "*IMAGINE* a college pushing a giant rock up a hill...."

The *IMAGINE* campaign was a setup from the start. It was completely non-specific to Marlboro. Its presentation was manipulative. There was not a paragraph of research attached to it. It missed the mark so wildly I was unsurprised months later at some CASE conference (that's the Consortium for the Advancement of Secondary Education, all about fundraising and advancement) to notice the *IMAGINE* campaign had been foisted off in its entirety to some other college.

From this experience I learned to quickly disabuse designers, marketers, or any consultant who insisted on conducting a show, as it were, with their proposal. It's a salesman's trick to get a group of presumed marketing novices to be awed and nodding approval at the detailed design and the concept, the *IMAGINE*.

So that was a waste of time and $5,000 we didn't have.

A decade later, Paul LeBlanc at Marlboro ran into a similar situation, while moving at his usual pace of about 1,000 miles per hour. I was on my way out, and nearby but helpless: Paul wanted what he wanted, and all I could do was watch it happen. Presidents. In any case, he had hired a large, successful, and slick marketing and "branding" firm from Atlanta called Mindpower (motto: *Mindpower for smart marketing*). He wanted something different, something to break through the white noise of college viewbooks, an admirable desire if there ever was one.

What he ended up with was an admissions brochure the front cover of which featured Langston Hughes, Eleanor Roosevelt, Jack Kerouac, and Janis Joplin as "nonconformists who "might have fit in" at Marlboro. "It's a good fit... " the brochure concludes, "for people who don't want to fit in."

The quote is from a May 2000 *Chronicle of Higher Education* story headlined: "Marlboro's Campaign to Attract Unconventional Students Is Derided as Phony and Hypocritical."

Okay. That hurt.

The Marlboro community, faculty, staff, students, nearby alumni, cats, dogs, the kitchen crew, the bread delivery man, they all went nuts with indignation, which of course eventually led to the *Chronicle* article, which felt like salt to a wound, thank goodness, instead of fat to a fire.

Now, just on the surface of things, only Langston Hughes graduated from college, and only Eleanor Roosevelt died what might be a normal death; the other two from drink and drugs. And while I don't believe we should judge people by how they died instead of how they lived, it does affect the mind under such circumstances.

The *Chronicle* story also focused on the college's hypocrisy in the marketing and the process leading up to the publication and within it, especially regarding the stories of individual students. What a mess.

Paul gave a spirited response, including saying, "Given the value system of a place like Marlboro, some students would like to see us not market at all. That's not the reality that our marketing and admissions people face." Hear hear!

In addition, he pointed out, the piece increased the response rate from 2,400 to 2,850.

This is all a much meatier marketing issue than Commencement, or even wiping out New Jersey and replacing it with Pennsylvania.

Let's, briefly, take a look at some of what Libby Turner, the founder of Mindpower and the chief designer of the publication, had to say to the *Chronicle* reporter, Ben Gose.

"Many colleges say, 'We want a national reputation.' One of our first responses is, 'How far out on the limb are you willing to crawl?'"

"How do you choose what gets in and what gets left out? Should we take photos of the back ends of buildings where the trashcans are? They (the students and faculty) felt like a line got crossed — to tell you the truth, I'm not sure where that line is."

Of course, this statement, these kinds of statements, are marketing claptrap, devoid of any actual meaning, and representing an attitude of bluster, of aggressive determination and ruthlessness, of a level of self-assurance so stunningly undeserved as to be borderline silly.

That is, if you cannot distinguish where that line is, why in the world would I trust your marketing judgment — or is there none? Did you determine a goal of, say, 450 new student inquiries, or were you just shooting in the dark hoping to hit something?

What would you propose for a viewbook if the goal were 2,500, or 5,000 new inquiries? I mean, how long is the limb, how far out are pictures of starving children, giant drainpipes spewing toxic wastes, zombies with spikes in their heads?

Did you think for one minute and review with your client the possible reactions within the institution? Do you understand there are internal ramifications in proportion to a desired external affect? What sort of marketing research did you do to determine how effective the piece would be, knowing, you had to have known, that the four famous dead people chosen would be unrecognizable to many in your target audience of high school juniors? You must have come up with something, you must have known where your cutting through the white noise would land with the biggest bang. Or were you just all excited, imagining how far out on that limb you had crawled and dragged your client behind you?

Did the viewbook do harm to the college's admissions effort? No. The viewbook performed as expected, inspiring a relatively small percent of the recipient high school juniors to respond, just as had the previous viewbook, and the one before that. Of that response pool of 2,850, I'm guessing, about 60 would eventually apply to Marlboro, 50 would be accepted, of which 25 would choose to matriculate. So, still plenty of white noise around.

Did the viewbook cause any harm to the college's public relations? Not much. Only people in the higher education industry, our colleagues, read the *Chronicle*, so a little annoying to be featured on the wrong side of a cautionary tale, which, by the way, noted a number of other colleges slapped down by their own engagement in what might be termed hubris-based marketing.

The issue is waste, loss, and mistrust. A president and an administration caught in suddenly ramped-up internal politics, internal backlash, cannot dismiss or avoid the issue but has to get right in there and deal with it, which takes a lot of time, of which presidents have little enough to employ effectively, in a world where nothing happens fast enough. Mistrust, of course, fades as other crises wax and wane across a campus, but it leaves a residue, each time.

It's not hard to increase the inquiry pool. All a college needs do is buy more ads, buy more addresses, visit more high schools, send out more stuff. Stuff, in my opinion, that actually informs. Then, let the real admissions marketers take over, the admissions counselors, in the admissions office, who talk to prospective students and their parents. They sell your college. And the better they are, the higher the yield. However, the challenge of investing in people and training is that it is boring and apparently expensive compared to the thrill of conceiving and creating really cool marketing materials that will alone be the force sweeping a new crop of students to your doorstep.

12

Vince, Me, and
Rod Gander's Ghost

April 2009 and Vermont State Senator Vince Illuzzi is sitting at the head of a heavy wooden conference table, in a small conference room in the back half of the Vermont State House. Vince, 58, a Republican, has represented the Northeast Kingdom since he was first elected at 27 years old, the youngest person ever elected to serve in Vermont. I'd met him some weeks earlier at the Eastside Restaurant, in Newport, on the shores of Lake Memphremagog, where the coffee came lukewarm out of plastic tubs and the giant muffins had the heft of cannonballs. It was a legislative information gathering, which Vince and Bobby Starr and regional representatives conducted at the Eastside every couple of months. I was there to meet him and ask for help. I had little expectation of what to expect; no expectation of the wild ride I was about to step onto.

Vince is thin and his suit hangs on him like on a rack of twigs. The crisp collar of his white shirt is a size too large; his light brown hair is swept back and flat, so he looks even thinner than he is. Even sitting still, Vince seems to be in motion.

In the State House Vince sits at the table's head because he is chairman of the Senate Economic Development Committee. Other member senators take up both sides of the table, and include Senators Tim

Ash, Douglas Racine, and Bill Doyle. As they arrive, individually but right on the hour, Vince waves at me at the other end of the table and introduces me, whether I've met them or not, as the president of Sterling College. Then — this is the important part — says, "Will worked with Rod Gander. Fifteen years. At Marlboro College. Rod was a mentor, right?"

Yes, Rod was a mentor and a friend, and a former journalist with a healthy ambivalence when it came to the honor and integrity of politicians. But also as a journalist, he had a fascination with what it would be like on the other side, politics, so he ran (slogan: *Send a Gander to Montpelier*) and won a whirlwind campaign in 2002, after retiring from the Marlboro presidency. He discovered that he loved everything about being a politician, especially the scheming and infighting while doing good things for the public. And they loved him, all the Democrats and most of the Republicans, from what I observed in the State House.

Vince's introduction, repeated many times over the ensuing weeks, was not only nice to hear about Rod, but completely calculated to help our cause, to provide me and my proposal with some special status slipped from Rod's brief service, two terms, the second of which he could hardly complete before having to quit to battle cancer.

With that introduction, we all had something in common, a shared and respected dead person. So the arriving senators took immediate note, turned to me, and we had something to talk about. I, in the meantime, had sat Rod's ghost down in one of the empty seats. I could see him there, hunched over his papers, his murky reading glasses hanging on his face, stub of a pencil in hand, joking around, and commanding without anyone knowing it or even feeling it. I felt this whole process, whatever it turned out to be, would be better with his company.

Vince has invited me to meet with the committee and explain to them and to him why I think the State of Vermont should give Sterling College $350,000 of the public's money so we can build a new dormitory. At this early stage I am unaware how brazen a request this is. The State of Vermont has never given money to a private college. The very idea had probably never occurred to anyone, because it was ridiculous.

But this was March 2009, and the economy was crashing all around us like a terrible winter storm, like a huge, crazed, rampaging gorilla wielding two giant clubs. The American Economic Recovery Act, President Obama's stimulus money, was beginning to pour into New England and Vermont, but there was no money in that stream for private colleges. So what was I doing here?

I notice Vince has in hand the two-page letter I had emailed him a few days previously, detailing the situation Sterling was in, in as positive a manner as I could express it. I outlined the economic blows Craftsbury and that corner of the Northeast Kingdom had already absorbed: the famous Inn on the Common, bankrupt and closed, now owned by the bank; the Historic Craftsbury General Store, belly up. Local unemployment up. Local farms down. Real estate frozen like a glacier. And the college, as small as it is, a vital economic driver in the region, struggling, and unable to find resources for expanding residential space. Without expansion, without building the dormitory we were in the process of designing, Sterling could be in real trouble.

I also notice Vince has not distributed copies of my letter to his committee, but instead keeps glancing down at his copy as the members settle into their seats, chatting and waiting for the chairman to call them to order. I realize Vince is reading my memo for the first time.

He calls them to order and suspends other agenda items in order to let me speak; but first, from the head of the table to me at the foot, he asks, in essence, why the State of Vermont should give Sterling College $350,000 that could be well spent in any number of areas of need, if spent at all.

I begin: I begin talking about the college and its economic and social impact on its community. I talk briefly about the critical need to expand. I talk about danger to the college....

Vince interrupts me.

"Not good enough," he announces from the far end of the table. The man who I thought was on my side, tentatively at least, has just tossed me away, probably for some unfathomable political reason only he knows.

I start again, turning to the seriousness of the situation, the thin line the college is trying to negotiate through this recession. I'm looking at the senators and they are motionless, noncommittal. I keep going.

I know what Vince wants and I am incapable of giving to him.

So he interrupts again and asks, "If you don't get this money, is Sterling College going to close? That's the question. Is Sterling College going to close?"

I've gone too far, I'm thinking. I can't answer that question. I can't say the words. To say the words could do Sterling more harm than the public relations pummeling this open and public quest for quick money is sure to produce.

"You've got to know. I mean, right now we're not going anywhere," Vince says and the senators, though hardly moving, seem to concur. I'm lightheaded. I'm staring at Vince. I look around at the other senators and after what seems like minutes but couldn't have been but seconds I say it. "Yes. If Sterling can't find the resources to build this residence, given all the other fiscal punches the college has absorbed, then, yes, the college will be threatened with closure."

"When?" asks Vince.

"Too soon," I say, or something to that point. The committee members ask me a few questions and I answer in detail and Vince doesn't interrupt, which I interpret as a good sign. But all I can think about is what I've just said aloud, that Sterling College is in danger of closing. I feel sick. And I brought it on myself.

No college president wants to say what I said under any circumstances. It can be an irretrievable pronouncement, a game changer that you would use only after careful consideration, which can take on a life of its own and travel to places where no good can come of it, to donors and alumni, to faculty and staff, to the surrounding community, to prospective students — to your banker. To speak it feels like crossing a roaring nine-lane highway blindfolded, at night, wearing dark clothes.

Worse, I knew where this had to go. I'd been working with Vince long enough already to know there were lots of people in this State House who would need to know what I said if this was going to work, if there was to be any chance of success. And the press, of course, they're in the State House, as well.

Was it true? Of course it was true. It was so true I didn't even know whether it would be the lack of beds or if one of the other teetering catastrophes that would spin reality in a way no one could ignore any longer, and we'd be done.

The very existence of a place like Sterling hangs on a thread where one false move too many and snap! When it happens, it happens that fast. Colleges don't close themselves. The reality of closure arrives unbidden, like a cartoon Death at your doorstep, with his hooded robe and scythe. Before you know it you are negotiating with NEASC on how to shut down, or sell off, or merge, or find, as it is sometimes called, an alternative future.

Vince's committee had other things to talk about, and I saw him fold my memo and slip it into his inside breast pocket. He thanked me for being there, and I thanked each committee member, then departed to drive the hour back to Sterling and await Vince's call.

———

My strategy of survival fit well with the increasingly close yet unpredictable relationship with Senator Illuzzi. The strategy requires seeking out and chasing down every possible opportunity to strengthen any one of the critical areas of need, those Sustainable Sterling Campaign goals I spoke of in Chapter 5, *Whores and Slaves*. The strategy did not include knowing or even predicting the outcome. Imagining various outcomes, however, is permitted. The trick is to back away from things not shaping up quickly enough to have effect. Getting out before going too far and missing some other opportunity. Which in reality was difficult to impossible to determine before having done so. As a strategy, it was still one large step behind Paul LeBlanc's just-in-time-planning operational method, which kept things exciting and freewheeling, but back then we had money to burn.

At Sterling, meanwhile, a number of resources had come within our reach, or at least our imaginations. Think of them as I did, as individual ceramic pots containing both money and ideas, floating in the air just out of reach, and carefully watched over by their owners or administrators. How they were all going to come together, now, in the summer of

2009, I couldn't yet see. In fact, as these pots floated about in my mind and I tried to get them to align themselves and be employable, I could not.

But they had to. Because if enough of them actually happened, and happened in the best possible order, I could imagine the end of the campaign, success, and survival. If they didn't — if I couldn't manhandle them or persuade them into the order I needed — well, the least of it would be I'd look like an idiot.

The Canaday Family Charitable Trust, based in New York and represented by Christine O'Donnell, provided Sterling with its first major grant of my tenure. I had called Christine after sending her a package of Sterling materials and we spoke at some length and she agreed to come to the college and look around. She arrived in little flat shoes, said she wanted to see the Sterling farm, and trudged through the barns and greenhouses amidst the chickens and pigs and the guard llama without hesitation.

The foundation was started by Ward Murphy, the man who led the design and manufacturing of the Willys Jeep, the ubiquitous work pony of WWII, and his wife, Miriam Coffin, a poet and art lover. Today, Christine informed me, the entire family gathers once a year to review the grant applications and vote or decide on who should get what. Everyone has a vote, she said, down to the youngest, a six-year-old.

I kept that six-year-old in mind when I wrote the request and Sterling received $75,000 for the design and permitting of a new 20-bed student residence. That floating pot, at least, appeared secured.

It was a terrific boost and immediately launched our ambitions to build. Vice president Ned Houston and an architect who had worked at Sterling in the past created a special topics course and with eight students spent a spring semester designing our new eco-maxed dormitory. Where the rest of the approximately $650,000 was going to come from I hadn't exactly figured, per the strategy of course. The question was, to me, in our situation, when was the soonest I could go back to Canaday and ask for more money, write to that now-eight-year-old?

The next floating pot belonged to the Gladys Brooks Charitable Foundation, also based in New York. At Marlboro I'd applied twice for what they normally awarded, a $100,000 endowed scholarship, and had been turned down twice without comment, without notification even. I'd have to call and be told. No. You didn't get it.

When I arrived at Sterling one of my first tasks, hand delivered by the college dean, Perry Thomas, was a half-completed grant proposal to Gladys Brooks, due in a matter of weeks and in need of immediate and extensive attention. As far as I could tell, the Gladys Brooks Foundation operated with a board of three men, all of the family, supported by a staff of two or three. One, apparently, had died or retired since my Marlboro days and was replaced by a much younger family member, from New Hampshire, not New York City, who had attended Sterling in the final years of its prep school days. The eventual award, a $100,000 endowed scholarship for a Northeast Kingdom student, was a welcome addition to Sterling's endowment, although it was soon downsized by almost one third at the start of the 2008 recession.

However, when you are starving for cash a gift of endowment is like receiving an extravagant frosted cake from which you may pluck just one small sugar flower a year. But by 2009, working with our alumnus on the Gladys Brooks board, it appeared the foundation might, maybe, support something other than an endowment. That's what was in the pot, an idea of money.

My initial try at addressing deep academic needs in student writing and communications was an application to the Davis Educational Foundation. I'd written successful Davis proposals from Marlboro and Montserrat, but struck out at Sterling. They liked the writing center idea, the renovations, new computers and courses, but they did not like helping for a couple of years to pay salary for the new writing center faculty member. We hired anyway, and the next year I returned with a new application — risky, I was told by the staff. The foundation did not like seeing a rejected proposal resurface. But I said this is what we need, and chose to stick with the second attempt, minus the wages. Remarkably, they came to see the college, Peter Davis, the son of the founder, a trustee, and the executive director. Then they awarded the college a two-year $100,000 grant. It addressed a critical need, and

Sterling's new dean, Pavel Cenkl, a mountain-climbing, marathon-running, Dante-quoting and ambitious young man, had a base of operations to keep reforming Sterling's curriculum.

So far, so good, and also pretty ordinary as foundation relations and grant writing goes. But next, Sterling entered a world of money and opportunity wholly unordinary, sometimes unfathomable, even mysterious, but with potential to complete the campaign and raise Sterling to the edge of solvency. That world had come upon Sterling and as many as 100 other American colleges entirely unbidden and, due to the money, if not the direct largess, of one of the nation's most prominent early industrialists, William Wallace Cargill, and his hugely philanthropic granddaughter, Margaret.

But first, before Margaret Cargill, and before I became president, Sterling was awarded a $225,000 share of a $2 million federal Department of Energy (DOE) earmark for six of Vermont's smallest colleges. This now old-fashioned practice of congressional grants (referred to as earmarks) via U.S. senators and congress members had all been worked through Vermont's two senators, Patrick Leahy and Jim Jeffords, some years previously, then it stalled and was presumed dead, but suddenly was reborn in 2009, to the great excitement of the receiving institutions. Still, especially for Sterling, there were problems, ones that like so many problems at Sterling revolved around its small, but muscular I liked to think, stature.

First, the money was restricted to projects directly related to energy conservation. Second, each federal dollar had to be matched. That meant the college had to raise or find another $225,000, independent from the annual fund, in order to secure a total of $450,000. The only way to spend that amount of money on energy-related projects was to build the new dormitory. In a stroke of good fortune, the DOE program manager had visited Sterling and had some understanding of the college's need for housing and its scale. So when I wrote him and asked whether the eco-dorm project could be considered an energy conservation project in its entirety, he said yes.

There it rested, a huge pot of federal money with our name on it. But energy conservation projects don't wait. They are part of that deferred maintenance issue I discussed earlier, so our DOE money was actually being whittled away in new windows, solar panels, and efficient heaters, small expenditures we matched in operations money, while I anxiously watched the cache shrink. To match that we needed big money. If we could not find it, eventually the DOE would declare our share up for grabs and our partner colleges would be delighted to divide up our unspent cash.

That's where the State of Vermont and Vince Illuzzi come in.

But who could know the outcome of my blundering into windmills, armed with a stick. And anyway, if it worked and the State of Vermont used federal funds to support Sterling, then those federal funds could not by law be used to match other federal funds, like those of the DOE. Take away the stick.

What about Gladys? The wait-out period still had over a year before we could reapply. Canaday, maybe they'd help fund the project they helped design and permit.

We had submitted other grant proposals, of course. Rejected ones. From one foundation, twice. Rejection always takes the stuffing out of you. First you research, then you contact, with their permission you construct the proposal and orchestrate all the bits and pieces that make the final a perfect-as-it-can-be document. It takes 2 to 10 people to write a worthy grant, and as much time as you can afford, given that grant writing for presidents is more a passion, or a compulsion, than a designated task. Then you package it up and send it aloft. Then you celebrate. Oh, yes. We always celebrated upon submission, never chancing the opportunity to the whims of grantors.

Finally, Margaret A. Cargill, the granddaughter of the founder of what is today the largest privately owned corporation in the nation, and thus under no obligation to tell anyone how much they are worth (billions and billions) or much of anything else, for that matter. After a life of heavy but almost always anonymous philanthropy to the Nature Conservancy, the Red Cross, the Smithsonian, and hundreds of other nonprofits, Margaret Cargill died, in San Diego, in 2006.

Shortly thereafter, I and about a hundred other college presidents received a communication such as none had ever received before. It came from the law firm representing Mrs. Cargill's testimonial wishes, which included gifts to mysteriously selected "environmental colleges," which Sterling and Marlboro were among. It was going to take some time to settle, we were informed, but in the meantime we would all be receiving $10,000 a year for five years, while the Cargill people figure out how to value the gift, needing to perform various business/banking maneuvers to create stock, then sell the stock, establishing actual monetary value. Then, in language even more obtuse, it appeared after five years, or sooner, the recipient colleges would be paid off in one lump sum, the amount undeterminable at present, and that would be that. Don't call back.

No one knew what to think. Queries to the Cargill managers were met with polite vague answers. But everything they said would happen did happen exactly on time. No mistakes. Minimal communication. By 2009 it was becoming clear the payout would probably come in 2011, but there was no indication yet how large a payout. I couldn't help it: I assigned it a place in the strategy, alongside the other pots full of money, and pots wishing to be filled, or pots waiting with someone's name on them, like "Margaret."

─────

When Vince called that night after my pummeling at the hands of his Economic Development Committee, he asked what I thought of the meeting.

"I could have been more specific," I said. "It required a leap."

"I'll bet," said Vince. "But it's got to be done. You need a better letter."

"I'm working on it already," I said.

Then for 15 minutes Vince discussed a list of senators and representatives who were important to this effort, real important, he said. And I had to call them and email them and ask for their support. And I had to comb the halls of the State House, two or three times a week as the end of the legislative session in May approached. And, finally, I had to use the best stuff I had.

I did all those things.

I rewrote the letter, and said right off the college was in danger of closing and thus further deepening the effects of the recession in the Northeast Kingdom. I gave them numbers, and included our economic impact report. Then I emailed the package to a growing list of senators and representatives on a new spreadsheet, and followed up with phone calls. In Montpelier, I tried to meet as many politicians and staffers as possible, learning the hallways and conference rooms in the labyrinthine Vermont State House.

But really, the best stuff Sterling and I had was Vince Illuzzi.

And the best thing I could do was keep him engaged and responsible. When he called at night and said some senator or representative was going to be at some meeting tomorrow morning and maybe I should be there to catch him — but it's not that important — I went. Every time. Sometimes I'd be able to hand deliver my documents, sometimes not. It didn't matter. What mattered was Vince.

When I didn't see him at the State House, we'd catch up by phone between 10 and 11 at night. I'd be in bed, sometimes asleep, and I'd respond with "tell me" and "who said that?" until I'd woken up enough to participate. In the morning, I'd find emails from Vince posted at 5:30 am. The man didn't sleep. Sometimes we'd speak for half an hour, sometimes just a few minutes. Then Lulu would turn over and mumble, "How's Vince tonight?"

Vince didn't let up, and consequently neither could I. In fact, I became more committed the more I learned the process, although I was excluded from the hallway conferences and cups of coffee where Vince worked his committee and anyone else he deemed useful or necessary.

Straight through April that's the way it was: back and forth to Montpelier, waiting around this meeting or that one to grab this person or some other. The closer to May and the end of the legislative season, the more frantic and crowded the halls of the State House became. Everyone was wrestling to cut money or to get money, to balance accounts between the ravages of the recession and the largess of the federal stimulus. And I, more or less standing in the middle of these surging tides of legislators, citizens, lobbyists, and green-clad legislative clerks — high-school students absorbed in their duties as messengers and retrievers. The money Vince and I were looking for wasn't in the stimulus plan, wasn't in the state budget, and didn't hold any sort of priority or status because it wasn't there being fought over, but in the end, if this worked, it had to appear. Didn't it?

This concept worried me, but it wasn't my job, I thought. My job was to stay focused and keep Vince in the ring with me like a corner man for a boxer with a long shot at the title. Then, in the last week of April, with commencement weekend and the spring board meeting just three weeks away and the State House boiling over with committee votes working their way into the proposed state budget, came the day for the two senate committees I was concerned with to vote on Sterling's request.

First, Vince's Economic Development Committee met and voted unanimously to support giving Sterling $350,000. I didn't attend this meeting because it was Vince's committee, after all, and I wasn't invited. My job was to pound the State House hallways looking to buttonhole any member of the Senate Appropriations Committee I hadn't yet nabbed at least once. That committee met at two in the afternoon. If a majority of the seven members voted yes, then Sterling's $350,000 would take its place — singularly — amidst hundreds of other items that made up the budget, at least from the senate's side.

If they voted it down, then this adventure was over, with the consequences to be fairly distributed upon my head and the body of Sterling College.

I didn't know Vince's schedule other than he seemed to work all the time, nor did I know how he worked the hallways as a politician. But once, at least once, he must have felt the pressure of his advocacy for Sterling because in an evening phone call, well after 10 in Illuzzi time, he said he thought we should reduce the request. It was too much. What about $200,000?

That woke me up.

The problem was this: while one set of plans focused on building the eco-dorm, another set was honing in on buying the bankrupt Inn on the Common. So we were proceeding with building inspections, permitting issues, and financing negotiations, at the same time we were plotting the details of the eco-dorm.

Matching the Department of Education money, down to about $175,000 by this time, with Vince's low-balled $200,000 and then focusing on a few of the other pots of money, we still would not have enough to build what we needed. We would need to begin an entirely new campaign just for that. But if we bought the former inn, we'd need at least $350,000, because the inn had only a few thousand dollars' worth of environmental problems so the DOE funds could not help.

Receiving only $200,000 would leave a big hole no matter which way we went, and would cause all kinds of problems.

The hour was late. I wasn't thinking clearly. This was all new from Vince. What was going on? Had he cracked, had the pressure got him? Impossible. He grew up in the State House, said so himself.

I paused, then said no. I think I said, "No, that would just makes things worse." An absurd statement: $200,000 to Sterling could never make things worse.

"You want to stay with $350,000?" Vince asked.

I said without hesitation. "Yes. I do."

And Vince said okay. We'd be back at it in the morning.

And I lay awake, again, thinking what have I done now? Maybe he was right. He's been right about everything so far.

It's crazy, you know, thinking back on it. Once the whole show was rolling along unstoppable, once the press had got hold of it and the editorials flew like darts. I never contemplated what would happen if it didn't work. If the legislature simply voted no and the whole business sank like a stone in the ocean, soundless and irretrievable. I would have led the college on a ridiculous quest. I would have announced to everyone within hearing distance that Sterling was about to close. But I would have been left with a large, permanently empty pot, and a strategic plan suddenly floundering for lack of resources. I would have been depressed. I would have achieved idiocy. I would have hurt the college. I should have gone with the $200,000. I never should have dragged us through this in the first place. College presidents are supposed to increase their institution's status, not diminish it.

On that day, the day of the Appropriations Committee vote, Vince and I arrive at the conference room a few minutes before two. It's empty, which is what Vince wanted, I think, so he could choose the seating, which placed me at the end of the table, facing the chairwoman, and him to my left in the center of the table.

The senators begin arriving, and Vince begins talking, making sure everyone knows me, which they do but some more than others. He mentions Rod again, how he was on this committee and how he and I worked together for 15 years, and he was a mentor. Senators Dick Sears, Diane Snelling, and Jane Kitchel were seated, then Peter Shumlin, the next governor of Vermont, came in and slapped the back of the chair next to mine and announced, "I'm in. Rod used to sit right there in this room. Of course I know Will, he's from Marlboro; I'm from Putney."

Then right there in the empty seat next to me, Rod. The old pro, the old pol, seated and paying attention. Already enjoying himself.

While they talked about Rod and how he was "one of the best" (Rod nodding in thoughtful agreement) Senator Miller and the chair, Senator Bartlett, arrived. She took her seat, signaling it was time to get things underway. She also turned toward Vince and Senator Kitchel and said quietly, shaking her head, "You know I can't vote for this," then called them to order.

A formality or two, then Chairwoman Bartlett looked down the table and said to me, "Tell us what it is you want, and why this committee should support your proposal."

This was now weeks and many drafts after Vince had been slamming the table and saying, "Not good enough!" A phrase, unfortunately, I have carried in my mind ever since and which rises up whenever I think I've done something well. Or well enough. I began, because I'd learned my lesson: "There's too good a chance that Sterling College will close and the recession will deepen...."

Very little discussion followed after I finished. Other than the senators and myself, and Rod, I don't recall anyone else in the room; usually the benches and chairs along the walls are filled with people like me, waiting to get their say to the committee. Maybe others were there, but my concentration was on the senators and I'd already witnessed one vote go down. In a moment, from an unseen signal, the senators began talking across the table, as if I had vanished: it seemed all abbreviated, like a practiced and foreshortened language to let everyone around the table know what each was thinking about the business at hand. There's an important point here, shown in this conference room, that I forgot to mention. Vince was not just chairman of the Senate Economic Development Committee, where the Sterling proposal originated; he was also a member of this appropriation committee, which meant he could carry a proposal passed by his committee into another and even more powerful committee, of which he was also a member. Hard to turn down your own committee member.

Then Chairwoman Bartlett says something like, "Let's see where this goes." I expect to be asked to leave, but no one seems to be paying me any attention, or Rod for that matter. I put my hands under the table and start to count off the votes — a yeah, a yeah, Shumlin says again, "I'm in." Then Vince and Senator Kitchel vote yes, and the chairwoman quickly votes no. And that's it. Passed in Senate Appropriations, 5 to 2.

Rod has vanished. I stay pinned to my seat as the committee breaks up as quickly as it had come together. I was almost last out the door and Vince was already surrounded by people in the hallway. The best I could do was wave and say, "call," which was unnecessary.

———

Meanwhile, back on campus, where I spent the remainder of my waking hours, commencement was approaching and with it the board meeting. Our speaker that year was Joal Salatin, the "Christian libertarian, environmental, capitalist" farmer who was featured in Michael Pollen's book *The Omnivore's Dilemma*. Heavy rain was unrelenting as we squeezed 300 parents, family members, and faculty and staff into the dining hall, our largest indoor space. Joel Salatin, a big man with farmer's hands and a preacher's cadence, and I were to follow the seniors in, last in line. And we had to meet them outside, so we could all enter and march down the narrow alley between the seats. As the seniors filed past us in the rain, we noticed their feet.

"Look at that," he said, as we entered the hall. "They're all barefoot."

"If that's the only strange thing that happens in the next two hours, I'll be eternally grateful," I said.

"Amen!" Salatin exclaimed with authority.

In addition to the commencement festivities — rain at Sterling dampens nothing of the spirit — there was an anxiousness among the board and senior staff members about what was happening in Montpelier, what was happening with the Inn on the Common, and what was happening to the college's reputation, as regional reporters and editorial writers came to understand that the state was about to deliver $350,000 to the tiniest private college in Vermont, in New England, maybe in the country.

Even as the students in the special topic course were presenting their ideas for the eco-dorm, we were turning more attention to the inn as a new student residence. We were already spending money on building inspections, appraisals, and loan negotiations. By then Vermont's Lt. Governor Brian Dubie publically suggested to Vince that the college buy the inn and kill two birds with one stone, gaining dorm space and saving a historic building and grounds. I've no idea whether Vince planted this idea in the Lt. Governor's head, or he thought of it himself; either way was okay with me.

Sterling's bill, Sterling's "bailout" as a regional paper editorialized, still had to be voted on by the House, where I'd done much less work and where there were already rumblings about giving $350,000 to Sterling when the state's public colleges and high schools were pinching pennies, and everything else in the session was about cutting spending.

Finally, the last hurdle is the governor, said Bobby Starr, the other senator from northern Vermont. "There's always the possibility he will veto the budget, then it is back to the drawing board." Where Sterling, it was clear, would probably have the honor of being the first appropriation penciled out.

Spring 2009 was crazy. The sheer intensity, compelling me to duck, swerve, jump, return the shot, respond to the idea, finish the proposal, meet with a dozen faces, mouths, voices, pick up the phone, pick up the email, and decide, choose, determine, negotiate — all that is, don't forget, just the reality of the job — so driving to the State House, mind-melding with Vince, working the back channels of legislative persuasion, and entering into failed negotiations to purchase the inn, to our eventual advantage, I suppose that was all extra, all new and exciting and anxiety-producing and worth every effort because there was indeed a pot of gold for the prize, first prize, the only prize.

I was feeling pretty good back at the college after the Appropriations Committee vote. I'd run into Bobby Starr again on the way out. I said I was worried about the rest of the senate and the house, especially the house. "Pretty hard," he said. "Pretty hard to knock something like that loose, after Appropriations." He added, "Vince, you know."

It was still nerve-wracking but for the first time in weeks I dared imagine success, in so far as that would prevent personal and institutional humiliation. But something else was bothering me. All along I'd ignored something. I hadn't asked. Why would I have asked? The chances of it being a relevant question seemed remote, like Pluto, the disgraced former planet. Vince would have to know by now. When he called, I asked, and he told me where the $350,000 was coming from.

"Vee-sack," he said. The Vermont Student Assistance Corporation.

Jesus, Mary, and Joseph and all the ships at sea! Where did this come from? How could it be? Now, at the final stage, the final drive?

VSAC was Vermont's own student loan corporation, highly respected among all the colleges in Vermont, public and private; almost every student at Sterling received loans and grants provided through VSAC; they were dedicated nonprofit pros; their leader a feisty, knowledgeable man who fought every day for his organization, for what he believed in, and over decades built VSAC into about the best, most progressive independent student loan agency in the nation.

The money Vince wanted, if he got it, would have otherwise directly supported Vermont students going to college. What we would appear to be doing, if not doing in reality, was the higher education equivalent to taking food away from hungry children. I thought VSAC was sacrosanct; everyone did.

But, I guess, over the years, fighting the legislature for money for Vermont students, you can create enemies, or at least you can create a body of people, politicians, who might think less of you and your organization than do college presidents and all the students and families who have benefited from VSAC's service.

The feisty VSAC leader called me at home, angry, accusatory. It was clear what he thought of Senator Illuzzi. He wanted me to withdraw. Come out and say it was all a mistake, and be done with it. Then he said he was going to kill it in the house.

"You can do that?" I said.

"Oh, yes," he said.

"Well, I hope it doesn't work out that way," I said. But that business of singlehandedly killing what I had nurtured from nothing struck me the wrong way. Withdraw? Not a chance. Instead I doubled the number of emails to house members and leadership. And I got on the phone.

"Sterling Aid Ruffles Feathers" was the *Burlington Free Press* front page headline on May Day. It was followed by a slew of regional editorials, including in the *Free Press* (where once, briefly, I was a reporter) all of them questioning, when not mocking, the absurdity of the idea, the cleverness of Senator Illuzzi, and the forthrightness of President Wootton. Newspaper stories, as you would hope, were more even-handed, but did spread the word Sterling was in immediate jeopardy of closing, at least according to its president.

The most upset people, the most legitimately angered or confused people, were those closest to the institution, who liked, loved, or admired Sterling. So I wrote an email to the faculty and staff and shared the "dire letter" with them, and said I wasn't going to back off, and I thought things would smooth out soon enough. By that time, too, I was able to say that VSAC was backing off some, and the senate was looking for other ways to fund the college.

Somewhere in here Vince called Wilson Ring, an Associated Press reporter, and Ring called Kate Camara whose job at Sterling included media relations, and the next thing I knew he's on campus, interviewing, and pulling information out of Kate's office, including what she had tagged the "dire letter."

It was the same letter used all along, and dire it was because it said what had to be said. The faculty, staff, and trustees had it, Vince and the senators had it. Pretty much anyone who wanted it could have it. The Vermont press had it, and now the Associated Press had it. And the letter's first sentence — I should have seen this — provided a perfect sublead for every paper in Vermont, of which there are many.

It read: "I want to bring your attention to a critical economic situation that if not successfully addressed in the near term will result in the closure of Sterling College and a deepening of the recession in the surrounding Northeast Kingdom communities."

Except for reporter Ring. He wrote the details of the $350,000, its course through the legislature and collision with VSAC, all interspersed with descriptions of Sterling, its buildings and barns, its curriculum, and quotes from students, and from me, like "Some people are terrifically angry at me in this state." And, "You ask for help and you see what happens." It was the best press Sterling had had in decades, to my utter astonishment.

The AP headline was *"Recession Gives a Small College an Economic Lesson"* and dozens upon dozens of newspapers across the nation carried the story, with some or all of the four photographs.

"My god we are everywhere!" Kate Camara emailed Wilson Ring. "Stunned at the power of the AP. President Wootton's traveling but he just called in and I told him to find a computer just for the thrill of seeing us on nine Google pages. Tizzy indeed."

And Wilson Ring emailed back, sounding like a true and veteran AP reporter: "When it's a happy story, like this one, it's a lot of fun. After 17 years it never ceases to amaze me."

I'd stopped trekking to the capital. The full senate voted 25 to 5 in Sterling's favor. I didn't hear the count in the house, but just like Bobby Starr said, it was hard to dislodge, we'd done our part, and the measure passed easily. By the time the AP story hit the wire, the story was over in Vermont. The governor hadn't lifted a finger. The legislature was going home. Summer was upon us, and the auction of the former Inn on the Common.

———

To enter the inn you come down the short stone walk from North Craftsbury Road, the only paved street in the village, and through the low picket fence to the wide front door. Immediately inside you see the dangerously steep 19th-century spiral staircase up to the rooms on the second floor, but you step right into the parlor, with its fireplace and wainscoting. The old wood floors creak and the ceiling is low. To the left are the double doors to the dining room and the wall-size glass panels facing the deck, with its blue and white striped awning with a large tear in it. From the deck you can stroll west through successive squares of formal lawns, with hedges, trees, bushes, stone walls, and flower beds, each leading to the next as you descend the gentle hillside watching the far off ridgelines of the Green Mountains and Camel's Hump unfold before you.

Some 80 people, most from Craftsbury and nearby towns, were in the dining room on the mid-June day of the auction, 2009. The door to the deck was open, and the crowd spilled out there to get some air. The auctioneer had set up in a corner next to the kitchen. The bankers, Ken Gibbons and his vice president and one or two others, hung near to the door to the deck. Everyone else sat at tables or arranged chairs in half circles facing the auctioneer.

Understand that 97 percent of the people who show up at Vermont bed-and-breakfast auctions have no intention of bidding so much as a nickel. They're there to tour, to peek into the closets, and watch who bids. If it happens that the contents of a B&B are to be hauled out to tents on the lawn and auctioned off in a daylong event where there might just be an item or two to bid on, you never know, then people bring their own chairs, their own lunches, sign for a bidding paddle, and settle in with neighbors for the entire experience.

In this case there was only one item of interest, and everyone was interested in it. Lots of people in the village wanted the inn to continue being an inn, ignoring the fact this was still 2009 and country inns all over New England were up for grabs. Most everyone also believed the college was going to buy the inn. The chance of a mystery bidder was always a possibility, some wealthy outsider who could afford to spice things up. Most significant to me, the bank also expected the college to buy the inn. The bank president, who was, I wrote earlier, as nice a bank president as one could wish for, was relaxed and cheerful, anticipating an easy and pleasant morning.

For my part I took a seat where I could see the bankers better than the auctioneer. Over the past week I'd paced the porch, running columns of money in my head, moving the stuff from one column to another, thinking about the bank's financing of the inn, the college's opportunities, and the eco-dorm. The bank held a mortgage it desperately wanted to move; it was like a sore to them, a bad loan right from the start that had now been festering for months.

We had the $350,000.

We also had plans to build a new residence and the money, the Canaday grant money, to design and permit the new 20-bed residence.

And finally, we had a growing nervousness around the condition of the twin dorms, Hamilton and Jefferson, built in the 1960s and occupied without interruption since. We were beginning to estimate renovation costs for replacing all the large north-facing, single-paned windows that sweated the cold into pools, then icy pools, that eventually leaked into the walls and floors. The Department of Energy money would match that project, reducing what could be spent on a new dormitory, but this project was just as necessary — maybe more necessary.

So we had choices. And we had money.

In the bank's view, the college was going to buy the inn. In my view, the bank was expecting around $500,000, because months earlier we'd bid that much and were rejected.

Even without the third appraisal completed, I'd already counted up at least $150,000 in needed renovations, so even if the bank were to settle at $400,000 in the auction, Sterling would still be looking at $550,000. Add to that an unknown penalty for any college willingly purchasing another 200-year-old structure, and we were up to $600,000, about half of it borrowed, from the bank.

So, over the course of the week we — some board members, Ned, I, and others — decided that at the auction I would not bid above $350,000. I'd become hesitant even at that.

There was only one other bidder, from Albany, Vermont, our neighbor just to the north. He bid $100,000. Then I bid, $200,000, I think. The bank bid to $250,000. The fellow from Albany was shaking his head when the auctioneer pointed to him, his eyebrows raised in anticipation. Then the bank said $300,000. Then I said $350,000. Then the bank said $400,000. Then I shook my head and thought, "I'd better call Vince and tell him we're building."

13

Regulate This!

Like spring warblers that are difficult to get a good look at but whose flickering presence in the low foliage is undeniable, two areas of importance in higher education administration have thus far escaped my attention. They are regulation, on the one hand, and death, on the other. Not a college's death, in this case, but the death of a donor. Given the influence of regulation and death on my career, my lack of attention is odd, while mission statements and marketing and stories just tumble out almost unattended. Perhaps it's because they are painful subjects, one literally, the other emotionally.

Remotely related in the industry, both, for instance, are imposed and unavoidable, death and regulation function very differently upon the mind and body of a college. Regulation is experienced on a regular and intrusive basis, but of varying intensities from that of a mild itch to that of a psychotic breakdown. The other is experienced just once, per constituent, and for an institution that once can be rewarding, or a sad, lost opportunity, or a kick in the pants.

This is as good a place as any to tuck them into the curriculum, almost as an aside, a discussion over a light lunch. Think of it as material worthy of consideration at a later date. Regulation because it's a rant, and death because it and the life of an institution is a deep and rich subject.

We are all familiar with how the for-profit world whines incessantly about the federal and state regulatory burden they endure and battle against, bitterly and vocally, and politically with everything they have. Meanwhile, higher education grumbles and acquiesces without much fuss, yet, I believe, is doubly burdened. We both endure the behemoth of federal and state regulations on just about everything we do or have done. Death and Taxes, yes, but it should be *Death and Taxes and Regulations*. We all agree. However, complementing the federal Department of Education, the principal but not exclusive federal regulatory agency affecting colleges and universities, are the six national regional accrediting associations. In New England that is the New England Association of Schools and Colleges: NEASC, "Nee-ask," the agency I've mentioned previously.

The U.S. Department of Education generates its blizzard of new and improved regulations and their reporting requirements, exceptions, and extensions in cycles of four and eight years as each administration does what it can to tear down previous efforts and implement their own plans, to be torn apart by the next administration. Hence we have bureaucracies, where un-dead legislation of past presidencies can be kept walking in circles, endlessly.

The federal regulatory process reaches near hysterical levels once about every 10 years when the Higher Education Act comes up for "reauthorization" where everything is up for grabs like a giant educational policy piñata. Pounded upon by bat-wielding congresspeople, secretaries of education, unions, and public and private lobbying entities, the results are changes and adjustment, sometimes clear and sometimes distorted, but law nevertheless, and that means new rules, requirements, and regulations by the trainload.

NEASC, however, claims not to be a regulatory agency because colleges are "members" who pay a "member's fee." But it's a membership a college cannot withdraw from. Without the accreditation bestowed upon colleges public and private through the regional agencies, the federal government would not recognize us, and our students would be ineligible for federal Pell Grants and other funded programs. Our faculty would not be able to apply for federal grants. In the nation a handful of colleges are wealthy enough and libertarian enough to forgo all federal aid; the rest of us would be out of business. So NEASC counts. It is vital to our existence.

NEASC's mandate is to certify and to assure the viability and integrity of the mission and performance — academic, financial, and budgetary — of its over 2,000 member institutions. It accomplishes this mandate through a never-ending accrediting process. And it manages this enormous task, or did in my day, as an essentially paper-based mini-bureaucracy in an electronic world. They send stuff through the mail. When Sterling developed one of the first online catalogues, for instance, NEASC was so flummoxed they insisted we print out each page, number them, make 15 copies of each, and mail them with all the other bound paper reports.

At Sterling, I seemed to be writing for NEASC about every four months: the annual report, the interim report, the special notice report, year after year because Sterling was less than perfectly secure, and that called for increased scrutiny, increased reporting. But for all colleges and universities, the process culminates every 10 years in the super-large Ten-Year Report, which is preceded by the merely very large Fifth-Year Report that unfortunately landed on my watch.

NEASC takes the Fifth-Year Report so seriously they send a designated staff member who does nothing but visit colleges to see if they need any help, conceptual help, in pulling together the report. There's little wiggle room, actually. So his visit to me and our team was just another afternoon in a long meeting with this fellow telling us how to organize something we were all used to organizing already. Yet the pain was only starting.

To conclude this primer on regulation, in preparation for the February 2011 Sterling board meeting, I ended my introductory remarks in the Board Book, perhaps somewhat inappropriately, with this:

Finally, between the first week of November and the middle of January a large handful of staff and faculty worked on what amounted to a second job, conducting the research and then writing Sterling's Fifth-Year Report for the New England Association of Schools and Colleges (NEASC).

The 49-page narrative of the report is included here in the Board Book. And in the Academic Committee report there is a more succinct rendering of our response to NEASC Standard Four: The Academic Program, and Standard Five: Faculty.

Trustee readers, we all hope, will learn something of the college or find parts of the report interesting or useful. But I have to say that no one who worked on the quasi-massive document found the exercise even remotely edifying, satisfying, or intellectually anything but frustrating or confusing. Here's what we were up against:

There are 11 NEASC Standards to which colleges and universities are required to respond to in writing, called the "Narrative," which is then supported with reams of data. Sounds easy enough, but attached to those 11 Standards are 178 numbered sub-standards; and each of those sub-standards include between 5 and 25 sub-sub-standards. Minimally, this adds up to 886 data points that must be, or can in theory be, reported on in the Fifth-Year Report.

This count does not include the additional 50 some pages of "data forms," which must be completed electronically by the comptroller, registrar, academic dean, and financial aid director, then printed out. Nor does the count include two special reports, "Series E" and "Series S," each a significant piece of work the point of which we were too sick of it all to even wonder about.

The standards themselves, indeed the entire process, is a stunning bureaucratic achievement, not too surprising from an organization that in a recent workshop discussed for a solid hour the title of some sub-standard or other bit of ephemera, asking, critically, "Is it planning and evaluation, or is it evaluation and planning?"

Any discussion that includes the federal Department of Education and NEASC leaves me often a little light-headed. After that, like a hangover, it brings out the worst, my anti-authoritarianism; the bristling when put upon by the higher ups. In contrast to that, however, my second short subject, *Death and the Liberal Arts College*, is positively refreshing. It is grander than that even: in the wide, sparkling firmament of institutional development, "Planned Giving" is the most serious enterprise we've got.

Dark suit and tie, conservative skirt and jacket, that's planned giving. There are no jokes, or no good ones. And in a universe where nothing happens fast enough planned giving requires Herculean patience on the part of the institution and the planned giving officer who does the deal making.

Here's as good a definition as I've come across: Planned giving is *"a systematic effort to identify and cultivate a person for the purpose of generating a major gift that is structured and that integrates sound personal, financial, and estate-planning concepts with the prospect's plans for lifetime or testimonial giving."*

It's the "testimonial giving" that hints at the reality of the practice, because planned giving is all about death. At the same time, it is all about money. Money and death — or death first, then money. Is it a wonder nobody's laughing?

As I wrote earlier, once a month on a Wednesday, from 1985 until 2001, I'd drive from southern Vermont to 57 Stuart Street in downtown Boston to attend a meeting of the Planned Giving Group of New England: PGGNE, pronounced without snicker. In the early years we started with a half hour stand-around at the bar, followed by a relatively intimate lunch and usually a lively and informed speaker.

Over the years they closed the bar and the number of attendees grew like, well, like whatever it is that grows like knotweed but produces Suits instead. From fewer than 50 attendees at the start, mostly from Boston colleges and organizations, the monthly luncheon grew to 250 or more by the time I stopped.

As membership soared in the 1980s and 1990s so did the economy, so did wealth, and so did the application of ever-more complex financial planning techniques, while death I suppose continued apace. As the conference filled to capacity, the luncheon speakers focused more and more on how to begin and sustain a planned giving program, the basics; not like the old days when we listened to presentations on how to calculate charitable remainders by hand, and wondered at detailed descriptions of tax provisions as they applied to philanthropy and death, or did not — that was supposed to be the fun, brain-twisting part, when the IRS ruled up or down, or more commonly sideways, with a letter that just complicated matters.

Back in those old days, too, the capital gains tax was 28 percent. Can you imagine? That meant for the wealthy to turn stocks and bonds into cash they had to forfeit 28 percent of the growth to the IRS. For old fortunes, that could be 28 percent of just about everything. Or they could transfer the whole lot to your organization, avoid the tax, and also take a charitable deduction. You can imagine how it was being on the receiving end of that now long-gone bit of federal tax code.

You can imagine, too, hundreds of development directors across New England trying to figure out how to add planned giving to their programs. So they came once a month to PGGNE, but not to learn the intricacies of tax law, or be quizzed on bizarre financial machinations to make estate taxes disappear and nonprofits a bit richer. Instead, the speakers and experts had to keep returning to the basics of starting and maintaining a program. When they looked up, they saw dozens of large round tables full of entire staffs from small and midsize organizations eager to hop onto this money train. But most of them were fundraisers, which was a problem. Fundraisers smile a lot and are generally happy and eager, or appear to be. Planned giving officers are different. They never appear eager. If you cannot understand why that is, don't get into the planned giving business.

One spring day not too long before I left the group, our speaker was an overweight, older, white, balding, rumpled-suited senior development officer of the old school from Baylor University in Texas. He spoke with a gentle, deep, slow Texas drawl that New Englanders can't help but pay attention to. He was there, he said kindly, to explain how it all worked, what it was all about. The how-to-right-now about planned giving. Mystery over.

With our complete attention, he said, *"It all comes down to this. You walk into the hospital room or nursing home or wherever your prospect lies and you say, 'When you dah, can I have all'ya stuff?'"*

I'd never heard the place so quiet. Stunned is a better word. Forkfuls of lemon cake suspended midair. Then, after a deadly warping moment, laughter. Acknowledgement. Then uproarious laughter. Laughter that beyond some decibel point served to muffle the uncomfortable reality of what this crowd actually faced, talking face-to-face with people not about death, but about their death and their money; everything else is ancillary, the systems and spreadsheets, written communications, prospect identification, and fancy techniques, and tax law.

It may sound cynical, but the Baylor fellow had it right. It's not complicated, not for us anyway: let the dying die, and let the lawyers figure out the details. You, planned giving officer, need to concentrate on the living and you need to combine the idea of philanthropy in a world without them, with their own notions of death and wealth. There is no convincing in planned giving. No persuasion. Some prospects will not discuss the idea of their death and their potential for post-death philanthropy. Others will, carefully, fully.

But you the planned giving officer will need to ask, and you need to be comfortable about it because those who can imagine the future of their wealth are already comfortable, or as comfortable as one gets in the matter. If you're all shook up about it, if you can't listen, if you just want to market and sell, then you should probably focus your career on the annual fund, or auto sales.

Just as with mission statements in their simplicity, and just as with trustee issues in all their complexity, when it comes to deferred giving the Web is a universe of information, certification, recommendation, essays, case studies, program development matrices, encouragements, ads, and warnings, all of it a swirling dust devil around that Texan's one question.

For fundraisers who are unbothered by the dying part of a planned giving program, the other part, the when of the dying part may be of some concern, especially when an organization is trying to determine whether to condition up for a full-fledged, long-term program. In the mid-1980s when I began taking a day off a month to drive to Boston for lunch — with travel costs, membership costs, and luncheon costs to Marlboro, which was, of course, broke — there was consternation by the board as to where the staff was putting its resources. After all, when a huge charitable remainder trust comes due upon the death of the donor but your college had shut its doors a decade before, one could opine you should have stuck with the annual fund, with cash today versus cash in the undeterminable future.

These were not meaningless concerns on the part of some board members, but I probably should not have produced a sample planned giving brochure for Marlboro's trustees in the shape of a coffin. Only Jerry Aron and Rod thought that was funny.

It's true, too, that although Marlboro's program survived its infancy and then grew in investments to its pooled income fund, in bequests, in the creation of trusts and annuities, and in the transfer of real estate upon death, not a single deferred gift came to the college while I was there. If that's the rule, it means when one begins and sustains a planned giving program the expectation should be no monetary return for at least a decade or more, unless you are lucky as a planned giving officer and someone dies suddenly, which is not funny but it is good for your school, college, or university. Marlboro eventually collected the pooled income funds, charitable remainders, houses and properties committed years before to the Ramona Cutting Society — many planned giving programs are called societies, I don't know why. In this case, Ramona was a longtime employee of Marlboro, a secretary who I knew well as a student. She had little money, but willed everything she had to the college, $60,000.

For those institutions unable to mount a long-term initiative into money and death, there is comfort that planned giving works all by itself, slowly, without a plan or staff or any of that, in the form of bequests that arrive unannounced, sometimes from people you've never heard of, and will cause hours of digging through the files until the relationship between your unknown benefactor and your institution is discovered.

Hoping and waiting, I'm afraid, was about the extent of Montserrat's deferred giving program, and Sterling's as well. It's not that such a planned giving program would have helped either one of them in their immediate need, but that they — we — were missing an important piece of a genuinely comprehensive advancement program. Montserrat replaced the missing piece with a billionaire, which worked pretty well for a while. At Sterling, we, like many others, had to do without.

14

A Twilight Zone for the Improbable

The Inn on the Common sat forlorn and silent through the fall of 2009 and deep into winter 2010, the auctioneer's signs replaced with a green and white For Sale sign from the local realtor. Inside were more than enough sheets, towels, blankets, and pillowcases for the six bedrooms and baths. The kitchen and cupboards, plates, bowls, glassware, silverware, wine carafes, pots, pans, chef's knives, walk-in, wine cellar, and Hobart — all there. Your complete turnkey country inn, or college dormitory.

At the time, there were probably a dozen Vermont country inns up for sale, some by their owners and some, like ours, by banks. It was a buyer's market, if there were any buyers, but nothing was happening. Nothing.

Then, one afternoon in March, that changed when Sterling's eco-dorm died a silent death on the Porch of Worry.

In fall 2010 the eco-dorm was alive and well, when vice president Ned Houston and an architect who'd worked for the college in the past co-taught the special topics course, with students designing and un-designing, learning the restrictive qualities of budgets, and arguing over the merits of Vermont's strict environmental laws. The course culminated in a presentation where each of the four student teams presented their best design and talked through it persuasively. What better way to start?

The money? Well, the money was a combination of what remained of the Department of Energy matching funds, about $150,000; a wonderful Canaday Family Foundation grant of about $75,000 for design and permitting and, of course, State Senator Vince Illuzzi's $350,000. I'd also had a close conversation with the Gladys Brooks trustee and Sterling School alum on whether his foundation might abandon their tradition of giving to endowments — what was the point in this economy? we agreed — and instead help match those federal dollars. "No one," he said, "likes to leave money on the table. Let's keep talking." That was enough for me. On top of all that, our bank was still more than willing to loan us the couple hundred thousand we'd negotiated when bidding on the inn, so we had room to maneuver.

Things could go wrong, stuff happens, but I figured I had enough rabbits and hats and smoke and mirrors to outmaneuver whatever those minor gods who had made Sterling their personal object of attention bowled at us. That's how I begin to think on the porch.

The eco-dorm site was the large field just on the other side of a thin hedgerow from Hamilton and Jefferson residencies, the two long dormitories built in the 1960s, with bathrooms that would disgust monkeys and mold you could eat with a spoon. I looked at them, Ned looked at them, our deepening concern masking our dread.

So it was a lot more exciting, in the architectural phase, to design pathways, driveways, and landscaping to tie the three dormitories, Hamilton, Jefferson, and the yet unnamed eco-dorm, together, especially as we imagined how we would renovate them or burn them down and rebuild. The plans looked great on paper, lots of paper. The emerging design itself was simple but dramatic, for us anyway. Over weeks, Ned and I drove to the architect's office in Stowe, Vermont, and he and his assistant came to the college. We worked at large tables, rolling out large prints of the developing design and landscaping plan, holding the corners down with miniature sandbags designed especially for the purpose. But Ned and I were growing wary because nothing we proposed was rejected out of hand as too costly. In our minds the comprehensive

$700,000 budget was beginning to look like an already overstuffed plastic bag into which we could endlessly jam ideas without ripping it apart. So we called for a detailed cost estimate to be conducted by an official architectural cost estimator, who, we were informed, took into account everything from the number of sheetrock screws to the wide pine boards and the shingles on the roof, plus labor, plus an estimate at engineering and septic costs. While that was being done, I paused any further work under the guise of caution instead of what we really felt, which was growing disillusionment. The architect became only slightly nervous; after all, he'd been here dozens of times, he knew everyone on the senior staff, he was already being paid through the Canaday grant. Concerned clients were part of his trade.

The newest estimate was $800,000, not including the 40 grand we'd already paid him and the engineering company he'd recommended. But not to worry. It was all part of the process. There was a solution. It was called — I love this phrase — "value engineering." It means first throwing out all the cool stuff we'd already paid to have designed, then it means shrinking the dimensions, then removing whole body parts.

Worse than that. The college had purchased the land a decade previously explicitly as a building and septic site for a future residence, after being assured it would withstand Vermont's stringent environmental protection law, Act 250. But that was previously. Laws change. We learned that our site was now marginal for a septic system, very marginal. We also came to understand whatever septic system we built had to include Hamilton and Jefferson, thus tripling the system's size and cost, also not included in the estimate.

More tests were needed it was decided by our engineer in consultation with state officials. We'd already dug a dozen test holes and had watched groundwater swell and recede. Now another dozen $600 holes were required and these had to be measured and watched over for an entire year. A year during which nothing could move forward and all we'd have was water rising and falling in holes, and Ham/Jeff continuing to deteriorate. All this, understand, has to happen even before getting into the Act 250 process. It's a commendable law, really, protecting

Vermont's environment, but it is also dreaded, disparaged, and endlessly argued over.

There was no way Sterling, in this case I, could hold onto all that money while keeping engaged but at bay those who controlled the money, especially the Department of Education, where we'd already extended our allotted time by a year, and a couple of foundations, Gladys Brooks, most important.

As for the $350,000, given the condition and needs of the college and, in reality, the vagueness of the statute's wording, there were plenty of ways to legitimately spend it.

We felt stiffed by the architect; we should have known, Ned and I. Neither of us were amateurs when it came to maintaining, renovating, and building new on rural campuses. But we took the ride and ended with an estimated cost in the neighborhood of $65,000 per bed.

We had two meetings and a bunch of phone calls with the architect during the value-engineering phase, each one chillier than the last. Then one evening the architect called me and asked if we could do without the common room, leaving us eight doubles and a handicapped accessible bathroom for a million bucks.

When I told him it was over, we were pulling out, he blanched, something I'd never actually seen before. Ned was subdued, contained. I was bitter, but presidential, meaning I said it was a "set of circumstances" that had done in this project.

But the architect could not let go. He had to save face, reputation, I mean, because northern Vermont is a small community and word travels not fast but around and around like an endless winter endlessly remarked upon.

The end was polite, I guess. The architect and his now completely silent assistant wanted to come over to the college and help us make the transition from something to nothing. He wanted to help us plan for the future, which he wanted to be a part of. We let him come and we listened. That was the polite part.

Thus back and forth, back and forth on the Porch of Worry, where in midstride the eco-dorm died before anyone else knew it, with a thud as opposed to a rattle.

The mind is never blank on the Porch of Worry, the porch, as often, also of scheming. When the eco-dorm gave up the fight in my mind, all the pots of money began shifting position again, and sacks of cash were flying from one pot to another. A little cigar and another dozen turns and I had Vince's $350,000 solidly in the inn's corner. That's where it would go, and I would go back to the bank. All I had to do was humble myself a bit before our banker, who was still annoyed at me for not borrowing the money from him to buy the inn in the first place, and make a lowball offer he couldn't refuse. It wouldn't feel good, losing the proffered loan and taking less for the now even lonelier inn, but it would offload the place and no bank likes sitting on a bankrupt property they probably shouldn't have financed in the beginning.

And that would leave Ham/Jeff, that ever-swelling institutional disaster that we had to fix before students and parents revolted, before the bathrooms rose up and hurt someone and the wind blew unobstructed through the both of them. Could we swing the DOE's attention away from the approved eco-dorm and, instead, use it to renovate what we already had?

And if we could do that, could we persuade Gladys Brooks to forgo endowment giving and support Hamilton and Jefferson with $100,000, thus securing another $100,000 from the DOE? And could I convince the ever-understanding Canaday Trust, having already wasted most of their first grant on design and permitting, to shift a newly awarded grant completely away from its target and towards the DOE match?

Such are the machinations of the Porch of Worry. It's just out the kitchen door at the rear of the house, overlooking the lawn, the small hoop house, a marshy field, a stand of cedar, and the winding path through the forest to Hamilton and Jefferson. Worry, one comes to understand, is the precursor to scheming and concocting, of rolling the dice with the left hand instead of the right.

***

Months later, in early summer 2011, sitting in a comfortable wooden chair on the front porch of the president's house, I am remembering the long winter's pacing on the back porch and of the moment, alone in my mind, I killed the eco-dorm but rescued a beautiful old inn and its lovely old gardens and shrubbery. Sitting there, I realized again I had secured the money and the contractors to pull Ham/Jeff back from a certain and messy death that in the last moments would have metastasized through the college, a cancer of failure. It all felt like I had crossed blindly a foot-wide precipice during a furious blizzard, then in clear weather looked back at what I had done, where I had led everyone short-roped together with a bit of frayed clothesline — what was I thinking? Did they understand how close it was? What danger we were in?

But now I'm watching the summer evening descend on the common like a soft breeze and the well-set sun light up the far ridgeline, and I'm thinking how twisted a course it was, *to buy the inn, to not buy the inn, to build . . . to not build, to finally buy the inn,* and what little control we had over it, how with all that pacing and all that reacting to stuff we were only marginally in control of, how unlikely it was that Sterling, would, at the end of that brutal little race, come out about as well as imaginable. It made me think, the evening quickening, that these presidential porches, one for sunrise and one for sunset over the common, one for pacing and one for watching, slip me in and out of a twilight zone expressly for the improbable because, it turned out, we could do all those things. The pots of money aligned like obedient planets, and the bickering, conspiratorial spirits for once backed off and admired what they assumed to be their handiwork. But it wasn't. It was in spite of it.

———

Thus The Inn on the Common, soon to be renamed Houston House in honor of Ned, joined the half-dozen other 150-year-old white clapboard buildings on campus. There were only six rooms, 12 beds, not quite half the number I had told everyone the college needed. The early 19th-century spiral staircase that descended like a still life waterfall into the narrow front lobby had a reputation of dumping cascades of guests at its foot: it had to go, said the fire marshal, and be replaced with a fire-rated staircase — what's another 30 grand? The rooms had to be rewired, the crawlspace and cellars insulated, the roof patched, the fire alarms and exits updated. The bank had tacked on a face-saving $20,000 to our $300,000 offer, which I accepted gladly.

The six bedrooms, it is notable, were better than anything else we had, just a little out of character, with lace curtains, poufy chairs, flowered wallpaper, and furniture that couldn't take a beating. All had private bathrooms, and one had a Jacuzzi — Illuzzi's Jacuzzi, I couldn't help thinking. The grounds included a beautiful but unused grown-over clay tennis court, enclosed by a really expensive 10-foot-high fence. The agriculture faculty and students immediately wanted to fill it with animals. After all, it was full of weeds and someone — everyone knew who it was — had shoveled out a large hole's worth of clay court to rebuild the pitcher's mound at Craftsbury Academy, the village high school. I locked the gate and declared it to be the presidential/community tennis court, and I'd raise the money to restore it, and thus it remained for many years unused by man or beast, until, inevitably at Sterling, the beasts and their faculty won out.

<hr/>

Beautiful grounds and six bedrooms. That left a small professional kitchen, a dining room, wine cellar, and sitting room. To me, that part of the inn represented opportunity already expressed in our campaign, to build income- producing programs. And the best place to do that was in a kitchen as part of a farm, as part of an agricultural community.

When I arrived in 2006, even on a day-by-bay basis Sterling's dining services were extremely uneven, to be nice about it. Except for its philosophy, in principle organic, local, simple, and healthy, little in the Sterling kitchen was working very well: the food was inconsistent in flavor, quality, and quantity; menu planning appeared entirely ad hoc, which is nearly impossible, I'd thought, if you want to serve 300 meals a day. The equipment, too, was consistently old, the sanitation practices subpar, and the entire budget inadequate. And the staff was ever-changing, except for Paul Sweeney, a quiet, longtime seasonal cook who I was soon to persuade into a full-time position. Thank the chefing gods for Paul Sweeny.

At the start of my fourth year, 2010, I'd hired my third kitchen manager. The first had inherited the job and struggled to combine kitchen management with teaching nutrition and a couple of outdoor-related courses. The second was an excellent cook, a good manager, and a quick learner, but after a year or so quit to help run a new non-profit startup in nearby Hardwick, *The Town That Food Saved*, according to a new and engaging book about how local agriculture was beginning to drive the local economy. It didn't hurt that the *New York Times* writer Marian Burros wrote a single article that propelled the Hardwick/Craftsbury/Greensboro regional agricultural phenomenon into a national one, however briefly. Nor did it hurt that a gang of young entrepreneurs, cheesemakers, farmers, organic seed growers, bakers, and brewers were driving the entire region with ideas, like a new nonprofit in the center of Hardwick, 10 miles from the college, the Center for an Agricultural Economy, to which I lost my second manager. The earnestness of this youthful bunch was as distracting as a room full of toddlers, and they knew lots about agriculture and regionalism, but squat about running a college despite their sometimes forcefully expressed opinions. Still, they put up their own money, and even better earned federal and state support in wonderfully disproportionate sums to their actual size, but not to their intentions and dreams, and significant accomplishments.

The third manager, it's almost embarrassing to admit, was a somewhat older student, but under 30, a driven, highly organized young man who had attended culinary school and was splitting his time between Sterling and Johnson State College, working toward a degree that combined the culinary arts and agriculture. Desperate to buy time until I could conduct a search for the impossible super-person Sterling needed, I persuaded him to drop out of college and take the job. The deal was if he held on for a year, he could return tuition free, anytime, at any age.

I was distressed he did not return for a second year. Instead, on a normal farm tour, which Sterling's ever-increasing numbers of agriculture students took on a regular basis, this young man locked eyes with a young woman working on one of those farms and that was that. It was love for the both of them, then marriage, then off they went to God knows where.

Why put up with all this, when a single phone call to your commercial dining and food service provider would provide the solution?

Because I disdain the food service industry, especially its near death grip on educational institutions and its profit-driven manipulation of "producers," meaning farmers and ranchers. And because that same industry has completely distorted people's already tenuous grip on what food is, literally.

I put up with all this also because I wanted to turn Sterling's kitchen into an academic component of the college, just like a biology lab, a library, or a writing center, except everyone would benefit three times a day.

Despite its managerial and culinary limitations, Sterling kitchen's was independent, completely corporation-free. It was not a "food service" and, unlike in the huge majority of higher education institutions, not beholden to any corporate food service providers, the Sodexos and Aramarks or their subsidiaries.

From a college management point of view, or at least in my view of college management, the only value of corporate food services is they are largely headache and hassle-free. If the chef comes in drunk and raging, if the manager behaves inappropriately with female employees, if a knife fight breaks out at the dishwashing station, you get on the phone and the next day a new manager, chef, or dishwasher appears. That's the entire good part. The bad part is the food. It is industrial, sourced from wherever, and fatty, salty, sugary, processed, overcooked, unimaginative, and usually an insult to whatever animal it came from or farmer who grew it. And it's expensive, environmentally exploitive, agriculturally damned or doomed, and boring to the eye and palate.

The contracts with these giant food service organizations (there are only giants) usually run for years and are almost impossible to extricate from, legally and logistically. If the equipment is inadequate, they will front the money for new stuff; if the plumbing needs work, they'll front you the money for that. And they will offer a price spread based on any menu selected, from the $1.55 per meal county prison menu of white bread, mayo spread and bologna sandwich, pancake, pizza with industrial cheese and a skim of tomato paste, to the incredibly wasteful cornucopia model of food stations where students choose from dozens of options at each meal, like hotel conventioneers and cruise ship patrons suffer through. Whatever the menu, the profit margin hovers around 20 percent.

Finally, the college loses control of its kitchen, which for some is another good feature of signing on with a corporate food service. But not at Sterling and not for me.

I selected a kitchen manager/chef/teacher search committee of a trustee, two staff members, two faculty, a student, and our young uneducated chef, all of whom assumed we would have the candidates cook a meal for us and from that we would gain a basis of comparison. This is what the giants do — in they come in their whites with their shining knives in briefcase-style cases, accompanied by a salesman/chef, and cook a really fine, upscale meal, high quality and good looking. And it's free, of course, and served with a practiced ease. It's all very impressive. When that happened at Marlboro, the hiring decision was made over dessert. That committee never had a chance against those fellows.

So my committee at Sterling was put-off and pointedly disillusioned to learn I was doing the cooking and their job was to interview the candidate. Because, I emphasized, our new manager was not going to be cooking much of anything, but shaping our kitchen and our curriculum to fit our agriculture program, to create a local sourcing methodology, and, in my vision, to link the liberal arts, agriculture, and culinary arts in a way the rest of higher education hadn't hardly thought of, where we would eat better and less expensively than at any college or university in the nation. That's why we needed a super-person who happened to be a chef, a nutritionist, a professor, and potentially a center of our little community.

It came down to three candidates: one from Colorado, in fact, from the very culinary school from which I had stolen at least half of the draft curriculum for the summer course I envisioned at Sterling. One from upstate New York, and the third from the Boston area. The fellow from Colorado pulled out before the interview, and we were down to two almost immediately.

We scheduled the two women a week apart, with interviews starting at four, dinner at six, then the following day more meetings with various groups of faculty and students.

The woman from New York was tall, good-looking, smart, funny, and knowledgeable. She'd run her own farm, owned a small restaurant, and talked the talk about local food sourcing, higher education, students, and teaching. She had appropriate degrees so as not to discourage faculty, nor overwhelm them. We learned, too, that she was single.

It's understood a hiring committee cannot at any time come out and ask a candidate his or her marital status, sexual orientation, religious beliefs, political affiliations: any of that sort of thing because it is regarded as discriminatory and has the potential to get you in all kinds of trouble. Hiring a single person of any persuasion to come to northern Vermont for a position that will underpay them, isolate them, and essentially lower the odds for emotional fulfillment, and thus a chance of becoming a longer-term employee, is a risk to the college, the curriculum, and potentially to the new employee. But in our experience that is not as risky as those who bring with them a suddenly unemployed and, in the remoteness of the Northeast Kingdom, now often unemployable spouse, where the slow misery of that deteriorating relationship will be apparent to all.

So after months of work, wrapping my mind around curricula I had only a rudimentary understanding of, barely a basic knowledge, I was delighted with this woman. We all were.

The next week came Anne Obelnicki, all five foot three of her. I noticed her from the president's house kitchen, where I was preparing a dinner of salmon and rice and vegetables, wandering back and forth in front of the post office, pretending to read the posted notes. She was early. Across her shoulder hung a satchel, the best word for it, large enough for her to crawl into, if necessary. The committee members were in the living room, waiting and discussing the former candidate and the questions they might pose to this one.

Anne had a great résumé, including working at a number of well-known restaurants, a degree from the American Culinary Institute in Hyde Park, NY, and a graduate degree in nutrition from Tufts. Her cover letter, long at four pages, was presented in a sort of script font, somewhat unprofessional, but very well written. Her current position was with a startup organization called The Chef's Collaborative, which was attempting to bring together chefs and farmers.

Eventually she decided to knock on the door, and once in the living room, looking like an undersized puppy among a wolf pack, she shook hands and looked confused, a little disheveled, even distraught.

"Can I have just a few minutes in the kitchen?" she asked me.

And I thought, "This woman's going to have a hard time competing with the last one."

In the kitchen, as the committee was taking its place at the table, she started unloading the satchel. Out came a large bottle of what turned out to be crème fraîche, finished in her room at a nearby B&B, a wrap of butcher's paper containing 10-month cured prosciutto she'd made in her cellar in Massachusetts in an old refrigerator she'd converted into a temperature-controlled environment, then a jar of jam from sour cherries she'd brought back from Michigan, and homemade crackers.

"You brought snacks!" I said.

"I did. I hope that's okay," she smiled, for the first time, not at me but at the pile of foodstuffs on the counter. "I'm not sure that crème fraîche is just perfect yet, but it will have to do."

Over the course of dinner, where Anne held forth on cooking, teaching, working with farmers, as well as the chemistry of crème fraîche, the various techniques for curing hams into prosciutto, and the beauty of sour cherries, she had the committee quite literally eating out of her hand.

Our super-person had landed, improbably and undoubtedly.

15

Lulu, a Grand Idea,
a Mother of Irony

Labor Day 2008, and the backyard of North House is filling up with faculty and staff families and their children. The back porch, without a rail and low enough to the ground to make a good seat, is lined with men and woman younger than I. Of the college's 50 or so employees only Ned Houston is older than me, by a year, and he's only 60.

At the back of the narrow well-worn porch are buckets of ice with beer and bottles of white wine. All the beers are Vermont brewed except Bud Lite — certain people are distressed, almost disoriented, at having to drink anything other than Bud Lite. On the lawn in front of the porch, 10 feet off, are two long tables with white tablecloths and bowls and platters of food: corn chips and salsa, a pyramidal stack of dinner rolls, a green salad, a potato salad, a cheese platter, a large aluminum bowl of potato chips. No one was eating yet. People were still arriving, delivering potluck contributions, baked beans, three-bean salad, green beans with onions, and drinking beer from the bottle and wine from plastic cups. Two big charcoal grills were heating up and near them stacks of raw hamburgers, hotdogs piled up like logs, and squares of orange cheese still in their wrappers.

The backyard then dipped and flattened out to circles of steel chairs with padded red seats and backs that formed islands of seated people around which circled pods of children, free to drink as much soda as they liked, ignored by their young parents for as long as possible.

I had brought the Labor Day party for faculty and staff with me from Marlboro College, where Rod Gander started it both as a way to introduce new people to old people, and because Rod had a cultural and professional attraction to the cocktail hour in all its forms. At Marlboro, like at many small colleges, the entire faculty met every two weeks around a long table — for 19 years I studiously avoided these meetings — but unlike at most colleges, Marlboro's ended with a cocktail party at the president's house. These I attended religiously. Rod also threw a large Christmas party, with roast beef and platters of shrimp, and commencement was similarly robust.

The only party tradition Rod did not bring to Marlboro was the even more remarkable Senior Dinner. This occurred off campus and was for graduating seniors and their faculty sponsors, or tutors, which is how Marlboro worked. No dates. No junior faculty. Part of that occasion, completely out of character today, was the "Loving Cup." Owned by one of the wealthier, more Harvard-than-Harvard local board and faculty members, the Loving Cup was a helmet-size sterling silver double-handed mug that would hold about two bottles of wine. It was passed as the dinner was winding down, tutor to student, student to tutor, through the room, among the tables, symbolizing, we like to believe, the transition of student to colleague, until at last it reached the president, Rod, who was to consume the remaining portion of wine and then lift the cup above his head to the cheers of the assembled.

As a new president, the stuff you bring, the ideas, experiences, philosophies, and practices that will equip the changes you put upon your new institution, is really all you have to offer. It comes out as knowledge, wisdom, expertise, leadership — or passivity, confusion, ineptitude, and incompetence. And it perseveres to the moment the next president opens the office door, his or her office door, for the first time. That's what presidencies are all about, the stuff you bring, and the stuff you leave behind.

You figure if some practice, some idea, worked at one place maybe it will work at another. Or even, if it didn't work particularly well there, maybe here it would. In either case, it requires overlaying the comfort and sure practice of one institutional culture on a differently formed culture of another. So, in fact, whatever it is — a cocktail party, a governance change, a managerial overhaul — is sure not to fit but instead must be fitted by hand, your hand, until the new wearer is comfortable and, eventually, feels what was new is now normal, at least for the present.

Our second Labor Day party was shaping up well, despite that compared with Marlboro the Sterling faculty and staff were relative teetotalers. This was one remnant of a number of Sterling phenomena that had survived the decades since it was a boys' prep school where the faculty, like all prep school faculties, drank clandestinely.

Lulu was in the kitchen, just off the back porch, watching over a pot of steaming mulled cider, directing small children to do small tasks outside the kitchen, "Would you take these three plastic forks and these little blue napkins and put them carefully anywhere on the table down by the hoop house? And you, and you, go with her. Off you go."

I was on the porch, standing aside for the troop of determined-looking children on their way out the door, the lead child clutching her three forks and paper napkins. From the doorway the kitchen was crowded with adults, everyone talking and helping, or not, really, just talking. Lulu turned around and looked at me just as the wall-mounted phone rang. She widened her eyes, "I'll get it," she mouthed. Who calls in the middle of a Labor Day picnic?

So we bring with us what we were, the achievements, the lessons, the failures, refreshed, remodeled, reconsidered: except for wives and partners, through whom, if we are lucky, we bring everything we need in personal human relationships, because college presidents have no friends, no confidantes, and no (inevitably scandalous) lovers. And because this is the case, your number one companion needs to be all those things. Some great job, too: your partner is unpaid, without definition, and faces high expectations on campus and among trustees, on the street, in town. The position comes with an exposure quotient relative only to that of the president.

The grill was ready. The yard was full of running children, the teenagers grouped, cross-legged, in their own circle. From around front more faculty and staff were arriving. Here is our anthropologist, and our art teacher/psychological counselor. The GPS instructor whom I hardly know. Then Deb Clark, our new comptroller with the narrow comfort zone, and her husband, a farmer and member of the Barton road crew. Someone slapped a dozen burgers and a handful of hotdogs on the grill. Children, like sappers, closed on the serving tables, plates in hand. The late afternoon sun shading the lawn and lighting up the hoop house.

I turned to the kitchen door. Inside Lulu was on the phone, listening intensely in the noisy kitchen. She looked up. Her face blank, worried, annoyed; she mouthed silently, "Dr. Schwartz" and put down the phone on the counter, for me, and turned back to the stove and sink and cluttered countertops and mingling guests and seemed for a moment to disappear.

Dr. Schwartz, you may remember, was an oncologist, Lulu's oncologist, at Dartmouth-Hitchcock Medical Center, in Hanover, NH. In 2001, he was the one who urged her to commit to a mastectomy followed by 16 weeks of chemo and five years of Tamoxifen; the one who said, "We fight cancer every day with everything we have in this building." That building, where after surgery, every two weeks Lulu submitted herself to the infusion room, where I'd sit uncomfortably next to the bed and where they poured the orange cancer-fighting toxins into her veins, making her not only bald but entirely hairless, and sick, sick for months with a mind-twisting, panic-inducing, vein-searing combination of drugs; the latest technology, the best hope. The only hope, really. Five years of biannual checkups followed that.

It had been no different this time. Lulu had driven the two hours to Lebanon, NH, on Friday for a day's testing: blood, mammogram, CAT scan. She had lunch with an old friend and drove back. I no longer always accompanied her. It seemed unnecessary. Outside of work, college presidents find almost everything unnecessary.

"Dr. Schwartz," I said on the phone.

"I understand you're in the middle of something..."

"That's all right. What's up?"

"It's not good, Will. The tests showed inflamed lymph nodes in Lulu's abdomen."

"And what's that mean?"

"Well, we don't know. But there are very few reasons that would happen."

"So you think the cancer has come back."

"Yes, I'm afraid I do...."

Yes I'm afraid I do. I'm afraid I do. I'm afraid I do.

That's all I heard. There was no noise in the kitchen, no sound. Just all those people talking and moving about and noshing chips and carrying bowls and trays of food outside, and drinking beer and pouring wine. Helping out. Being useful.

Yes I'm afraid I do.

"Are you available tomorrow?" I asked.

"Of course. I've already told Lulu to call. At one o'clock."

"But still, you think it's back."

"Yes, I'm afraid I do."

"Thank you," I said. "We'll call."

Lulu was facing the stove, facing away from everyone, stirring the cider. I moved to her side so it was just us, the stove, the steam.

"I can't believe this," I said.

"I don't know," she said.

"I want to throw everyone out," I said.

"No don't. Let's just get through it," she said.

"I'll go do something." I said. "Whatever it is," I said, "We'll just have to start all over again."

"I don't know," she said. "I just don't know."

Then she hefted the pot of cider and handed it to me. "Put this on the table. Let's just keep going."

―――――

The second-floor Trustee Room across the hall from the president's office was dominated by a 24-foot-long, 5-foot-wide, 2-inch-thick handmade wooden table surrounded by 20 school chairs, the type with the institution's emblem on the backrest. I was sitting at this giant table with

Sterling's board treasurer Pete Chehayl and Deb, our still relatively new comptroller.

The room's ceiling is gently bowed upward and the paned windows line two walls, the north windows overlooking the campus, and the east just feet off the road that bisects the upper village north to south.

The table's big for a meeting of just three people, but we had papers to spread out, three-ring binders to lay flat, Deb's laptop, and cups of coffee. It was distressingly possible other trustees, particularly the board chairman, might join this midmorning meeting, which was called by Pete without any explanation other than he and Deb had been reviewing a lot of numbers. A sure sign of trouble.

It is fall 2008, and with two years on the job I am no longer a new president. The full panoply of institutional crises — the swelling deficit, the crumbling infrastructure, the clunky curriculum — has been swallowed whole by the burgeoning, now global economic catastrophe.

Deb hadn't been sharing with me the content of the hours she and Pete had been working lately, and I didn't ask her: a comptroller, you see, is caught between two bosses, the real boss, the college president, and the other boss, the board treasurer, who has access to all the figures and spreadsheets and, importantly, speaks the same language from the same mindset as the comptroller. They are kin. In the colleges I'd worked at, comptrollers were like bankers in an alternative world, where, impossibly, the outgoing funds always exceeded the incoming. It was where they focused on how much money they did not have to work with. On the actuarial mind, this is wearing, constricting, and frustrating simply because in this universe numbers aren't adding up. It is a road that unlike most real roads comes to a certain end. A place where everything stops, including numbers, and begins to back up, uncontrollably.

That's what the meeting was about. Deb and the treasurer were running numbers, projections, reaching further into the future and they didn't like what they saw and thought it was time I should know.

Having two bosses to keep in line, Deb said little. So Pete the treasurer laid it out in a clean narrative. First, however, he took a short, deep breath which clearly said, what I'm about to tell you is the truth and it's going to hurt. Then he spoke: "Sterling has, you have, two years. In two years the college will be broke, with no reserves, and closure will certainly be the subject at hand."

He went on, using numbers now, to explain why. There was a good bit of, "even if this happens, then this other thing happens, and there's no change from the downhill slide." Unless a miracle donor appeared, always a possibility for a college like Sterling, the future according to Pete was preordained.

Two years, I thought. Two years and we'll be talking about closing the college. That would make saving the college even more difficult. Talk about closing the college would discourage those very people determined to save it, making everything harder. The treasurer and Deb seemed disappointed in my lack of response. Their problem was I didn't believe a word of it, or a number. However highly I thought of the treasurer, the best I'd ever worked with, and however much I was thrilled to have a clear thinking genuine CPA in the comptroller's office, neither one of them knew what they were talking about, outside of their own numbers, I mean.

Back one day in the fall of 1994, at our flower farm in Marlboro, I was sitting on my 1960 Ford 600 tractor at the top of the driveway when a Marlboro alumna and former short-time employee pulled in, having seen me from the road. She had graduated earlier than I, in the early 1960s, and was now a social worker in Massachusetts. I'd gotten to know her by being the alumni director, and a fellow member of the Marlboro faithful, a true believer.

"How are you, Will, how have you been?" She said, climbing out of her car. She had been attending some alumni function at the college.

The old Ford was so tricky to start I didn't turn it off to speak with her. I couldn't climb off, either, because the brakes didn't work, and I didn't trust the hydraulics enough to use the bucket. But none of that dissuaded her from leaning in, resting an arm on the rear tire, looking up and speaking loudly over the chugging motor.

She asked mostly about the old time faculty, many of whom were still in residence.

Then she asked what all alumni from back then asked. "How's the place doing? How's the money?"

At that moment the money looked better than it had in years. Not that the college was making money, but for the first time in years it was not aggressively losing money. Speaking over the engine noise wasn't working, and it was clear she couldn't hear much of what I was saying, which was that the old place was getting by pretty well.

"Yes," she said in a shout. "Once we were told we were going to eat canned food for a week to save money. But the regular food was so horrible we thought it was a good idea."

"Yes," I called back. "And not too long ago we were down to two paychecks in the bank."

"Good for you!" she said in surprise. "That's wonderful. We never came close to that. Having one payday was a major deal. Two paydays," she said again, in wonderment, "that should take you close to the start of school in the fall."

I wanted to say that was four or five years ago. Rod told only a few of us, very few, how suddenly desperate things were. Two pay checks. Two months. He was shaken. At that moment he looked like a man emptied of answers, shorn of ideas, a stage magician with no top hat, no cape, no rabbit.

But this alumna, back then, would have praised the Lord for two paychecks in the bank; now, she was instead amazed and relieved.

Marlboro, understand, had bred generations of people who could live on air and idealism and still show up to work; people who thought a few paychecks in the bank somehow represented a level of security on par with Harvard's endowment.

The Sterling faculty and staff were all of that. More so, in fact. They grew their own food and provided their own entertainment; they were infused into a larger community, they weren't going anywhere.

The treasurer and Deb had no idea about any of this. They didn't understand the effect of generations of experience with living on the brink. They didn't see how this institutional attitude, this fatalistic belief that life will go on despite terminal adversity, is absorbed into the woodwork, into the offices and classrooms of a place.

Pete, and probably the majority of the Sterling board of trustees, didn't understand just how little was needed to survive with a faculty and staff like this. They'd never imagined survival itself as a time-eating strategy, as unrelenting as winter.

But I had. I had seen it at Marlboro and I saw it Sterling.

The institution was not the problem. Two years was not the problem. The problem was personal — presidential. I was expected, I and I alone was expected to lead the way out of this roiling economic catastrophe and to bring everyone out with me. Everyone. That's the deal the way I saw it, the way I had experienced it. Whether it took 10 years in the trenches living on canned food, then another 5 years of rebuilding, or things worked and worked quickly enough, it was expected that I as president would be there as long as the board and the community were behind me. For better or for worse.

The cornucopia of problems, issues, and outright threats to Sterling's existence, however measured — 6 months, 2 years, 5 years — were by now fully displayed, except for those wounds to the body yet to be revealed, the Hamilton and Jefferson residences, for instance.

That sudden, alarming realization of the obvious provoked by Pete's spreadsheets reinforced the strange aloneness of the president's job, even while surrounded by, absolutely packed in by people who were focused on the president because they wanted something from him for themselves, or for the college, or for the community. Or, simply, because you were the person doing all the talking; you were doing all the writing; you were not at the bully pulpit, you were riding the bully pulpit, strapped hard to it when it was like a bucking bronco or when it was a tired old thing, swaybacked and barely able to put one foot in front of the other.

⁓

The relief in learning Lulu's inflamed abdominal lymph nodes was not the return of breast cancer lasted as long as it took Dr. Schwartz to say so, not even enough time for an atheist to thank God.

The procedure to examine those enlarged lymph nodes, performed in the unapproachable surgeries of Dartmouth-Hitchcock, involved a tiny video camera and a miniature pair of garden snippers probing her insides, inserted down her throat. We hadn't waited long after the Labor Day party to get there, and we hadn't told anyone at the college, we hadn't told our children, we barely spoke of it ourselves but let the intervening days roll by wrapped in a shared, contained, and private dread. Without speaking of the mastectomy and recovery we relived it, the terrible months of chemo, the understandable but uncomfortable publicness of the whole thing, the uncertain future suddenly upon us.

Back then, after the mastectomy, except to Lulu's sisters and most intimate friends, whom she spoke to as much as her energy allowed, my job was to answer the question, "How is Lulu?" There were the unabashed who would push. "No really, tell me, how is she?" And those who were medically oriented, "What drugs will she be taking? Why aren't you doing radiology?" And, almost the worst, those offering alternative advice, delivering books and articles on herbal solutions, cosmic remedies, mystical/spiritual pathways to finding your own power, your own healing power. But the worst were those who disparaged the course we'd chosen, fallen upon, ended up with, issuing warnings on how chemo was actually killing her, enabling the cancer, how the cancer itself was caused by one's own negative, unenlightened emotions.

The benign were those who launched into their own stories, their mother's cancer, their sister's, who died and who didn't; long, detailed stories I listened to in the kitchen as Lulu slept or hid in the bedroom.

I suppressed the feeling of utter unimportance in what was happening; my place was as a service provider, not a lover, or husband, or even friend. Anything that was bothering me, I understood, was to be suppressed. Once I had a dream there was a knock on the door. When I opened it, I was standing in the doorway but something was wrong. I'd been in an accident while mowing the lower field using the Ford 600 with the unprotected drive shaft to the mower. This kind of accident happens very rarely, and then usually in the Midwest somewhere, and not with a mower but with a bailer. Somehow my jacket had been caught up in the drive shaft, but instead of yanking me around in its unstoppable spin and killing me pretty much instantly, I'd fought back, violently, and it had, literally and completely, torn off both my arms. So in my dream I was standing in the doorway, no arms, covered in blood, shaking, dying, staring down at this woman, who looked up at me frightened and concerned and said, "How's Lulu?"

"Good," I replied.

"Are you sure she's good? Really good?"

"As best as can be."

"Can I come in?" she asked, starting to squeeze by me.

"It's not a good time," I said.

"Oh, I'm sorry," she said, offering a tinfoil covered dish. "It's meat-loaf."

———

What Dr. Schwartz said was that the lymph nodes were not cancerous, merely and apparently harmlessly a little enlarged. Without pause he added, "The doctor who did the exam did notice an aberration on your pancreas. He took a sample and that has turned out to be precancerous, a condition called...."

Steve Williams, the longtime maintenance director at Sterling when I began, a large man, big bellied and strong, who could occupy half a morning jawing in the post office parking lot adjoined to the maintenance shop, came into my office one morning while Ned the VP and I were talking, sat down, put his hands to his face and cried, two huge heaves of cry, then breathed deeply, looked up red-eyed and said, "I've got pancreatic cancer and six months to live."

A decade earlier, Marlboro's full-time carpenter didn't come to work one day and we soon learned he had been diagnosed with pancreatic cancer and had six months, at the outside. And that's exactly what happened in both cases, six months from diagnosis to grave.

That's the rep of pancreatic cancer. You got it, you died.

Except, maybe, for Lulu. After the diagnosis the hospital's medical elite, all surgeons, weren't sure which direction to take. There were a variety of options, none of which were "good" and none of which led to a "cure." Operate and cut out the cancerous or precancerous half of her pancreas? Treat it with powerful drugs, instead? Impossible. Radiate the thing, also impossible. Do nothing for a while? You see, in this case apparently no one really knows how fast this cancer grows, or how it grows. Is it essentially dormant for decades, then ripens like a melon in a matter of days? Or does it grow slowly, steadily, as its host body ages and weakens and finally succumbs?

But we, including Dr. Schwartz, were now in the hands of surgeons and, naturally, in the end they recommended going in and cutting it out. The only remaining question was when was the best time, how long could it wait?

We needed a second opinion. Not that it represented the hope that some other surgeon would look and say you don't need surgery, this isn't cancer, there's nothing to worry about — that wasn't going to happen. The second opinion seemed more for the doctors than for Lulu, checking their thinking, their proposed procedure, their team versus some other team.

Dr. Schwartz gave us some names, we selected one and drove to Boston.

———

I didn't believe that in two years we'd be broke and shutting down. But Pete Chehayl, with Deb's analytical efforts, created part of the subtext of anxiety that wore at me, already, early in my tenure. I mean, in the saving colleges business, at Sterling there is the requisite tenacity and spirit and even food on the hoof, but there is also the New England Association of Schools and Colleges. It is when they decide there is not enough money to carry on that you understand your institution is in deep trouble, and it is not yours any longer. Pete's terminal analysis was like a sheet of glass, no irregularities, nothing hidden, there for all to see. It wasn't going to change shape or form. It was incapable of change.

But institutional cultures aren't like that. Instead, they are everything people are, all jumbled together on one playing field: charming, weird, predictable, stupid, bright, passive, aggressive, and stubborn. They are not necessarily rational. Their pasts are food for the present. Their ambition is primordial; only life matters.

Pete's path to oblivion did not account for Sterling's culture, and it was that culture I employed to balance his thinking: it's a culture that endured multiple and complex changes, absorbed them, adapted them, tried and rejected them, yet somehow retained its principles and characteristics, the central aim of things next to life itself, over 40 years, not a single one of which had been a year of plenty.

Amidst all the other plans, initiatives, campaigns, schemes, moves, and desperate ventures honed on the Porch of Worry, there was one idea that circled in and out, dispersing the chorus of chattering spirits, fending off the Molotov cocktails of financial projections. It fit the strategy of survival, but looked more like an exercise in bob and weave! Bob and weave! Like a boxer, you know, frantically avoiding the knockout punch.

My idea was to create a year-round college. I'd been carrying that notion around in my head for 25 years in higher education administration, longer, in fact, if you include my undergraduate years, where summer vacation meant an absence of something — classrooms and books and art and intellectual discourse and community — when we were tossed off the Marlboro campus and replaced by a music festival. For four months the college disappeared. Then it started up again one day in early September as if nothing had happened. As if it had been there all along.

I guess everyone understands that residential colleges and universities of every type pretty much shut down in the summer. Researchers research, and the administration grinds on; in fact, life is marginally better in a college even temporarily without faculty and students. There's more elbow room, fewer distractions, less controversy. It's also lonely, its pathways and hallways nearly unoccupied, its campuses like mothballed movie sets. But whatever little does go on — summer programs, music festivals, the occasional three-credit course — undergraduate education across our nation and effectively around a good portion of the globe stops cold one day in early May and doesn't stir again until Labor Day looms.

I'm sure that schedule once made sense, but as community colleges and for-profit colleges discovered years ago the academic side of the human brain has yet to be permanently reconfigured despite centuries of being turned off in May and booted up again three or four months later. Remarkably, their discovery that students will go to school between May and September has remained pretty much lost to traditional residential colleges.

At Sterling, the entire campus for 10 weeks of summer was rented to Circus Smirkus, a children's circus camp. Over the summer we had to hire students as farm interns to help the agriculture faculty keep things going, plant gardens, work the draft horses, fix fences. What we needed were tuition-paying students, not a camp for children, not programs in adult education, not a music festival.

At Marlboro, the famous and completely independent music festival had a death grip on the college. They were born in each other's arms, but grew as cousins, not siblings. The festival was never going to go away. But at Sterling no one had deep feelings about the circus camp, the shouts and singing of happy children aside; it was too off mission, incongruous, and it didn't pay enough money to instill dependency.

Instead, the situation was closer to a unifying principle in the theory of survival: not just summer courses, but a whole and seamlessly integrated third semester, a year-round college, unloaded from my mind upon this place at this time. We'll start with the farm semester and work to broaden course offerings until we had a contingent of students fully engaged. Why not? How complicated could it be? Especially here, at Sterling? I could see how this old and not unique idea could be tugged, pushed, and levered into existence, if not for a long life, then maybe just long enough.

From northern Vermont to Spaulding Rehabilitation Hospital in Boston is a four-hour drive, straight down Rt. 93 through New Hampshire, crossing into Massachusetts near Montserrat College of Art, pushing quickly east over Somerville, nearly sideswiping our graduate school apartment of 35 years ago, still there, a shingle-sided three decker with six apartments in the then-slummiest neighborhood around Austin Street, and finally across the Charles River on Boston's newest bridge, the Leonard P. Zakim Bunker Hill Memorial

Bridge, the first exit from which lands you at the door of Spaulding Hospital.

The doctor we were going to see occupied two offices, one at Spaulding and one at Massachusetts General. His was in the old section; we saw little of the hospital, just the shiny, linoleum floors, the oversized elevator with room for a stretcher and doors at both ends, and hallways cluttered with lifesaving paraphernalia. Finally we eased through a pair of swinging doors into a quietly lit reception area with an immediately attentive receptionist.

We were escorted into the doctor's office, and seated in comfortable chairs in front of his large wooden desk. Lulu's better at these things than I am. She asks lots of questions. She asks questions the answers for which appear obvious until she's extracted a new bit of information, or achieved a correction, or a partial retraction. Me, I was paying attention to an extended collection and display of antique, white, ceramic bedpans the doctor had placed around his large, carpeted, cluttered, oblong office. There was a row of them up toward the high ceiling on an extended slab of molding, like crenellations. The deep windowsills each had its assemblage of four or five. Others milled about on a long table cluttered with an assortment of book stacks, journal piles, and yellow legal pads.

The doctor reviewed the obvious, saying all the same things his colleagues at Dartmouth had said. These guys all knew each other. Serious surgery gets their competitive spirits up. So it wasn't a matter of merely agreeing on the procedure prescribed by Dr. Schwartz's colleagues, it was a mild but oddly pointed declaration that they here, at Mass General, really did know about how to perform such delicate operations a little better than the very, very respectable surgeons at Dartmouth.

Poor fellow. Lulu and even I, distracted as I was by the apparent difference between ceramic bedpans and ceramic bed urinals (male urinals by the shape, a sort of reverse and presumably hollow phallus-shaped protrusion identifying them) bore down on the notion the Dartmouth guys were any less on the case than these Boston fellows.

To his credit, he had some persuasive evidence about why neither the Boston nor the Dartmouth surgeons knew what was going on. For instance, only two percent of autopsied bodies have pancreatic cancer, though that might not include anything but the immediately obvious pancreatic cancer, as opposed to Lulu's "immature" pancreatic cancer. And, of course, autopsied bodies are, in the full scope of dying and death, which goes on unremittingly, a rarity. And thus, just like the Dartmouth doctors, he had no idea how quickly Lulu's condition might change.

And that was the only question we really had.

Lulu having softened him up, I asked, "So, should we be immediately concerned? Should we rush to get this operation done?"

"No, no, no," He said. "Nothing like that."

"So we could wait a year?" I asked.

"Well. . . ."

"Could we wait five years?"

"On, no. Certainly not." He declared and sat up. "Not five years."

"But a year. . . ." Lulu asked.

"Not a year, it's something that needs to be taken care of."

In the end all the surgeons agreed on surgery. It wasn't unexpected. Sunrise in the west would be unexpected.

———

There we were, two years after Dr. Schwartz's Labor Day call, Lulu, Pete Chehayl the treasurer, and I, on a sparkling early summer night in Chicago, 2010, standing at the rail in the owner's box at Cellular Field, home of the White Sox. In front of us, around us, the metallic and glass enormity of the place, the booming music, the banks of lights and the announcer's voice an excited, shouting god from above. Lulu and I pressed against the rail, suspended over home plate, the packed stadium stretching away from us like the inside of a giant interstellar spaceship, the towering banks of lights illuminating the playing field, its brilliant green grass, perfect brown dirt, and white-pointed diamonds. The crowd roared, the players emerged, the national anthem started up and the giant circle of expectant humanity rose as one. Lulu laughed and spread her arms. I leaned toward her and shouted to be heard, "It feels like Rome, the Coliseum...." She put her arm over my shoulder and spoke close to my ear, "Yes, but nobody dies here."

Pete, Lulu, and I, had already finished dinner in the owner's dining room, a cafeteria-like space leaning toward a sort of low-end county club manliness and exclusivity, except for the children darting around the tables, and college-age sons, daughters, nieces and nephews of the owners reassembling after their school year. Red and white wine was being served in plastic cups from carafes on the tables. A serving station provided thick slices of rare roast beef, filet of sole tucked up next to a mound of steaming crab, or a chicken Florentine and mushroom risotto. Ethnically diverse but mostly African American, the servers, the cooks behind them, the few waiters carrying trays of empty dishware were all smiling and laughing and joking with the millionaire owners and their wives and progeny.

Shortly after Pete's gloomy prophesy, I engaged, or was engaged by — that's what it eventually felt like — a hyperactively persuasive consultant and his team of suited consultants. They were all PhDs and in their suburban Boston offices referred to one another as "Doctor Jones," or "Doctor Desjardin." Usually employed by public colleges, they didn't know anything about Vermont and not much about small private colleges, which was part of the reason I thought, desperately, they might bring a new perspective to Sterling's multiple problems and be of help.

I was constantly being invited to their headquarters for meetings and dinners with people they thought I should meet. People from China selling students and recruitment programs, and people who were knowledgeable about our accrediting agency, NEASC, and could provide assistance were those overlords to take an even greater interest in Sterling. They pitched a few ideas, like beginning a firefighter course and a program in law enforcement, which they deemed perfect for rural young men with a partial community college education. Not helpful, but I kept trying.

Eventually, three of these thoroughly professional doctor-level consultants came to Sterling to conduct an afternoon-long student retention workshop, a field they had broad experience in and which is underpinned by established protocols. Still, the Sterling faculty and staff absolutely hated this commitment I'd made for them, believing, as faculties and staffs universally do, that their institutional uniqueness negated the expert advice and critical observations of people who actually knew what they were talking about, that whatever might have worked at one place could not possible apply to theirs.

The doctors served the point admirably, and made good dinner companions. But after a few months with this unusual, entertaining, but ultimately inapplicable firm, I called up the boss and said it was over, which he didn't like and offered up half a dozen reasons it would be a great mistake to pull away, now, just when things were beginning to roll. A great salesman, I felt, just lacking a product for Sterling.

But there was, in fact, one more thing I wanted that could draw out the relationship for another couple of weeks. I wanted their youngest associate, Michael Reinsdorf, from Chicago. He was their numbers guy, the analyst, who without spreadsheets and figures wasn't sure what he was doing with these consultants. He also happened to be the son of Jerry Reinsdorf, the owner of the Chicago White Sox and the Chicago Bulls.

What I wanted was a three-semester spreadsheet and his take on the long list of assumptions we would need to model the financial aspects of a year-round college. And I wanted Pete the treasurer involved.

I understood people can make numbers do anything, and how important it was for me to provide Pete with a second, very different set of figures that took the college in an entirely different financial direction. Figures that added up to a level of hope that dampened his two-years-and-we're-out conviction before it affected other board members, particularly the financially challenged, panic-susceptible ones.

In a strategic sense, engaging young Doctor Reinsdorf was just a variation of a classic managerial maneuver, which relies on a psychological soft spot common among trustees, corporate officers, and others exercising power and responsibility. It goes like this: the influence of the outside expert is double, sometimes triple, the influence of the inside expert with exactly the same knowledge, opinion, skill, or recommendations.

The spreadsheet, too, was nothing spectacular — it worked identically to one built to project expenditures and income for two semesters; we simply added a third. Its uniqueness was what it represented and how, as we filled in the blanks, a rough model of our year-round college would emerge.

Thus the board of trustees, faculty, and other staff would be able to follow the development of the idea in the sure knowledge that our ever-calm and competent treasurer was on the case throughout, and, even better, an outside expert had shaped the basic approach and modeled a unique financial tool to help get us there.

But don't be fooled. Such a maneuver can backfire seriously. You could choose the wrong outside expert whose figures subvert your imagination. You could choose the right one who reveals something you hadn't seen, like the White Cliffs of Dover or the Rocky Mountains that not only block your way but make you look like an idiot for not being expert enough to see what lay smack in front of you.

⁓

During the interminable drive back from Spaulding Rehabilitation Hospital in Boston to the president's house in Craftsbury Common, instead of anything else about our immediate and grim future Lulu and I talked about who to tell, how much to tell, and when to tell all the people who would want to know.

You have to tell people. The irrational notion that it's none of their business can wrap you up for as long as you like. Your cancer is none of their business. But it is the business of small communities, akin to gossip, and fed by compassion and the fear that if not for the grace of God they're next. And there is your own family, where communal ownership of disease, suffering, and death in all its forms is taken for granted, even expected.

All of it made for good conversation.

"Who did you tell today?" I asked Lulu, after we were back in North House.

She told me. "And how did she take it?" I asked.

"She told me about her mother's battle with brain cancer."

"And how did that make you feel?"

"Better, actually."

"I told the senior staff at the meeting this morning," I said.

"You made an announcement?"

"At the end of the meeting. It was that or pick them off individually, which would have been torturous."

"What was the reaction?

"Stunned, I think, in a word."

"How stunned?

Eric closed his eyes and dropped his head to his chin like at a funeral at the command, "Let us pray." Ned, who I had told earlier, stared straight ahead, sitting up straight, rigid. Deb sucked in a deep breath and her eyes unfocused. Micki, who had just months ago lost her younger sister (and became an aunt/mother to two young nieces), her eyes reddened, her lips firmed; she knew all along something was wrong. Maybe I even told her. I can't remember, and I don't remember the others. I could hear my own voice as I spoke.

We are going to take a week off, then go into surgery, I said after a while.

It didn't matter what you said, how you told people, about the operation; the words "cancer" and "pancreas" were heard as "pancreatic cancer" and that meant to just about everyone that Lulu would be dead in six months, maybe a year.

It was fall 2008, well into October, the warmth of the summer drawn out of the ground, replaced with a penetrating dampness winter can hardly freeze. The intense numbing green of Vermont, a thick, waving, multifarious, unrelenting greenness overspreading the mountains and valleys, the towns and gores, was all turned yellow and red, the leaves dropping in swirling piles either dry and crackling or patted down and soggy already. Across the hills huge stands of conifers offset the stark and leafless maples and oaks and even the shining white birches, except for a couple of weeks when the patches and strings of tamaracks turn a flaming gold and glow in contrast to the dark pine and spruce. Then no more color until spring.

Dartmouth-Hitchcock Hospital reminds me of Disney World,

even though I've been to Disney only once and to Dartmouth dozens of times, as a patient of inconsequence once and as a moderately capable advocate for Lulu through her breast cancer. While you're inside there's an air of suspended belief, suspended personhood, an imposed feeling of otherness, where your choices of action are pro-scribed to conform to this separate, specialized reality of subdued anxiety and dread.

The operation was going to be rough. No example of precision sur-gery; instead, a scar like a saber slash across her abdomen. Four days in the hospital, four days showering in a motel and nodding off in the bed-side chair, days on pain killers that make Lulu mildly paranoid, freaked out, and scatterbrained.

First, though, we fled. To lower Cape Cod. Where we always flee. We rented a little house on Lieutenant Island. I caught a few undersized stripers casting off a collapsing wooden stairway pounded by the high tide. Lulu locked us out of the house — while the kettle was on. We found a ladder, climbed up to the second story where a window was ajar, and standing a first floor window bump-out, I heaved her up and shoved her through, with a thud. We ate. We slept. We walked the beaches. We didn't talk about surgery.

———

In Jerry Reinsdorf's owner's box 20 or 30 guests could be comfortable, standing around the bar and kitchenette behind the 16 seats along the rail over home plate. But it was just the three of us occupying the dark leather seats, plush but upright, not lounge-like, no beer holders sunken in the arm rests. Behind them was space large enough for a buffet table and a stand-up bar that could have served a midsize restaurant, from which, Jerry's son told us, we were welcome to help ourselves. At one point a dessert cart was rolled in from the hallway, and later a man came by with a shoeshine cart. Best of all were the two oversized cigar boxes on a shelf next to the bar, in which lay an arrangement of $30 cigars; posted above the bar was a No Smoking sign.

Inside this exclusivity was another, more exclusive chamber. Set apart by thick glass walls and entered through a glass door from the rear, just beyond the bar, were another 8 or 10 leather seats, in two rows, fronted by its own rail.

Of the various people who briefly stopped by the owner's box as the game progressed, one fellow proceeded directly to the cigar box, then into the empty glass room where he took a seat in the second row, and lit up, taking big drags of smoke to get the thing going. Then he settled back and watched the game, alone in his smoke-filled but well-ventilated glass box.

"Who's that?" I asked Michael Reinsdorf. "How come he gets to smoke?"

"That's my father. He shouldn't smoke at all and especially not here. This is a public building. There are laws."

"But there's the cigar box."

He shrugged, son of a strong-willed father. "But there are privileges," he said.

"Can I go in there?"

"Sure. I'll introduce you."

"No, no," I said. "I'll grab a cigar and introduce myself."

So after a while, there we were, just the two of us, the owner of the White Sox and Chicago Bulls, Jerry and me, puffing on our cigars as the players came on and went off the field and the crowd roared and cheered, until they groaned and fell silent.

But we were smoking contently and talking. I'm not sure what it is, but if you tell businessmen or politicians that you are the president of a college, even, or perhaps especially, if you tell them you are the president of a very small college in northern Vermont, you get an automatic credit of some kind, an attention boost. It may be because you appear to them as a kind of hybrid creature of interest among the other businessmen, corporate bosses, politicians, and booming entrepreneurs college presidents sometimes mingle with. And, if you are a listening sort of president, these encounters often become one-sided conversations as the businessman, corporate boss, or booming entrepreneur recalls his or her college experience, revealing levels of psychological change and growth, if you think about it, that are more personal and informing than educational.

Jerry Reinsdorf was all about the liberal arts, their importance for being human, as I understood it, and the relative lack of attention they are currently receiving in colleges and universities. As I described Sterling, he nodded, puffed, and recounted turning points in his own somewhat uneven undergraduate experience at George Washington University. I have no idea what this powerful man would be like sitting opposite you at the negotiating table, or from behind his desk, but in his glass cubby inside his owner's box he was a comfortable man, easy to talk to and easier to listen to, without anger or sarcasm, thinking back to his undergraduate days and where they took him and how he wouldn't mind going back that way, to feel, I guess, what he felt then.
We watched the game.

The White Sox were losing. We were watching their first loss after a nine-game winning streak. In the eighth inning the other team, I've no memory which team, relieved their pitcher, who was doing great, who was in fact the most interesting athlete on the field, and sent in another one. "Looking for a save," Jerry Reinsdorf informed me when I asked why.

I asked. "What is that exactly?"

We puffed.

"If this new pitcher holds onto this lead of theirs," Jerry Reinsdorf said, "he gets credited with a 'save,' not a win, but a save, which is sort of next best, an essential part of a win, and a whole lot better than a loss."

Self-made powerful men like Jerry Reinsdorf are learning machines, men who suck up education, emerging from undergraduate college like starving predators who swallow business school like they'd down a shrimp on a toothpick, and finally land at the ultimate dining experience, law school, where they consume with gusto.

Who knows what they learn? Of the weighty ephemera of higher education, doctorial education, postdoc, law school, who knows what these sorts of people extract from it all. What changes them? Influences them? But whatever it is, it seems to happen most frequently between the freshman and senior year in a baccalaureate environment, at that age, with those people, upon that ancient notion, often contested, that all learning is effective, especially upon the pulsing, uncontrollably individualistic young mind. It is there, somehow, where these boys and girls realize they can become who they are. And that changes everything.

———

We huddled down back into North House. Lulu as beat as I've ever seen her, her confidence in life shaken, her energy zapped, her nerves twisted by narcotics. Outside, the college moved around us like a herd of happy beasts, the common out the front door of the president's house shone in the early sunsets.

This time, the women who knocked on the door were older women, some survivors themselves, and not hysterical with either fear or compassion. One in particular, Susan Flynn, just sat in the bedroom, or out in the living room, waiting for Lulu to wake up or not, just being there.

I stored the containers of gifted food. I slept. Lulu paced at night. Our children, my sisters, my brother, my mother called regularly until a week, 10 days, and Lulu emerged and sat in the kitchen looking pale and weak but conscious.

"I thought I was going to die. These drugs are too much."

"You've been overly dosed."

"Whatever pain it was masking is pretty much gone."

"Everyone's worried, of course. There's a line outside the door. Your closest protectors have kept them at bay, and the freezer's full."

"I think I'm going to live."

"That's good to hear."

"You need to go back to work."

"I still can't believe you've had to go all through this again."

"I'll be all right. I need to call the kids. I can barely remember speaking to them."

"They understand you're a temporary drug addict."

"I am not."

"That's the spirit."

———

I was very happy how the year-round college idea took hold: the best argument was based on Sterling's major in sustainable agriculture: if you are going to teach a full agriculture curriculum in Northern Vermont — animals, plants, soils, policy, economics, and business — you'd better be up and running in the summer. We started with a summer semester in agriculture, four miserable but willing students, sleeping in tents, eating leftovers from the circus camp. A couple of summers later, the circus camp having moved to new quarters in Greensboro, we filled in other areas of study, froze tuition and fees for those who stayed enrolled. In the summer of 2010 we had 60 full-time students.

Besides their academic classes, what those third semester students learned, what they experienced, was summer in Vermont. Think of the thousands and thousands of Vermont students decade after decade, the majority of whom were not Vermonters, who were forced like migrating voles each May to depart at the end of the school year, at the very moment summer was beginning its brief, glorious, annual rescue of the hearts and souls of those who live through winter and the doldrums of spring. A spiritual loss if there ever was one.

In colleges and even universities, in a business sense, summer brings financial drought, with no tuition payments until fall and the paltry income from summer programs hardly enough to buy lunch.

At the same time those 60 students were spending the summer at Sterling, and maybe because of the recession, or because every pundit and politician knows better than anyone else how higher education should be run, the subject of year-round education was all over the national news.

And I, somewhat irrationally, believed Sterling deserved national press coverage for already having embarked on something everyone else was just talking about. *Newsweek* featured "The Three-Year Solution" on its cover to describe the accompanying essay by Senator Lamar Alexander, a Republican from Tennessee. *The New York Times* published a stack of letters in response to an article, "A 3-Year Degree: Can Less be More?"

My favorite was a *New York Times* commentary that included this quote, "Switching from four to three years would be simple; it would mostly be a matter of altering calendars and adding a few more faculty members and staff."

In response to all this I wrote a snappy commentary for the *Chronicle of Higher Education*, the standard of higher education journalism, which they headlined, "We Designed a 3-Year Degree... and Survived."

It did fairly well, but did not spark the national attention on Sterling College that I hoped it might.

But the program was a fragile thing, too. The faculty were only marginally in favor, except the agriculture faculty, who were highly in favor. The distorted rhythms of academe, like rhythms of sleep, proved hard to adjust to for staff and their various management systems and schedules, as well. And it did not help that we had no money to put behind the idea and its implementation. We'd developed it on our own dime, marketed it as best we could externally and internally. That was as much as we could handle. And it was enough.

May 2011, sitting with Deb and her spreadsheets, we determined that at the end of the fiscal year in two months Sterling would have a surplus. We would not have a deficit for the first time since the day I arrived.

The balanced budget wasn't pretty, you understand. Nor was it large, or even medium large. It was relative pennies. But it was real. And it had an effect on me like being mildly, pleasantly drunk for about a week. And after that wore off and the surplus still existed, the effect became more profound and would in not too long change everything, again.

⁓

Slowly Lulu became human again. She had two recoveries: first from the surgery; it took months, really, for the physical and mental trauma to recede. And then slowly she recovered from the threat of pancreatic cancer, as much as one recovers from the threat of something that retains a right of return, and can be suddenly upon you with a simple phone call from Dr. Schwartz.

After six months, after a year, the intensity of the question, always to me, always an aside, in private, "How is Lulu?" also receded. She hadn't died, after all. She was looking all put together. Things were back to normal. Except normal meant a return of the private background anxiety of remission versus certainty. That, too, changes how you think about things.

————

I suppose the answer is out there someplace, what the thinking was behind Margaret Cargill's critical role in Sterling's survival and even its current level of fiscal stability and relative strength. Presumably, at a minimum, she had heard the name Sterling College, but that is as likely as not.

Margaret Cargill was one of those who inherited all her money, every penny of it, as the heir to the Cargill Corporation fortune, which her grandfather began in 1865 and which by the 21st century the family has grown into a privately held, multinational corporation in agriculture (think chemical agriculture) commodities, food production (think industrial scale), and industrial products and services.

The corporation's other products, also international in scope, include environmental damage and degradation, human rights abuses, and contamination.

Margaret Cargill's stock, all of which was left to her two foundations when she died in 2006, was worth about $6 billion.

The first foundation, the Anne Ray Charitable Trust, started with a mere $100 million in 1997, supports the American Red Cross, Berea College, the Nature Conservancy, the YMCA and a handful of other deserving places. The Margaret A. Cargill Foundation, established at her death, supports lots of efforts, like animal welfare, care for the elderly, children, the environment, and, who would have guessed, Marlboro College and Sterling College.

Since 2006 Sterling had been receiving $10,000 a year, on a certain and predetermined date, from the foundation because, we had been informed tersely, Sterling had been deemed an environmental college by Mrs. Cargill. That was Sterling and dozens, perhaps a hundred or more — there was never a list I saw — of other mostly small, relatively obscure colleges.

Sterling qualified as an almost extreme example of an environmental college, but Marlboro, not really. Goucher, Guilford, Wofford,

Rhodes, who knows what the working definition was of an environmental college in the minds of Margaret and her advisors. When you have some large portion of $6 billion, I can only imagine, you have to get creative to spend it all.

As those $10,000 checks arrived over the years, the brief, one-way, lawyerly communications indicated that at the conclusion of this five-year program there was to be an undetermined payout to the participating institutions. Once a year upon the arrival of the Cargill check we'd scrutinize the accompanying documentation for indications of when and how much.

Then, in 2011, we learned, we discerned, the payout would be $400,000 and would arrive in 2012.

And that gift, from a mother of irony to a college that fed on the stuff, meant to me a second year of balanced budgets, with some left over, which could mean three in a row.

So all this, the deficit dog slinking away, dead to us, the inn secured, Hamilton and Jefferson under repair, the economy of Vermont and the nation stabilized, the summer semester established, it all meant Sterling *would* survive; the terrible storm of the past six years loosening, the air clearing.

Only then could I clearly see the weaknesses of the strategy of survival, that it was not a shared strategy. It was all singularly in my head. On the other hand, had it reached the light of day, it would not have proven a particularly uplifting, confidence-building strategy, as such institutional efforts attempt to be. But its worst feature was its sudden uselessness once confronted with the success it fostered. And now confronted with that success, the strategy of survival was as dead as the dog it had killed.

16

The Hill You Will Die On

A new college president arrives, one morning, and occupies his new office. The old president has cleared out, though traces of occupation remain like barely perceptible wafts of perfume. The bare, picture-less walls radiate silence. The desk and chair are his, the carpet, the positioning of the furniture. On the bookshelves are a few leftover volumes you suspect he left because he thinks you should read them. Not really. They are left because someone else thought he should read them, which he didn't, but left them for you.

You pick up the phone, his phone or her phone, punch 9 to get an outside line but nothing happens. It's early in the morning of your first day. You are surrounded by the office space. It feels like a prison cell, you feel completely alone in there. It is not the seat of power because you don't know anything about power. You can't even use the phone. You try the computer but it just glows, inert.

A dark green metal file cabinet sits in one corner. You slide out a drawer, read the tabs; they are meaningless and for the most part will remain meaningless. Out the window you see a few people crossing your view. It's the middle of summer, at the start of the new fiscal year, they're not students or faculty, and they're not headed your way.

In the hallway cardboard boxes line one wall, and there's another rack of never-read volumes on an otherwise empty bookshelf. These are nonprofit management books, autobiographies of college presidents you've never heard of, and thin, self-published novels and books of poetry by alumni and faculty. A sign taped to the shelf says, "Free."

The phone rings. You pick it up and say "Hello." It's someone calling the former president. He's confused because you don't sound like him. "You must be the new guy," the voice says. "Do you know where I can reach…?" A pad of paper is in the drawer and a few scrappy pens in a plastic holder. You sit in the old president's padded fake-leather chair and take a message. "Thanks and good luck," the voice says.

You hang up, having completed your first official presidential action. You are alone already.

Six years later, midsummer, my second floor office is nearly empty: the pictures are off the walls, the bookshelves are empty except for a small collection of poetry books, a thin hardbound book about canoeing, a children's novel, and a collection of essays one of which begins, "Our world is falling apart…." The phone works but almost no one calls. The computer works but my email is mostly junk. A single cardboard box holds the contents of my desk drawer, pencils, pocketknives, business cards, paper clips.

The campus is humming around me. Students are just emerging from breakfast in the dining hall, filing off in different directions to classes, their barn chores having been completed before eating. The draft horses are on their first morning tour of the common, Rick Thomas the instructor and two students on the logging arch. The little parking lot is filling up, faculty members are heading for their classrooms and labs. Staff members are gathered on the porch across the way. The summer semester in full swing.

Life is humming around me as if I am not there. And I'm almost not. All I have to do is pick up the box, walk out the door, and there will be no excuse for returning, except, I guess, to drop in on the new guy and wish him luck. Then go home and see what that's like.

———————

I wasn't six weeks into the job when Sue Bryant, then chair of the Sterling board, dropped this wonderful nugget of leadership practice on me. She had asked whether it might be possible for the faculty to wear academic regalia at the October presidential inauguration ceremony, like in a real college.

Sure, I said. We can try that. I told Ned Houston the vice president, who muttered an oblique caution, something like, "Well, it could happen, I guess."

But when I suggested robes and hoods at my second faculty meeting the silence that followed, and followed, still rings like a hurricane in my head. Within the week, every faculty member, each in his or her own way, informed me that wearing robes was just not going to happen. It never had. It was out of character. Everyone would hate me.

Sunk before I had time to fire a shot, I called Sue Bryant and told her. I said that if she felt strongly about it I'd go back in there and try again, but the odds didn't look good.

"Oh, don't do that — not for me," she said. "You get to choose the hill you will die on."

It was more comforting than disturbing, the notion that I had a choice, that the choice was mine. But that also meant I had no one to blame, that whatever hill this was, it had been a solo climb.

Every year between late spring and early summer some large percentage of college and university presidents face the choice of whether to stay on the job or announce their resignation. The exceptions are board-compelled resignations and those rare instances when a president is fired outright. Once you have a contract and have settled into the job, there is no fanfare to staying on year after year. It's all been fixed up behind the scenes anyway, between the president and the board leadership. By the middle of June everything is settled for another year, or there's another three-year contract. That's the way the stars move and everyone knows exactly what's happening. But not so for me.

I cruised into my seventh year confident of the future: we'd bury the damn dog for good, firm up the year-round program, end the campaign having achieved the goals, and with any luck build a new horse and animal barn with help from a recently revealed major donor. Everything was looking good. I was ready.

Until I wasn't. Staying for a seventh year and informing the board of my resignation toward the end of it meant staying for an eighth year, the inescapable lame-duck year. I'd managed to forget that fact and to convince myself I was feeling one thing when, come to realize, I was thinking the opposite. If I wanted out, the opportunity to say so was now. Without bidding, reasons and rationales to stay or to go swirled around me, as interrupting and bothersome as the porch-dwelling spirits of the president's house.

Rod Gander once told me I saved Marlboro College. The Title III grant I'd gotten on my third try brought in such a flood of money, technology, and new curricula that, combined with a strengthening economy and increasing fundraising and recruitment success, Marlboro did indeed turn a corner, balanced a few budgets, steadied itself. Because of me, he said.

But Rod saved the college, too. He's the one who faced the $750,000 deficit the day he arrived. He's the one who pushed and pulled and tip-toed the college though a minefield of crises and threats, who cajoled and pressured wealthy people to give up even more of their money. He's the one who could live day-by-day, hand-to-mouth, and bring everyone along with him.

And Paul LeBlanc saved Marlboro. He took all that was delivered to him, remixed it, energized it, made it whole, and brought in millions of dollars in endowments and hard cash, which he spent with abandon and intellectual drive that propelled Marlboro from quaint to competitive. A definite save.

My predecessor at Sterling, Jed Williamson, who left the not quite empty office and the free books, saved the college, no question about it. He brought Sterling from a two- to a four-year institution. I knew his kind. When it came to determination he was unbeatable. He'd beg and borrow from his own family. Which he did. Then he passed the best of them onto me, and I begged and borrowed.

That's how I began to see this college-saving business, when it came to dishing out credit. As in baseball, in my kind of institution opportunities to post a save happen with sometimes frightening frequency. Think of it like this: the ball game's in progress. Your team is in the lead. You are sent to the pitcher's mound to preserve, at the very least, the lead. If you do, you are credited with a save. With institutions of higher education, my sorts, the game is also in progress, your lead is that you have not succumbed, your job is to strengthen and preserve. If you do, you are credited with a save. It's just that easy.

Lots of people can earn saves, multiple saves. One a month sometimes. The closer to the edge, the more opportunities. But no one ever gets to save Middlebury or Amherst or Harvard or Yale or Stanford. They and the land-grant universities are the continents on the globe of higher education, apparently unmoving and permanent. I wouldn't know what to do at such a place. Take up squash, perhaps. Create cool new programs upon which to leave my mark. Collect lots of money and build new vaults to pile it in. No, the college-saving business is for certain types of people and certain types of colleges. I was one of the people. My colleges were of the type. And that was now another part of the problem.

I had created (by default, out of necessity) a strategy of survival, and we had survived. I understood — it became obvious to me — that my whole career had been built around saving colleges, helping to save colleges. The lessons I learned, the moves I'd developed, the professional people I employed, the very person I seemed to have become — not bred in the bone — required crisis and desperation to be effective. It's only at the edge of the cliff that I seem to know what to do. If there's no crisis, if there is no threat — I might as well go trout fishing, or go to Cape Cod and see if there are any stripers running.

My worn and ragged strategy of survival, if draped over a college whose survival was increasingly assured, would make a sorry-looking garment. Yet it was the only cover I had. And my thinking was backed up by my long-established wariness of overstaying. I'd seen it too often; I'd heard the stories. I feared the self-assurance that accumulates like confetti around a president's feet. Where I had been merely uncomfortable living life and job in a fishbowl, now I felt two more years at that exposure level would rub me out, roughly, like a pencil eraser.

I would disappoint a lot of people if I quit. Or would I? Presidents who stay too long, which can be any length of time, up to the length of time it takes to cause serious damage, are blind to it. Their years pile up like a slow motion train wreck all around them, but somehow they never glimpse it, while appearing watchful and engaged. To the staff and faculty who endure it, their persistence is interminable and wearisome. The board, well, it's your board after all these years and it reflects you, so everyone's comfortable.

But leaving at the top of your game is so rare in college presidencies it can have the appearance of rudeness, or of having taken advantage and used the place as a jumping off mark to something better. The idea of planning one's departure to coincide with the good condition and increasing prospects of the institution has never been among the traditions of the presidential switch-out.

If I left I'd be broke, but it was not as if I'd made much money. Getting a raise and enduring a salary cut occurred with the same frequency in my experience, and there were plenty of plumbers, carpenters, and midlevel fundraisers making a better wage than I. Within a few weeks the trepidation of being unemployed faded in importance, faded almost completely. It just didn't fit the equation I was constructing, while other things fit neatly.

There was something else, too, about finding the right hill to die on, which had to be somewhere along the verdant, ancient cordillera of higher education. The hill I was on I'd been hiking for three decades, I wasn't born on it: I scrambled up it as a young man and couldn't find my way down. And to live up there, to thrive on such rough ground, I had to exert what was for me an unnatural level of personal discipline and concentration — a work ethic, when really I am more a hyperactive person with an aspiration to achieve idleness. A truly idle person, not someone who attempts idleness, like me, or wishes after it, also like me, is not lazy or slothful. I admire them for their ability to experience a different measure of time, a different depth of place. But none of that fits at all with the demands of a college presidency, or really any senior level position in the industry, and especially not in places that generate commodity levels of stress. The result was by the summer of 2011 my long relationship with that self-imposed work ethic was in tatters.

I talked with Lulu. I confessed what I'd been thinking. It was difficult. Up and down. We talked about my resigning on and off for days.

I didn't want to completely retire, I said. I'd get another job. Former college presidents, young ones at that, I was 63, must be worth something out there.

I don't think she liked it. She looked at me with a gentle annoyed sympathy, like I was experiencing an unexplainable life crisis, or a psychological collapse long confined by a framework of competence and self-assurance.

Still, she was supportive. "I'm not going to leave you just because you're unemployed and we're living in the cold and dark," she comforted me.

September was a week away. I was past the deadline. If I held back much longer without telling the board it would be too late. I'd be committed to another two years.

Or I could write the one page letter and bequeath the thinly balanced budget, the rebuilt campus, well, parts of campus, the redesigned curriculum, the beefed up infrastructure, the whole reinforced *thing* capable now of further improvements, and operating outside of the zone of death-at-any-moment, safely away from the edge. A survivor, again. I could do this all in good conscience, the place running before the wind. New ideas wanted. Youth encouraged to apply. It is all for him. All for her. But if the presidential search goes south and I'm replaced with an incompetent, an ego, or a micromanager who effortlessly weakens my college unto death, and my leave-taking is condemned, then he or she can join me in the shadowed nether world where grave mistakes live like feral cats.

You do get to choose the hill you want to die on, and there I was, 29 years in, giving up the best job I'd ever had, one that I aspired to, the very one, I guess, that I deserved. But I was going to walk out, hike down, and no one was going to die.

17

Afterword

Publisher's Q & A with Will Wootton

In fall of 2012, unemployed, what did you concentrate on? What did you do? Or How did you adjust?

After resigning from the presidency, I didn't write a serious word for over a year. I'd been writing in one form or another pretty much every day for 19 years: during my six years at Sterling I'd accumulated 18,000 non-junk emails, produced a couple thousand pages of reports, proposals, and appeals; two-dozen letters a month; two magazines a year; a file folder of poems; three or four aborted runs at fiction; journals; notes. At Sterling, when I wasn't writing I was talking on the phone. I gave that up as far as practical, too.

I spent the year, year and a half really, reintroducing myself to a long subdued — but ever present — passion I'd been afflicted with since high school, through college, and into life — sculpture. In all its forms and directions. But my own is nothing complicated: old boards, split cord wood, stones, bamboo, copper, pretty much sums it up. But by fully engaging in art I could compensate my tattered brain for its sudden disengagement from the written, and for that matter the spoken, word. In my mind, my brain, after a while, was grateful for the change of scenery.

Eventually, however, the urge to write down words and thoughts reemerged, as I expected it would. I was ready. I knew there was a richness of information, experience, situations and characters rippling through my years in higher education. So I wrote.

All I was waiting for was a point of view, and a voice not constrained by audience, or compelled by institutional or governmental guidelines, journalistic form, or even chronology. To find it, I started writing, about mission statements, in fact. So my initial aim was simply to write about administration issues until that voice became clear. It took quite a while. (My sculpture in the meantime has maintained its wonderfully silent place, if not prominence.)

Where does the title, Good Fortune Next Time, *come from?*

I've had many working titles for this book. The longest lasting was The Dog is Back. Kill the Dog, and Other Stories in Higher Education Administration, though that wore thin after a year or so. Coming up with one that "felt" right occupied many hours of staring at blank paper. Sometimes I'd come up with four or five. Show them to my wife. Start all over again. One day I was telling a story from my days in Boston Chinatown, 1980, when I was the English editor of *Sampan,* the Chinese language newspaper. After our first edition hit the streets, I was sitting in a Chinatown restaurant talking with my Chinese editor, Klysler Yen, through his barely English-speaking wife — Khysler was also the paper's Chinese section typesetter because he owned the only Chinese typesetting machine in New England. In his first try at setting type with this remarkable machine, the worst thing that almost happened was my pasting up one entire story of Chinese text upside down.

"We'll have better luck next time," I said and his wife translated as best she could. They spoke back and forth.

"Luck like fortune, yes?" she asked me.

"Yes. The same," I said.

She spoke to her husband, and he said the only English words I ever heard from him, "Good Fortune," and raised his cup of tea.

"Next time," I said, and raised mine.

What were your biggest challenges?

The single biggest challenge — perhaps inevitably — had nothing to do with writing itself but with the conflict between writing about higher education administration, and writing about myself. I refer to this conflict in the book's beginning: in trying to write somewhat dramatically about college administration, I developed "memoirish tendencies." Meanwhile, I come from a family, a culture I suppose, where individuals are not comfortable talking about themselves beyond a certain relatively protected and comfortable psychological level. But I was advised by a critic-friend and I eventually understood that you can't tell stories, and write in the first person, and not get into areas of potential conflict with your own cultural/familial comfort zone, even one as narrow as mine. As many writers my age, my sex, my skin color, have already discovered, you write a memoir and one way or another you're going to end up writing about your father. In my case that led to interesting discoveries about him, and possible explanations about my own behavior. Which I explained in the book. But not too much.

Another challenge was a disruption. The first draft was almost complete when I temporarily suspended my retirement and took an interim position in Las Vegas, New Mexico, as the vice president for advancement and executive director of New Mexico Highlands University Foundation. That was an overwhelming and wonderful fifteen months in the Land of Enchantment, but it threatened the writing. I managed one chapter while living in my camper at the local KOA campground, waiting for Lulu to arrive and looking for a place to rent. But once engaged at the university it was all I could do to stay abreast of all the things I was supposed to do. A few months flashed by, and no writing, I thought maybe it was over — but it wasn't. I forced myself to sit and write in the mornings and on weekends, then the compulsion returned, and before sleep my thoughts turned to the next day's encounter with the manuscript. The same would occur during some meeting at the university, or while riding my bike out to the High Plains. It was a worry abated, I guess, more than a challenge overcome.

What was the easiest thing in writing — what did you enjoy most?

The easiest thing, the part I most enjoyed, was the writing itself. To get there, however, it's remarkable to me how much research was required, regarding both my lives, the professional and the personal. Times, dates, places, budgets, people, successes, blunders, and the sequence of events were, I discovered, all a muddle and had to be constantly teased out, researched, logged, and understood. Topical research became necessary, as well. Where did I read what I'd already observed, that new college presidents typically overspend their budgets? (It was an Association of Governing Boards research paper.) And which year exactly was Marlboro College's winter of discontent with only two paychecks in the bank between it and oblivion? (I almost had to choose among two or three very similar years). Chapter by chapter, notes, references, and reprints of articles filed in folders. To map the overall construction of the book, I made maps of timelines and story ideas on large sheets of paper, over which I'd spend hours, doodling but also uncovering facts and recalling stories.

Then, with more material than I could employ and the illustrative story or stories shaping up in my head, I could finally write. And rewrite. And insert and extract. And when I dropped my lead, I could follow for a time and see where that went. That's what I enjoyed most.

Were there surprises for you in the writing — subject-wise, thematically, literary?

Yes, in all those ways. I was surprised that I wrote about dyslexia — my dyslexia. My ever-probing editor maneuvered me into it. Everything in the book I'd written about before, in various forms, or told in the stories I'd recounted over decades, except anything about dyslexia. That was new territory and I didn't feel at all confident even skirting its perimeter, which is about all I accomplished. It's just not a subject I've ever cared to discuss... unless it's your dyslexia, in which case I'm all ears.

Going back that far in my personal history, to that place occupied by the dumbest, loopiest, slowest-reading kid in the lower school, and then bringing it forward to my sister's Christmas party just a few years ago — was not the mental struggle I'd imagined it would be. It was enough, however, for the time being. I couldn't go on about it, anyway; too off topic. Which was another surprise: all the material — on paper or in my head — that couldn't be fit in, or that had to be jettisoned along the way as too burdensome, or not essential. But that's the nature of a literary excursion, or memoir. You start off loaded up one way, and return lugging an entirely different pack of different stuff, of the same or greater weight.

Given that the book is not a linear narration, can you say something about its structure?

Originally, I followed the standard sequence of subject matter in a college-level program on non-profit management. They usually begin with a discussion or assignment regarding mission statements, so that's where I began. Next, for me, was a chapter on boards of trustees. Because I used examples and stories from my own experience to illuminate these subjects, chronologically the text moved back and forth across three decades with relative ease. This worked well as I roughed out the book and began writing. However, a narrative developed, unbidden really, but not surprising as my career was, of course, chronological and called for identify and for clarity. The more I wrote about myself outside of my profession, the more I allowed the narrative to develop, the greater the need to strive for some level or order for myself and for the reader. The result is non-linear — and a compromise between the instructional and the personal — and it was as likely as not to fail and end up a jumble of scenes, opinions, funny stories, rants and raves; in other words, in a literary sense, an unidentifiable piece of work. I think I've avoided that. The concept of the book as an excursion, opposed to the idea of a straight-forward chronological memoir, provided considerable comfort to me as I worked to keep the reader and the writer informed, up to date, and entertained.

Did the writing of the book teach you something you didn't know when you started writing?

It was a complete revelation to me that throughout my life I have mirrored my father's proclivity for moving from place to place. It wasn't until I was writing about the importance of place to small colleges that

I began thinking about my own picking up and moving habits. It turns out my nineteen years at Marlboro are the exception, as are his many years at *LIFE* magazine. And because so many of my moves were linked to his, his problem — as good a word as any to describe the trait — became mine to carry on, and I never saw it until I wrote it down.

That's probably normal in memoir, the discovery of things smack in front of you; the more you look into the mirror the more you see. If I'd looked harder, I would have seen my wife, whose part in all this, this book, this moving from place to place, this life for the past 42 years, is not given fair, to say nothing of equal, play. But then, this is a literary memoir, an excursion, a singular one and at times a lonely one.

— Winter, 2017, Craftsbury Common, Vermont

Acknowledgments

It's hard, impossible really, to think what this book might have been without the critical reflections and suggestions of a small collection of persistent readers. John Elder's early intervention — I doubt he'd call it that — reset entirely what I thought I was writing by introducing me to the wildly variegated possibilities and limitations of memoir. His encouragement to keep writing — with the promise he would keep reading — was exactly the fuel I needed. My old high school hockey coach, Bill Mayher in Brooklin, Maine, a writer and artist himself, read early drafts and declared I'd developed a compelling "voice," something I'd searched for but wasn't sure I'd found.

I finished the book for the first time in January, 2015 and sought publishers and/or literary agents, learning the bits and pieces of submitting manuscripts to welcoming publishers who never wrote back. On a whim I submitted it to the Santa Fe Writer's Project literary contest. Months later I was excited to have made the "long list" of about 75 submissions. But I was not included on the short list, nor of course the finalist's list. Later still, however, Andrew Gifford, the SFWP director emailed me and suggested I submit the first chapter to the *SFWP Quarterly*, an on-line literary publication. With the help of the *Quarterly's* editor, Melanie Cordova, who was the first of a number of people to pare my attraction to ellipses, the chapter appeared in the spring, 2015 edition. I learned that this sort of third-person testimonial — an acknowledgement of your writing from someone who does not know you — carries considerable weight in the literary world, and I'm thankful to Andrew and Melanie for giving me that chance.

In summer 2016 my editor/publisher arranged for four "critical readers" to read, comment at will, mark up places they felt needed improvements, or deletions, and generally have their way with my again completed manuscript. John Elder joined this group, as did Jon

Larsen, a seasoned print journalist, editor, and writer; Ann Slayton, writer and editor; and Stark Biddle, a neighbor, teacher, and avid reader. To these good friends and colleagues I owe a deep thanks. Without their combined critique the non-linear construction of the book would have failed, succumbing to reader confusion. Instead, the writing became leaner, dates and places clearer, and, in some cases, order put to chaos.

There's a special thanks to Steve Wright, Sterling president from 1989 to 1992, for his photographs and patient photography when we didn't know what we wanted and when, finally, we did. Thanks, too, to Carol Hollander, an old friend and colleague from Marlboro days, and the only professional proofreader I know. Carol took on the unenviable task of fixing my em dashes, eliminating more ellipses, and correcting errors unnoticed or ignored by everyone else, which only a proof reader can do.

Merrill Leffler, publisher, editor, poet, and friend, without whom this book would occupy some deep drawer in an unused desk, deserves more than thanks, more than unabated gratitude. His steady confidence in the ultimate value of the manuscript, his creativity, his persistence, and his sometimes overwhelming absorption in literature and the literary life all drove me forward and simultaneously gave me the patience and determination to dot every "i" cross every "t" and eliminate more ellipses. It was Merrill who teased out stories I would have let be, who asked questions I would have preferred to avoid, and who took delight in a well-wrought sentence or a solid paragraph and went to the trouble to tell me.

It's amazing to me that over the three years it took to write this book my wife of 41 years, Lulu, read every word of every version of every chapter, pencil in hand. Her verbal critiques, long and sharp or short and sweet, never missed the point however much I resisted. My gratitude for her involvement, her willingness, her support, her frankness, is unbounded.

Index

Alice Lloyd College, 31

Aron, Jerry, Marlboro Board, 47, 61, 67, 68, 115, 220

Association of Governing Boards (AGB), 35-7, 121

Association of Vermont Independent Colleges (AVIC), 30

Ballantine, Bill, 13

Ballantine, Roberta, 13-14

Berea College, 30-2, 259

Beverly, Massachusetts, 73-4

Blackburn College, 31

Boards of Trustees, chap. 4; see under college administration

Bryant, Sue, 262-3

Burlington College, 17, 111

Burlington Free Press, 111, 173, 208, 281

Burros, Marian, 228

Calderwood, Louise, 180

Camara, Kate, 208-209

Canaday Family Charitable Trust, 196, 199, 211, 222-5

Cargill, Margaret, 198-200, 259, 260

Cenkl, Pavel, 198

Center for an Agricultural Economy, 228

Center for Northern Studies, 123, 126, 179

Champlain College, 17

Chehayl, Pete, 238, 244, 248

Chinese American Civic Association, 6

Christian, Clayton, 20

Christian Johnson Endeavor Foundation, 11, 58, 61

Christo and Jean-Claude, *The Gates*, 83-90

Clark, Deb, 236

Coffin, Miriam, 218

College Administration: accreditation, chap. 13; annual funds, chap. 6; boards of trustees, chap. 4; curricular development, chap. 14; endowment campaigns, chap. 5; finances, chap. 8; governmental relations, chap. 12; marketing, chap. 11; mission statements, chap. 3; planned giving, chap. 13; presidential searches, chap. 7; public relations, chap. 6 and 11

College of the Atlantic, 51, 110

College of the Ozarks, 32

Consortium for the Advance of Secondary Education (CASE), 260

Curricular development, chap. 14

Dartmouth-Hitchcock Medical Center, 105, 236, 241, 247, 270

Davis, Holbrook, Marlboro Board, 45

Davis, Jerry, President of College of the Ozarks, 32

Davis Education Foundation, 86, 197

Derr, Matthew, President, Sterling College, 99, 106, 110

Ecclesia College, 28, 31, 33
Elder, John 5, 9, 151, 275
Endowment campaigns, chap. 5

Farber, Lil, Marlboro Board, 45-9, 70, 101, 102
Flynn, Susan, 278
Freeman Foundation, 147
Frost, Robert, 75, 186
Fuller, Buckminster, 171
Fundraising, chap. 5

Gander, Rod, former President, Marlboro College. 11-13, 19, 22-23, 40, 45-49, 61, chap. 5 passim, 91, 101-103, 105, 185-186; chap. 12 passim; 234, 2400, 264; memorial service 103-105; saving Marlboro 264
Governmental relations, chap. 12
Gibbons, Ken, 136, 146, 210
Gladys Brooks Charitable Foundation, 197-199, 222-5
Great Yokahoma and Tokyo Earthquake, 169

Hampshire College, 110
Hardwick, Vermont, 228
Harvard Business School, 20, 114
Harvard Seminar for New Presidents, 31, 98, 107-14
Harvey Mudd College, 110
Hendricks, Walter, 74, 119
Houston, Ned, 39, 122, 144, 196, 221, 233, 263
Hunt, Mitch, 178-180

Illuzzi, Vince, 191-225

Judd, Dick, 159

Kaufman, Ted, 51-2
Kidd, Julie, 11, 22, 48, 58-1, 147
Klawa, Maria, President of Harvey Mudd College, 110
Kohlberg, Jerome and Nancy, 61-8, 148
Kuenruther, Fred, Marlboro Board, 48, 49
Kytle, Jackson, 117, 118, 122

LeBlanc, Paul, President, Southern New Hampshire University, former President, Marlboro College: 40, 48, 66-67, 91, 99-100, 108, 113, 183, 187, 195, 264,
Lennox, Jo, 76

Maine College of Art, 110
Manhattanville, College, 47
Marlboro College: brief history, 74-6; comparison with Sterling College, 259. cost of a board of trustees, 41-3; endowment campaign, 68; mission, 26; Marlboro and Sterling compared, 119; Title III proposals, chap. 5 passim; trimming a board. See under college administration
Marlboro Music Festival, 75, 140, 245-246
Mark Hopkins College, 17
Marketing and public relations, chap. 11
Martin, Micki, 127, 177-8
McCormack, Elizabeth, 47, 48, 61-2, 68-70, 100-101, 115
McKibben, Bill, 127
McLaughlin, Judith (Harvard Seminar for New Presidents), 109
Moby Dick, 9, 98

Montserrat College of Art: annual fund, 84-85; art auction, 81-83 18; board of trustees, 80-1; financial issues, 85; mission, 27, 77; on place, 92-96; see also Christo and Jean-Claude, *The Gates*, 88-90;

Morgan, Ross, 198

Mundell, Bill, Vermont poet, 75

Naess, Ragnar, Marlboro Board, 49

National Association of Independent Colleges and Universities (NAICU), 4, 29

New England Association of Schools and Colleges (NEASC), 71, 76, 137, 214, 215, 244

Norelli, Vince, 57

Obelnicki, Anne, 231

O'Brien, Carol, 56, 60, 67

O'Donnell, Christine, 196

Paris, Oren, President of Ecclesia College, 31-4

Pfeiffer, Sandy, President, Warren Wilson College, 31

Planned Giving Group of New England (PGGNE), 60, 217, 218

Planned giving, chap. 13

Presidential searches, chap. 7

Pride, Mim, President of Blackburn College, 31, 32

Reinsdorf, Jerry, Chicago White Socks, 250, 253, 255

Reinsdorf, Michael, 250, 259

Ring, Wilson, 208

Ringling Bros. and Barnum & Bailey Circus, 13-14

Ryan, Willy, 177-181

Salatin, Joel, 205

Schwartz, Gary, 95-6, 236, 241, 243-234, 247-8, 258

Sheldon Jackson College, 110

Shelton, Bob, 127

Shinn, Larry, President of Berea College, 30, 32

Shumlin, Peter, 204-5

Smith, Jonathan, 68-70

Starr, Bobby, 191, 206-209

Stepp, Joe, President of Alice Lloyd College, 31

Sterling College: origins, 76; Center for Northern Studies, 123-5; curriculum and community, 76-77; curricular development, 130, 143; food service, 230-2: mission, 76; Sterling College and Marlboro compared, 119; year-round college, 21, 140, 245-6, 250-1, 256-7

Stoner, David, Sterling College Board, 142

Straus, John, 45, 48

Sweeny, Paul, 227

Taylor, Dick, Marlboro Board, 44, 47, 48, 67-8

Thomas, Perry, 179, 197,

Thomas, Rick, 62

Title III, Strengthening Institutions Grant, 51-53, 57-66; *see under* Marlboro College

Trinity College of Vermont, 17

University of Vermont, 112

Unity College, 110

Vermont State House, 213-214,

Vermont Student Assistance Corporation (VSAC), 207-9

Warren Wilson College, 31, 33, 101

Whitehead, Mary Jane, Marlboro Board, 48

Williams, Steve, 243

Williamson, Jed, 39, 40, 117-8, 123, 264

Windham College, 17

Work Colleges, 28-34

Wootton, Clara (daughter) 13, 18, 127, 173

Wootton, Connie (sister), 8, 14, 902, 127, 155-157, 161, 176, 256

Wootton, Elizabeth (Liz, sister), 8, 14, 902, 127, 155-157, 161, 176, 256

Wootton, Lulu Ballantine: cancer, 2, 94-6, see also chap. 7; flower farm, 13, 18, 94, 239; *see also* Gary Schwartz

Wootton, Marie Core Duffy (mother), 8, 14, 91, 155-161, 165-171, 183, 256,

Wootton, Pete (brother), 92, 156, 158

Wootton, Philip (father): death, 154-5; East Dover, Vermont, 93, 168; Kobe, Japan, 92-3, 168; editor, *LIFE* magazine, 8, 93, 165-166, 171-173, illness, 173; Singing River Ranch, 8, 152, 159-61; T-Cross Ranch, 93; Yale, 165-167

Wootton, Russell (son), 13, 90, 127, 168, 173

Wootton, Will: Boston University and graduate school, 6, 14, 168, 173; cooking, 7-8, 167-168; dyslexia, 157, 272; editor of *Sampan*, 6, 14, 270; fishing, 18, 106, 132, 136, 152-4, 159-60, free-lance journalism, 173; hockey 14, 18, 19, 115, 158, porch of worry, 22, 29, 120-1, 129, 147-8, 211, 221-2, 224-5, 245, 264; *Potash Hill* editor, 14, 22, 48, 174; rescuing Sterling, chap. 12; Title III proposal writing, chap. 5 passim; undergraduate, 13, 158; wrangling, 8, 92, 160-165

GOOD FORTUNE NEXT TIME:
Life, Death, Irony, and the
Administration of Very Small Colleges
BY WILL WOOTTON
*is designed by Sandy Rodgers. The text is typeset
in Baskerville and the titles in
Baskerville Italic.
The book is printed on acid-free papers
by McNaughton & Gunn, Saline, Michigan.*